THE AutoCAD®
Productivity
Book

Tapping the Hidden Power of AutoCAD

Third Edition

A. Ted Schaefer
James L. Brittain

Revisions for Third Edition by George O. Head

Ventana Press

Chapel Hill, North Carolina

Library of Congress Catalog No.: 88-051343
ISBN: 0-940087-27-8

Book design by David M. Kidd, Oakland, CA.

Cover photograph by Dennis Bettencourt, San Francisco, CA.

Cover model by Don Bennett, San Francisco, CA.

Cover props furnished by Berkeley Computer, Berkeley, CA.

Third Edition cover design by Mary Votta, Chapel Hill, NC.

Typesetting by Johnna Webb and Wendy Wegner, Pixel Plus
    Desktop Publishing, Chapel Hill, NC.

Third edition revisions by George O. Head

Third Edition, First Printing
Printed in the United States of America

Ventana Press
P.O. Box 2468
Chapel Hill, NC 27515
919/942-0220

About the Authors

A. Ted Schaefer is president of Applied Technical Support, a CAD service bureau based in Tulsa, Oklahoma. A veteran CAD trainer, Schaefer heads the Tulsa AutoCAD Users Group and is a member of NGGA. He has written frequently on CAD and computer graphics. He can be reached at Applied Technical Suppport, Inc., 11740 East 21st St., Tulsa, OK 74129, 918-438-5311.

James L. Brittain, a graduate of Oklahoma State University School of Technical Training, has extensive experience on five CADD systems, including AutoCAD, and now specializes in writing LISP routines for CAD and computer graphics programs.

Acknowledgments

The authors and publisher wish to express appreciation to the following individuals who assisted in the writing and production of this book:

Greg Malkin
Robert Siletzky
Mary Votta
Johnna Webb

Limits of Liability and Disclaimer of Warranty

The authors and publisher of this book have used their best efforts in preparation of the book and the programs contained in it. These efforts include the development, research, and testing of the theories and programs to determine their effectiveness. The authors and publisher make no warranty of any kind, expressed or implied, with regard to these programs or the documentation contained in this book.

The author and publisher shall not be liable in the event of incidental or consequential damages in connection with, or arising out of, the furnishing, performance, or the use of the programs, associated instructions and/or claims of productivity gains.

Trademark Acknowledgments

AutoCAD and AutoLISP are registered trademarks of Autodesk, Inc. Any representation of the AutoCAD name and logo throughout this book and related promotion is not to be construed as an endorsement on the part of Autodesk, Inc.

Some passages in Appendix C, "AutoLISP Notations," were reproduced with the permission of Autodesk, Inc. All further rights to these passages are reserved by Autodesk, Inc.

dBASE is a registered trademark of International Business Machines Corporation.

MS-DOS, Microsoft and Multiplan are registered trademarks of Microsoft Corporation.

WordStar is a registered trademark of MicroPro International Corporation.

Norton Utilities and Norton Editor are registered trademarks of Peter Norton, Inc.

Lotus 1-2-3 is a registered trademark of Lotus Development Corp.

Contents

CONTENTS

Chapter Five   Improving Your Screen Menu

CONTENTS

Chapter Eleven   Release 10 Tips and Tricks

Section Two—The AutoCAD Productivity Library

CONTENTS

3D Macros

Foreword

Third Edition

Much has been said about the importance of "working smarter" versus "working harder," and nowhere is that more obvious than with CAD. Great leaps in productivity, job security and personal satisfaction can be gained by using AutoCAD as something more than an electronic drawing board.

The AutoCAD Productivity Book helps professionals perceive and use AutoCAD not merely as a function-by-function drawing editor, but as a powerful and vital new tool that can turn drawing and design into something approaching magic. Valuable techniques for increasing speed, power and performance lie just beneath AutoCAD's surface and within easy reach of any user.

The AutoCAD Productivity Book also addresses company-wide linkage and integration of CAD with engineering, sales, purchasing, desktop publishing and manufacturing for the ultimate in productivity and competitive advantage.

Beginners, the largest group of users, often realize less than half the benefits and productivity offered by their AutoCAD systems. They tend to reach a plateau after they get line work on paper a bit faster with AutoCAD than by hand. Yet they haven't learned many simple, built-in techniques that can save hours of drawing time each week.

Intermediate users generally know some AutoCAD commands and tricks. They're familiar with their computer's operating system, tend to own a word processor and have done some customization. Yet until now, they haven't had a comprehensive guide that quickly and easily translated these tools into powerful work-savers.

Advanced users have spent long hours working on AutoCAD macros and menus. They've read everything that references AutoCAD and are intrigued by "mainframe" CAD on a micro. Yes, this book is also for the whiz kids, who will be introduced to some complex AutoLISP™ routines and total drawing automation for Autodesk's latest version, Release 10. A quick scan of the book will reveal dozens of valuable programs that can save hours of programming and debugging effort.

Advanced users and trainers may also want to use this book to help answer questions from students and novices. An instructor guide and student workbook are available from Ventana Press.

The AutoCAD Productivity Book picks up where Autodesk's *User Reference* manual and beginning tutorials leave off. Regardless of your level of expertise, this book teaches you how to tailor your AutoCAD software and hardware to meet the particular needs of your discipline.

Acknowledgment of Autodesk might seem too obvious to mention. However, anyone who has followed the computer-aided design industry over the last decade appreciates the exciting new ground Autodesk has broken.

Prior to Autodesk, anyone who purchased a CAD system was dependent upon the CAD company for everything from service and training to customization and application development. Users could make productivity gains only with the expensive and often hard-to-come-by cooperation of their chosen CAD company.

Autodesk, on the other hand, asked not for your loyal servitude, but pioneered open architecture for CAD. AutoCAD allows you to easily rewrite menus and create powerful tools to suit your discipline. No longer must you wait for someone in a distant city to develop a new function or create a specialized application; no longer must you accept the man/machine interface dreamed up by a programmer unfamiliar with your specific needs.

Autodesk has created a universal graphics engine noted for speed, ease of use, 3D and customization tools—and this book has been written to teach you how to take advantage of these tools. By following the text and tutorials contained in this book, you'll be able to create routines so streamlined they seem like embedded AutoCAD commands written at the "factory" in Sausalito.

Each Autodesk software revision increases your ability to adapt AutoCAD to your own needs. With the release of AutoLISP, Autodesk created one of the most powerful and exciting internal programming facilities of any CAD system—AutoLISP. AutoCAD's potential is now limited only by your imagination.

Upon completing *The AutoCAD Productivity Book*, beginning and intermediate users should have mastered AutoCAD's many exciting new productivity tools. And I hope this book inspires advanced users and trainers to reach new heights of productivity.

Ted Schaefer

Introduction

Third Edition

AutoCAD is a powerful, easy-to-use Computer-Aided Design and Drafting program. With an elementary understanding, users can create beautiful drawings much faster with AutoCAD than by hand. Many use AutoCAD at this level, just as it comes from the factory, with a mouse or digitizer and AutoCAD's standard menu.

But why stop there? You can easily double your productivity by giving AutoCAD a new personality that makes it work the way you work! In other words, if you draw widgets, then turn AutoCAD into your own customized widget-drawing machine.

The real power of AutoCAD lies in the ease with which it can be customized to your needs and linked with other processes in your company, such as engineering, CAM and desktop publishing, or other Autodesk products like AutoSHADE™ and AutoSOLID™.

Always keep in mind that the reason to customize AutoCAD is to make it simpler, not more complex. AutoCAD is complex enough by its very nature, wanting to provide everything to everybody. But you shouldn't have to choose all the options all the time. You should make your CAD system do it your way.

Written to help you tailor AutoCAD to your specific discipline, *The AutoCAD Productivity Book* gives you not only instruction, but the concepts with which you can creatively solve any number of customization problems. These "thinking tools" are timeless principles that work for any version of AutoCAD. In this way, *The AutoCAD Productivity Book* remains current regardless of the latest release of the software.

The techniques described throughout this book help you evaluate your customization needs and teach you how to add to the AutoCAD menu and tablet for optimum efficiency. With *The AutoCAD Productivity Book*, any user in any discipline now can reconfigure and reorganize AutoCAD's commands (screen, pop-down or tablet), invent new commands and link with design calculations and other processes. This book can help you streamline work and save hours of design and drafting time every week.

WHAT'S INSIDE

The AutoCAD Productivity Book covers a range of AutoCAD enhancements—from DOS and better hard-disk management to simple tablet and screen macros and AutoLISP routines. Eleven tutorial chapters offer a step-by-step guide to creating and using these productivity tools—including total drawing automation.

The 80 macros and AutoLISP routines found in Section Two—The AutoCAD Productivity Library—are ready to use, allowing you to benefit from the enhancements while still learning what makes them work. (For an even faster start, a diskette that contains the entire library is available.) You will quickly learn how they'll save you time and money.

THE AUTOCAD REFERENCE LIBRARY

The AutoCAD Productivity Book is the first of four books that comprise The AutoCAD Reference Library from Ventana Press. The others are *The AutoCAD Database Book*, by Frederic H. Jones and Lloyd Martin, *AutoLISP in Plain English*, by George O. Head, and *The AutoCAD 3D Book*, by George Head, Chuck Pietra and Kenneth Segal. Together, these books form the most comprehensive body of knowledge on customizing AutoCAD, managing its database, and on using AutoLISP and AutoCAD's

3D capabilities to become more productive. *The AutoCAD Productivity Book* provides the framework for making the best use of the knowledge contained in the other books.

WHY MORE PRODUCTIVITY?

Several references to productivity have already been made, by which is meant the ability to achieve and maintain greater speed, performance and flexibility with your system. In a global marketplace, every company must bring better designs and products to market faster than ever. However, productivity is more than a few clever AutoLISP routines; it's a systematic, thoughtful approach to CAD and how it relates to all other functions in an organization. *The AutoCAD Productivity Book* offers many practical tips, but its focus is on the thoughtful approach.

The enhancements gained from *The AutoCAD Productivity Book* easily justify the one-time effort of creating a macro or AutoLISP routine. If you use only 10 percent of the enhancements in this book, you'll realize immediate benefits, including:

1. Lower Support Costs — AutoCAD is a universal CAD system that easily can be customized to meet the needs of many different departments and applications. Thus, a company can avoid buying and supporting different CAD systems to meet different needs.

2. Time Savings — By using the techniques covered in this book, you can combine many keystrokes into one pick from a menu. For example, with one pick, your initial blank prototype drawing can be called up and formatted just the way you want it, thus saving you setup time. AutoLISP programs can prompt you for input and then run unattended, creating the drawing itself. Feed engineering data directly into AutoCAD, and AutoLISP does the drawing without operator intervention.

3. Reduced Errors — Mathematics can be built into an AutoLISP program in such a way that all you have to do is answer a few questions (in plain English!) and never worry about incorrect calculations.

4. Consistency — Macros and AutoLISP programs combine groups of repetitive AutoCAD keystrokes into a few keystrokes, increasing consistency and saving time. For example, if your work constantly demands multiple filleting at a fixed radius, you can create a simple routine to do just that in two keystrokes. No more guesswork!

5. Less Expertise Required — Because otherwise complex functions can be dramatically simplified, less experienced users can do the same work that heretofore could be accomplished only by advanced users.

6. Better Designs — "What if" situations can be quickly explored when AutoLISP routines are used to create designs from user-specified parameters. To optimize a design, you merely respecify the parameters — almost instantly creating a new drawing!

7. Creative Motivation — CAD can become mentally fatiguing when operators crank out the same type of drawing and repeat the same keystrokes day after day. Knowledge of macros and AutoLISP routines encourages you to search for ways to automate systems and expand your knowledge of AutoCAD. As we all know, creativity brings job satisfaction and increased job security.

8. Linkage to Other Programs — Sharing the geometry and information in your drawing can break down departmental barriers and further increase productivity. You can often automate most of the drawing process by sharing data with other departments.

UPGRADING YOUR SKILLS

Before CAD, the greatest improvement in drafting was the electric eraser. CAD technology and use have evolved rapidly, bringing increased productivity and professionalism to the drafting room.

Just as doctors, lawyers and other professionals are expected to upgrade their skills regularly, so must CAD users continually explore new and better ways of employing the tools of their trade. The rewards for a knowledgeable CAD professional are great.

However, because most work is done "under the gun," there is usually no time for increasing productivity. That's where *The AutoCAD Productivity Book* comes in. It shows you valuable enhancements, saves you time in creating them, then saves you time each day in your work. Even if you must initially do a few routines on your own time, both you and your boss will quickly see the benefits!

HOW WELL SHOULD YOU KNOW AUTOCAD?

Though a thorough knowledge of AutoCAD is encouraged, it's not required or assumed. However, readers should at least know how to boot their systems and be familiar with basic AutoCAD commands.

By and large, most users aren't very enthusiastic about reading reference manuals and technical books. (It is hoped that this book will be an exception!) However, after reading Section One, please skim the AutoCAD *User Reference* manual. It will refamiliarize you with less frequently used commands and functions and help you make better use of this book.

It's always a surprise when I reread the reference manual—four times a year—and find two or three big time-saving techniques. (For example, did you know that you can reset the origin for hatching patterns? This capability has been there for more than a year, even before the UCS.)

HOW TO USE THIS BOOK

The AutoCAD Productivity Book is written for anyone who wants to save time and increase productivity. You need not be a crack programmer to use the programs here. In fact, no programming experience is required.

For ease of reference, the book is divided into two sections:

Section I—The Tutorial Section (Chapters One through Eleven) shows you, step by step, how to create and edit macros, how to organize your screen and tablet menus, and how to automate your drawings.

Section II—The AutoCAD Productivity Library includes 80 macros and AutoLISP routines. The purpose of each macro is explained, along with valuable tips on invoking, revising and using the macro.

After reading this Introduction, browse through The AutoCAD Productivity Library to see which macros and routines will be most useful to you. You may see one that might be useful immediately and want to enter it or pull it from the optional diskette. Then read and keyboard Chapters One through Eleven, particularly if you're a beginning AutoCAD user or have never created AutoCAD macros.

For further reference, Appendices on DOS, EDLIN, AutoLISP and Word Editors can be found in the back of the book. The menus, macros and AutoLISP routines are available on diskette using the card in the Appendices.

Treat this book as a workbook, not a library text. For example, when your directory names or macros differ from ours, make a note in the book. If you find a topic of interest, "earmark" the page. This book covers many different items for a wide range of interests—so you'll want to mark passages important to your discipline.

A NOTE ABOUT LISP AND AUTOLISP

The treatment of LISP and AutoLISP programming merits special mention. The purpose of this book is not to teach a programming language; that subject requires a book of its own, such as George O. Head's *AutoLISP in Plain English*, part of The AutoCAD Reference Library, published by Ventana Press.

The AutoLISP routines featured throughout this book can be used "as is" — typed directly into your computer. (You may want to purchase *The AutoCAD Productivity Diskette™* for a faster, "typo-free" start.) For those who want to dig deeper, we provide brief explanations on how the programs work. For further reference, see Appendix C.

Many users find they do well with AutoLISP if furnished with easy-to-follow examples, brief explanations and AutoCAD's *AutoLISP Programmer's Reference*. This book's goal is to give you enough exposure to AutoLISP so that you can create your own simple routines.

REQUIREMENTS

1. Your Version. Since tablet and screen routines are part of every base AutoCAD (Version 1.4 or later), anyone working with AutoCAD can use *The AutoCAD Productivity Book*. However, it doesn't specifically address early AutoCAD versions. In this edition, Versions 2.52, 2.62 and Releases 9 and 10, running under MS-DOS and PC-DOS, are the supported versions. The macros in this book are written to support only the highest version of software available. Features that belong to one version and not another are pointed out. In some cases you'll need to revise routines to fit your version.

Note: If you have AutoCAD on a workstation (such as Macintosh II, Sun, Apollo or Micro-VAX) the AutoLISP and menu systems are identical to AutoCAD's MS-DOS version. Because the operating system is different, merely skim the DOS information for concepts. To make full use of this book, you'll need to learn a text editor, such as the VI editor in UNIX.

Many of the more complex AutoLISP programs are included to fire your imagination and to demonstrate the power of AutoLISP. However, you still will want to use the simpler macros and routines shown in the tutorial chapters and the Productivity Library. Some of the simplest macros can save the most time.

Note: If you're planning to upgrade AutoCAD to the latest version, do it sooner rather than later—you'll get more use from this book and instantly increase your productivity.

2. Word Processors. All customization is prepared in an ASCII (American Standard Code for Information Interchange) file. Because MS-DOS (your operating system) comes with an editor called EDLIN, EDLIN is used as the word processor throughout this book. However, EDLIN is not a very good editor. An editor of your choice is recommended. Consult the Appendices for some possibilities.

You'll learn EDLIN just by reading this book. For further reference, a list of EDLIN commands and operations appears in Appendix B.

If you have a word processor, we strongly recommend you use it instead of EDLIN when creating macros and AutoLISP routines. Appendix D describes how to use word processing programs other than EDLIN to create and edit macros and AutoLISP routines.

3. Hardware. Using *The AutoCAD Productivity Book* requires no special hardware other than a functioning AutoCAD system. But let's consider for a moment why you bought this book in the first place!

Increasing AutoCAD productivity is often synonymous with increasing drawing and processing speed. If you have an adequate pointing device instead of arrow keys, you immediately double your speed. A mouse or trackball is fine, and a digitizer will give you yet another 25 percent increase in speed.

A "286" or "386" class computer or workstation for industrial use is recommended. Waiting for a computer to process your drawing means losing concentration and productivity. The closer you are to instantaneous response, the greater your productivity!

To avoid "diskette shuffling" and to speed processing time, a hard disk is a necessity. Also, AutoLISP will be disabled without at least 640K RAM. This book assumes a hard disk configuration. If you use a dual floppy configuration, please consult the *AutoCAD Installation Guide* to find where your customization files are located. Hard disks now are required for Versions 2.5 and later.

4. Printer. A printer is a vital tool for any type of programming. In long menus where it's difficult to keep track of what you've done, a hard-copy printout is a must. A printer also is useful for maintaining directories of your diskettes and hard drive.

GETTING STARTED

Beginning Users. If you've just started using AutoCAD, or want to increase your knowledge of DOS, EDLIN and AutoCAD menus, read Chapters One through Eleven sequentially before going to the Productivity Library.

Advanced Users. If you know your way around DOS and can create and edit macros and AutoLISP routines, you probably will want to skip the tutorial chapters and go straight to The AutoCAD Productivity Library. Afterwards, read or skim the tutorial chapters, which you'll find interesting and full of tips.

The book is designed to be used while you're sitting at your computer. Reserve at least an hour of uninterrupted time per session, particularly with some of the more complex AutoLISP routines. You'll gain far more from the book if you're relaxed and undistracted during the sessions.

RULES OF THE ROAD

To make sure we're all speaking the same language, the items below serve as a guide to the naming and notational conventions used consistently throughout the book. These rules must be followed carefully.

1. CAPS — As a matter of preference, upper-case letters are used for simple macros and lower-case (or upper-lower) letters for AutoLISP routines. In Chapters One through Eleven enter all characters as they appear. By the time you reach The AutoCAD Productivity Library, you can choose the style that best suits you.

2. 0's and **O's**; **1**'s and **I**'s — These are noticeably different in the text and cannot be used interchangeably. **O**'s must be typed as letters, and **0**'s as numerical values. The same is true of **1**'s and **I**'s. Your routines will not work if these are not entered correctly.

3. (ENTER) and **(RETURN)** — The **(ENTER)** key is used interchangeably with **(RETURN)** or **Carriage Return** or **[CR]**. Throughout this book, **(RETURN)** is used.

During an AutoCAD drawing session, a **space bar** can be substituted for **(RETURN)** when you enter a command or an option. Until **(RETURN)** is hit, you can change what's on your screen (CRT) by using the **backspace** key and retyping the command.

4. Type: — Whenever you see this word in the page margins, type exactly what's shown in the proper case and including all brackets, parentheses, forward and backward slashes, colons, semicolons, commas, spaces, etc. After **Type:**, explanations, reminders and other information sometimes appear in parentheses. Do not type these notes.

5. Response: — Following **Response:** you'll see the computer's response as it appears on the screen. This may be a close approximation because of differences in your version of software, brand of computer and how your files have been created.

6. fname.ext — Several generalized names for files and directories are used throughout the book. You're expected to supply your actual **fname** and extension or directory required. For example, **ACAD** refers to the directory where you save AutoCAD files. Your actual name may be different. **OLDDWG** and **NEWDWG** denote arbitrary drawing names.

Remember that AutoCAD automatically places a **.DWG** extension on your drawing files. A **.DWG** extension is assumed if you're in the AutoCAD program — or it may be shown in DOS, **NEWDWG.DWG**. Other names exist where you're to supply the middle part of the name, such as **ELECXXX.DWG**. The **XXX** part of the name usually refers to a number between **000** and **999**.

7. Directories—You always should be in the same sub-directory as the current step in the exercises. In Chapter One, you'll modify your prompt to show your directory. If your prompt, **C:\ACAD>**, shows you're in the **ACAD** directory when you should be in the **ROOT** directory, **C:\>**, then **Change Directory (CD\)** to the proper directory before proceeding.

8. CTRL-X—Where **X** can be any other key, **CTRL-X** means to hold down the **CTRL** (Control) key while tapping the designated letter key. Control (**CTRL**) keys used throughout this book include:

  CTRL-S and **CTRL NumLock**—freeze the display and the scrolling of a directory or other information.

  CTRL-C—cancels or **aborts** an action, such as a directory.

  CTRL-Q—toggles the printer **on** and **off**, valuable for printing directories and **README** files.

9. Command: This is the AutoCAD **Command:** prompt, which means you must be in AutoCAD to take the next step.

10. Indention. Because indention is often confusing to beginners, AutoLISP routines in this book aren't indented. All AutoLISP routines found in this book are properly indented in the optional *AutoCAD Productivity Diskette.*

Throughout the book, many other helpful rules and tips are prominently featured.

YOU'RE ON YOUR WAY....

...To a creative challenge, higher productivity and some fun. You'll be challenged to create menus, macros and AutoLISP routines to suit your needs. And you'll learn a new way to think about drawing and designing with CAD.

The road to increasing CAD productivity is travelled with many small steps. A macro today, a software upgrade tomorrow; a new menu, a hardware upgrade, a training class—all are important steps. A year down the road, you'll be proud of a major achievement made of these steps.

As you learn the routines outlined in this book, AutoCAD will never be the same. No longer a mere substitute for the large system you really wanted, AutoCAD will become mainframe CAD on your desk with you as the master.

Section I

Tutorials

Making Your First Menu

IN THIS CHAPTER

To start you immediately on the road toward greater AutoCAD productivity, here are some basic tools and concepts, including:

—An introduction to DOS (Disk Operating System), the internal, usually invisible program that runs your computer.

—An exploration of the hard disk, which places us all on the same playing field.

—Reasons for improving AutoCAD to suit your needs. We'll answer the questions "What is a macro?" and "What is the '20/80' rule in customizing AutoCAD?"

—The basics of EDLIN, a simple text editor, and how to use it to create your first macro.

You'll then put these and other tools to immediate use by creating your first two-selection screen menu!

MAKING THE BEST BETTER

The first time you used AutoCAD, you were probably wowed by the time you saved compared to using a drawing board or a more cumbersome CAD system. Yet you may sometimes wonder why AutoCAD didn't write certain commands or menu selections in a way that would make your work easier.

Part of the reason is that AutoCAD was designed to meet the needs of all its 200,000-plus users and includes more commands than any individual regularly can use.

However, the sheer number of available commands and options can often make your system cumbersome and slow your work.

In fact, the typical CAD operator uses only 20 percent of AutoCAD's commands and options to produce 80 percent of the work — the familiar "20/80" rule!

You'll see how to rethink your menu and modify it to make that important 20 percent work better for you.

For example, have you occasionally wished for a shortcut by creating an entirely new command from a series of other commands and options? Autodesk anticipated that. AutoCAD's screen menus, tablet menus, a macro facility, script files and AutoLISP provide easy ways for you to optimize AutoCAD — even to the point of making automatic drawings!

This book provides the thinking tools to elevate AutoCAD above an electronic replacement for your drafting board and eraser. However, to realize new levels of productivity, you must wage a creative battle with your CAD system to make it do more work, while you do less.

It's said that the best CAD technicians take the longest coffee breaks. Why? Because the computer does all the work! Which means they're working smarter!

GENTLEMEN AND WOMEN, START YOUR ENGINES!

What does AutoCAD deliver "fresh off the showroom floor"? A vehicle with a powerful engine, modest tires, rugged drive train and steering. What isn't included? A body and seats. So you strap a crate to the frame, and away you go! It sure beats walking. If you lived in a different time and place and didn't know any better, you might be perfectly content.

Taking the analogy further, suppose you needed to haul a load of rocks, plow a field or drive cross-country. AutoCAD's new productivity tools allow you to use the same running gear but change bodies nearly instantly.

If you work for a big company that has many different CAD needs, AutoCAD — with some customization — can meet those needs effectively. With AutoCAD your mechanics need service only one type of running gear, and you can stock fewer parts.

MEET YOUR FIRST BIG TIME-SAVER

Now, let's get down to some hands-on business. Turn on your computer, start AutoCAD. Be sure to configure your system for a screen menu. Create a new drawing called **JUNK**. If the **ACAD** standard menu doesn't appear on your screen, from AutoCAD's **Command:** prompt,

Type: MENU (RETURN)

Response: File name:

Type: ACAD

Response: Loading menu file...

When your standard AutoCAD menu appears on the screen, create three random lines. Now erase these lines, using your **ERASE** and **L** commands.

The best CAD operators go so fast they frequently make mistakes, usually on the last few objects entered. The AutoCAD **ERASE** command has a **LAST** option that allows you to go to the **EDIT** menu, select the **ERASE** command, then select the **LAST** option from the **ERASE** submenu.

If you want to erase the last three objects, you must select **ERASE**, then **LAST**, for each object you want to erase, a process that requires six selections, or "picks." How can this operation be streamlined to save you time?

Tip: There is, of course, the **UNDO** command. By typing **U**, you erase all line segments placed with a command. But how can you erase one line segment at a time?

Consider for a moment how the backspace key works on a typical keyboard. As fast as you can hit the key, one character is removed from the CRT.

Can AutoCAD's **ERASE** function also be accomplished with fewer keystrokes? Shouldn't there be a new command called **ERASE-L** (combining **ERASE** with the **LAST** options) that would "backspace" a drawing entity as fast as you could make a single selection? And wouldn't this routine be 100 percent faster than AutoCAD's "double-pick" **ERASE LAST** routine? Yes — on all counts! How can this operation be streamlined to save you time?

Consider for a moment how the **ERASE-L** command erases one line segment at a time. The proof lies in the **ERASE-L** macro that you'll create later in this chapter.

GETTING IN SYNC

Let's skip the formalities and go for some action by writing our first screen menu, thus dispelling the myth that menus are difficult. Do you have ten minutes? Okay, let's begin.

It's very important that you follow the procedures step by step. Because AutoCAD systems are often configured differently, we must bring all readers to the same starting point by using one common denominator: DOS. First let's find your DOS files and place certain files where needed.

Exit AutoCAD to DOS. If your DOS is menu-driven, exit the menu system as well. When you're at the DOS level, this prompt should appear on the left side of the screen:

```
C>
```

DOS doesn't tell you automatically if you're in a sub-directory. Subdirectories are like file drawers, but you don't know yet what "drawer" you're in. DOS does give you the means to change the **C** prompt to include the current sub-directory. To instruct DOS to give you a new prompt that includes sub-directory names (path),

Type: PROMPT=PG   (RETURN)

Response: Your C prompt now should look like this:

C:\>

The backslash, \, indicates that you're in the **ROOT** directory. If you're not, our new prompt will tell where you are. If you *are* in your AutoCAD directory, the prompt may look like this:

C:\ACAD>

which indicates you're one level down, in the **ACAD** directory, which is where you'll want to be later. If you're not in the **ROOT** directory (or whatever the name if it's a separate directory), you'll have to explore.

Type: CD \   (RETURN)

Response: C:\>

This puts you in the **ROOT** directory. **CD** stands for **C**hange **D**irectory. The \ identifies the **ROOT** directory.

Type: DIR/P   (RETURN)   (/**P** means Pause.)

This pulls up a screen directory of your disk with a pause, so you can see one screen full of information at a time. Look for (and make note of) the following files and directories: anything beginning with **ACAD**, **EDLIN**, **TREE**, **FORMAT** or **DOS**. If you have an AutoCAD directory, it might be called **ACAD**, **ACAD9**, **ACAD10**, **CAD**, **AUTO**, **ADESK**, **DRAW**, etc.

If **EDLIN.COM** doesn't appear on your screen, but you have a DOS directory:

Type: DIR DOS   (RETURN)   (or **DIR DOS/P** for Pause.)

You can recognize a directory since **DIR** appears in the line. During a DOS directory listing, DOS leaves out the period between the filename (the first eight characters) and the extension (the last three characters). The **EDLIN** listing would look like this:

```
EDLIN   COM    7621  8-30-87 12:00p
```

where 7621 is the size of the file in bytes (eight binary digits, or bits). The date and time are obvious.

You should find **EDLIN.COM** there. Regardless, you need a copy of **EDLIN.COM** in both the **ROOT** directory and in your AutoCAD directory. (We'll keep it simple for now; later we'll explain a DOS path.) You also need **TREE.COM** and **FORMAT.COM** in the **ROOT** directory.

If you can't find these files, let's copy them from your DOS system diskette. From the DOS prompt **C:\ >**, place your DOS system diskette in the **A:** or **B:** drive and:

Type: COPY A:EDLIN.COM C: (RETURN) (or B:)

Response: 1 File(s) copied

Type: COPY A:TREE.COM C: (RETURN)

Response: 1 File(s) copied

Type: COPY A:FORMAT.COM C: (RETURN)

Response: 1 File(s) copied

If you haven't seen an "AutoCAD type" directory, or the files themselves (**ACAD.EXE** and **ACAD.OVL**, etc.), then use the DOS **TREE** command to show a listing of the "tree structured" directories on the hard disk.

Type: TREE   (RETURN)

You'll see a listing of only directories. (A **CTRL-S** will stop the scrolling. Hit any other key to resume.) Make note of the most likely directory name that may contain your AutoCAD files. Now let's make sure they're in place:

Type: CD ACAD (RETURN) (Or your AutoCAD directory name.)

Response: C:\ACAD>   (You're now "down" one directory in **ACAD**.)

Type: DIR/P (RETURN)   (List the contents of the current directory, pausing at each full screen.)

Response: Volume in drive C has no label
Directory of C:\ACAD

ACAD	EXE	250784	6-05-86	2:06p
ACADL	OVL	68160	3-21-86	5:43p
ACAD1	MID	140	3-24-86	9:18a
ACAD	OVL	196234	4-04-86	12:31a
ACAD1	OVL	78154	11-01-85	10:40a

etc.

(**CTRL-C** will abort the scrolling.)

Now that you've done a little exploring, copy **EDLIN.COM** to your AutoCAD directory.

Type: COPY A:EDLIN.COM C:\ACAD (RETURN) (or B:)

Response: 1 File(s) copied

Note: Throughout the book, the directory of your AutoCAD files is referred to as **ACAD**. If your directory name is different, substitute it for **ACAD**, or change the name of your AutoCAD directory to **ACAD**. (To avoid confusion, you might want to incorporate the AutoCAD revision number into the directory, such as **ACAD10**, **ACAD9** or **ACAD262**.) Here's how to rename your AutoCAD directory:

From **C:\,**

Type: RN [Your Directory Name] ACAD

Let's continue. If you're not in the **ACAD** directory,

Type: CD\ACAD (RETURN) (Don't use this step if your **ACAD**
                              files are in the **ROOT** directory.)

Response: C:\ACAD>

(or **Type: CD\ (RETURN)**, if your AutoCAD files are in the **ROOT** directory. After reading on, you may want to create an **ACAD** directory, **COPY** your files to it, then **DEL**ete them from the **ROOT**. We'll give you the tools.)

CREATING YOUR FIRST MENU WITH MACROS

By now, you should be ready to write your first menu, called **MY1ST.MNU**. It will have a title that appears on the screen and will combine two often-used AutoCAD functions: **LINE** and **ERASE LAST** (discussed earlier in this chapter).

After you've created this macro, you'll be able to "erase the last entity" you drew in one step instead of two, saving time!

First, move down into the AutoCAD directory:

Type: CD\ACAD   (RETURN)

Response: C:\ACAD>

From the DOS prompt, **C:\ACAD >**, to clear your screen of all previous "garbage,"

Type: CLS   (RETURN)

Response: a clean screen

Now from the operating system prompt, **C:\ACAD**

Type: EDLIN MY1ST.MNU   (RETURN)[1]

Response: New File
           *

The asterisk (*) is the prompt for EDLIN, meaning that it's waiting for your instructions.

Type: I   (RETURN)   **(I stands for Input.)**

Response: 1:*

You're ready to enter your first line.

---

[1]As you're using EDLIN and creating macros, you'll undoubtedly make mistakes. For now, here's a quick way to cancel mistakes and start over:
Type: CTRL-C
Response: *
Type   Q(RETURN)
Response: Abort edit (Y/N)?
Type: Y(RETURN)
Response: C\ACAD>
    Now start over (For example: EDLIN MY1ST.MNU).

Type: [MY FIRST]   (RETURN)   (Always include the brackets, as shown.)

Response: 1: [MY FIRST]
2:*

You guessed it—time for the second line.

Type: [MENU]

Response: 1: [MY FIRST]
2: [MENU]
3:*

Type: [LINE]LINE
[ERASE-L]ERASE;L;;

Your screen now should look like this:

```
EDLIN MY1ST.MNU
New File
*I
  1: [MY FIRST]
  2: [ MENU ]
  3: [LINE]LINE
  4: [ERASE-L]ERASE;L;;
  5:*
```

To exit EDLIN's Input mode, type in a ^C (CTRL-C) by
holding down the **CTRL** key and tapping the **C** key, much
as you use the **Shift** key.

Response: *

To **E**xit EDLIN and save your menu,

Type: E   (RETURN)

Response: C:\ACAD>

LET'S TRY IT!

Run AutoCAD.[2] Open a new drawing (task 1 of the **MAIN** menu). Call it **TEST**. From AutoCAD's **Command**: prompt,

Type: MENU   (RETURN or SPACE) (AutoCAD's command for a new menu.)

Response: File Name:

Type: MY1ST   (RETURN or SPACE) (the **.mnu** extension is assumed.)

Response: Menu file loading ...

Now you should see something familiar — the screen menu you created!

Note: Unless otherwise specified, AutoCAD assumes a side-screen menu rather than a pop-down or tablet menu.

Pick the **LINE** function and draw a few lines. Hit the space bar, then pick **ERASE-L**. You just erased a line. Pick it as fast as you can until all the lines are erased. See how fast it works? **ERASE-L** is a true macro that combines a command with an option and two **RETURNS**.

Now draw a few more lines. Without hitting **RETURN** or **SPACE**, try **ERASE-L**. **Invalid**, right? You must cancel the **LINE** command before using **ERASE-L**. You can improve

---

[2]You may have to activate your screen menu by going into the **configuration task** from the main menu and giving a **Yes** response to the screen menu selection question during configuration of the video display. Type **0** to **exit** the configuration process. You should be back in the main menu, but sometimes you first must restart AutoCAD.

on that! But first, **END** the **TEST** drawing, saving it. And this leads us to Rule 1:

Rule 1: A menu command should automatically cancel any previous command. Menus—tablet or screen—are more productive if you can change your mind at any time without worrying about canceling a prior action.

REVISING YOUR FIRST MACRO

Let's edit **MY1ST.MNU** to correct the problem of having to cancel the **LINE** command before using **ERASE-L**. **QUIT** your drawing, **EXIT** AutoCAD and return to the DOS operating system environment, **C:\ACAD >**.

Type: EDLIN MY1ST.MNU   (RETURN)

Response: End of input file
              *

Type: L   (RETURN)   **(L** stands for **List.)**

Response: 1:*[MY FIRST]
              2: [MENU]
              3: [LINE]LINE
              4: [ERASE-L]ERASE;L;;
              *

Type: 3   (RETURN)

Response: 3:*[LINE]LINE
              3:*

EDLIN is waiting for you to type in a new line or corrections.

Type: [LINE]^C^CLINE   (RETURN) (See note on next page.)

Response: *

> **Note:** To enter the ^C, you must type **SHIFT 6**, which produces the caret. Then you enter a **C**. You can't use the **CTRL** key while typing **C** because EDLIN interprets this as a **CANCEL** or **ABORT**.

Type: 4   (RETURN)

Response: 4:*[ERASE L]ERASE;L;;

Type: 4:*[ERASE L]^C^CERASE;L;;   (RETURN)

Response: *

Type: L   (RETURN)   (List, to view your modifications.)

Response: 1: [MY FIRST]
                  2: [MENU]
                  3: [LINE]^C^CLINE
                  4:* [ERASE L]^C^CERASE;L;;
                  *

Type: E   (RETURN)

Response: C:\ACAD>   (If **ACAD** is your AutoCAD directory name.)

> To explain, while drawing, you can cancel any command in AutoCAD with a ^C (hold down the **CTRL** key while tapping the **C** key, **CTRL-C**). If you're in the middle of a dimension, you must do it twice. The first ^C cancels the dimensioning command, returning you to the **DIM:** prompt. The second ^C returns you to AutoCAD's

Command: prompt. That's why we use two ^C's in front of commands.

Reboot AutoCAD (type **ACAD**) and try this newly modified menu with your **TEST** drawing. See how much additional time and work you save! (Use AutoCAD's **MENU** command to load as before.) This time **end** your drawing.

When you load the drawing again, using task **2** of the **MAIN** menu, **MY1ST** automatically will be there. AutoCAD stores the name of the last menu used with the drawing.

You may want to keep **MY1ST.MNU**. If so, play it safe and put it on a floppy. While we're at it, let's consider another important rule:

Rule 2: SAVE your work often! **SAVE** whenever you're not willing to redo or redraw something. When you draw, keep a floppy marked "safety" nearby.

It's not good practice to save directly to a floppy disk. If it's a large file and you run out of floppy disk space during the save, you can be in trouble. It's best to save first to your hard disk then copy the file to the floppy using the DOS **COPY** command. This may be done outside of AutoCAD or by using the **SHELL** procedures.

Because you want to develop good work habits that prevent data loss (which nullifies your productivity gains), copy **MY1ST.MNU** and **TEST.DWG** to a new floppy.

Exit AutoCAD to DOS. Change Directory (**CD**) to either your **ROOT** or DOS directory where **FORMAT.COM** is located.

First, place a floppy diskette in the **A:** drive and

Type: FORMAT A: (RETURN)   (or B:)

Follow the prompts. When finished formatting,

Type: CD \ACAD   (RETURN)

Response: C:\ACAD>

Type: `COPY MY1ST.MNU B:`   (RETURN) (or A:)

Response: `1 File(s) copied`

Type: `COPY TEST.DWG B:`   (RETURN) (or A:)

Response: `1 File(s) copied`

   Note: If you have a 286 or 386 class computer, see below.[3]

SUMMARY

What did you learn in creating your first menu? First, you poked around in DOS to find the tools and locations of needed files, programs and directories. You then learned a few commands in EDLIN (**I** = Input, **L** = List, **E** = End, and that a line number causes a line to appear for re-entry).

   With EDLIN you created, used and edited a menu containing your first macro. (For a handy list of EDLIN commands, refer to Appendix B.)

   You used some miscellaneous AutoCAD conventions. As you must suspect, words within square brackets **[ ]** are titles that appear on your screen. The ^**C** must be entered with two keys, a **SHIFT 6** followed with a **C**. The semicolon (**;**) denotes a **RETURN** or **SPACE**.

   Finally, you learned Rule 1, which states that a good menu must let you change your mind by touching the next command, not a cancel key. And Rule 2 reminds you to save your work often.

   Some important DOS commands were used: **CD, CLS, COPY, DIR, DIR/P, EDLIN, FORMAT, PROMPT, TREE, TYPE** and ****. These essential DOS commands help you

---

[3] The top drive, A:, is a 1.2 Mbyte drive. It requires special "HD" diskettes. When a floppy is formatted or written to, in a 1.2 Mbyte drive, it's generally unreadable by the standard 360K floppy drive. If your AT has a second floppy drive, it's **B:**, and is usually a 360K floppy. If you want to communicate via floppy with other PCs and XTs, use **B:** drive.

increase productivity through the proper and informed use of your computer's operating system, bypassing some of AutoCAD's less flexible file utilities. For a quick reference, a list and explanation of DOS commands appear in Appendix A.

Fine Tuning
Your System

IN THIS CHAPTER

In trying to master CAD productivity, you may tend to ignore DOS and disk management. After all, DOS is largely
hidden, somewhat intimidating and doesn't actually make
drawings.

However, soon after you begin to use AutoCAD, strange
problems may crop up. For example, a hard disk that
shows two Mbytes of free space might produce a **disk full**
error. Or a 20-Mbyte hard disk or floppy disk with 50 percent free space might suddenly give you a **directory full**
error. Your system may become inexplicably sluggish.
You may lose drawings for no apparent reason or, worse,
delete or reformat the entire hard disk.

Proper use of DOS can prevent these and other
problems and save you time. In addition, certain DOS
routines are important in learning to create and edit
macros and menus.

In this chapter, you'll become more comfortable with a
number of DOS commands vital to system management
and AutoCAD customization. You'll cover:

— a general description of DOS and reasons why you
  should come to grips with this important productivity
  tool.

— tips and techniques for managing your drawings and
  data on a hard disk.

— how to fine-tune your system, including an easy way to increase your computer's speed by 20 percent.

Many users have lost drawings and data because of the lack of DOS knowledge. Just learning how to manage your hard disk can save you time and avoid catastrophes.

DOS—AUTOCAD'S MANAGER

To fully utilize AutoCAD, you must understand how your computer's operating system works. Simply stated, DOS manages your equipment. AutoCAD doesn't communicate directly with your hardware. It communicates with DOS, which then decides how to handle your request.

Because DOS is the controlling "middle man" and many procedures cannot be executed without it (such as formatting a diskette), you'll want to learn about it sooner or later. How about right now?

YOUR "HIDDEN" DOS FILES

DOS contains three parts: "hidden" system files, **COMMAND.COM** and *utility* files. Your hidden DOS "system" files don't appear when you ask for a directory of your disk. They're loaded into the working memory of your computer, RAM (Random Access Memory), with **COMMAND.COM** and take up about 65K RAM. These two hidden files and **COMMAND.COM** form the core of your computer's operating system. These files give you continuous access to frequently used DOS commands, such as **DIR**, **TYPE** and **COPY**.

When you **FORMAT** a diskette with the /**S** option, these three system files always transfer to the floppy, making it "bootable."

What does *"boot"* mean? Short for bootstrap, *"boot"* derives from the colloquialism "pulling yourself up by your bootstraps"—which is exactly what the computer does each time you turn it on.

On start-up, your computer responds to only two instructions: 1) "Go look at **A:**; if you find a disk there, pull in the operating system"; and 2) "If there's no disk in **A:** or no operating system on the diskette, then look at **C:** for the operating system."

DOS is a shortened name for PC-DOS (supplied by IBM) and MS-DOS (for non-IBM compatibles), both written by Microsoft Corporation. AutoCAD requires DOS Version 2.1 or higher.

DOS UTILITIES

We talked about the portion of DOS that resides in memory, part of which is the hardware management function (such as reading the keyboard or sending data to the plotter and CRT). The other part consists of frequently used utility commands, including **DIR**ectory, **TYPE**, **CD** (Change Directory), **MD** (Make Directory), **RD** (Remove Directory), **COPY**, **DEL**ete, **REN**ame, etc.

Because other DOS functions are used less frequently, they're not pulled into valuable RAM space, but reside on your disk in separate *executable* files. You can recognize these files by their **.COM** or **.EXE** extensions. (Files with **.BAT** extension, **BATCH** files, are the only other executable files. **BATCH** files are user-defined DOS macros.)

Let's get a listing of these "external" (vs. "internal," RAM-based) DOS commands. From your **ROOT** directory **C:\ >**,

Type:　　DIR

Response:　　Volume in drive C has no label

Directory of C:\

ASSIGN	COM	1509	8-30-85	12:00p
BASIC	COM	3400	8-30-85	12:00p
BASICA	COM	3400	8-30-85	12:00p
CHKDSK	COM	9435	8-30-85	12:00p
COMP	COM	4168	8-30-85	12:00p

DEBUG	COM	15536	8-30-85	12:00p
DISKCOMP	COM	4023	8-30-85	12:00p
DISKCOPY	COM	3630	8-30-85	12:00p
EDLIN	COM	7261	8-30-85	12:00p
FDISK	COM	15334	8-30-85	12:00p
FORMAT	COM	6957	8-30-85	12:00p
MODE	COM	5187	8-30-85	12:00p
MORE	COM	282	8-30-85	12:00p
PRINT	COM	8291	8-30-85	12:00p
TREE	COM	9740	8-30-85	12:00p
ATTRIB	EXE	7438	8-30-85	12:00p
BACKUP	EXE	21720	8-30-85	12:00p
BASICA	EXE	88640	8-30-85	12:00p
EXE2BIN	EXE	2816	8-30-85	12:00p
FIND	EXE	6403	8-30-85	12:00p
JOIN	EXE	8956	8-30-85	12:00p
LABEL	EXE	2750	8-30-85	12:00p
LINK	EXE	38422	8-30-85	12:00p
RESTORE	EXE	20320	9-12-85	12:56a
SETUP	EXE	31488	6-30-86	10:37p
SHARE	EXE	8352	8-30-85	12:00p
SORT	EXE	1664	8-30-85	12:00p
SUBST	EXE	9910	8-30-85	12:00p

The filename (**fname**, maximum eight characters) is left-justified, while the extension (**.EXT**, maximum three characters) is right-justified. DOS directories don't indicate the period (.) required to separate the filename from the extension.

Note: To execute a file, you need type only the filename, not the extension.

The files (executable programs) you'll use in this chapter are **EDLIN.COM**, **FORMAT.COM**, **TREE.COM** and **CHKDSK.COM**.

TUNING UP YOUR COMPUTER

Before you begin writing menus and macros, your computer must be running at peak efficiency. In achieving productivity, a top-performing computer is as important as a time-saving macro.

Let's continue to explore your disk to familiarize you with the DOS tools that make creating menus, macros and programs easier.

AUTOCAD'S FILE UTILITIES

Although Autodesk has provided the **File Utilities** menu as a convenience for the new AutoCAD user, a sound knowledge of DOS is a must for achieving peak productivity and maintaining your hard disk. In fact, proficient AutoCAD users will use the **SHELL** command to execute DOS commands while drawing.

Let's consider some special DOS functions important to your productivity with AutoCAD and to the use of this book. By no means are the following discussions exhaustive, but they provide a springboard for your continued learning. Some of the more commonly used DOS commands are listed in Appendix B.

If you turned off your computer after completing the last chapter, you may get the plain **C** prompt when you turn it on again. If so,

Type: PROMPT=PG

Response: C:\>

each time you boot your computer to show the directory path; it will then be directed to the **ROOT** directory.

FREE—A 20 PERCENT SPEED INCREASE

You can easily increase processing speed by 20 percent by 1) modifying the **CONFIG.SYS** file, if you have one, or 2) adding **CONFIG.SYS** file to your **ROOT** directory. Before you learn to do this, record the time it takes to boot AutoCAD (you may have to change the directory to **ACAD**). We'll retime it after the exercise is complete.

CONFIG.SYS is a file that your DOS operating system "looks at" during boot-up. Many AutoCAD systems don't have the **CONFIG.SYS** file. To find out if yours does, first use the **C**hange **D**irectory (**CD**) command to make sure you're in the **ROOT** directory.

Type: CD\ (RETURN)

Response: C:\>

Next, ask for a listing of the **ROOT** directory and look for the **CONFIG.SYS** file.

Type: DIR (RETURN)

Did that go by too fast? Let's tell it to **P**ause.

Type: DIR/P (RETURN)   (Use a forward slash.)

Now it stops for each full screen of directory information, waiting for you to **Strike a key when ready . . .** (for another full screen).
Another handy option is the wide directory that allows you to view four times the number of files at once.

Type: DIR/W (RETURN)   (**W** = **W**ide)

You can even type in **DIR/P/W** if your directory is really full. By now you should have determined whether you in fact have the **CONFIG.SYS** file. The direct approach to find a single file is:

Type: DIR CONFIG.SYS (RETURN)

Response: CONFIG   SYS   23   6-21-86 3:11p
             1 file(s)   9986048 bytes free

Or, if you'd like to see all the system files:

Type:　　`DIR *.SYS (RETURN)`　　　　(This lists all the **.SYS** files; the * is a wild card.)

    A **File not found** message means you don't have **CONFIG.SYS**, which has to be in the **ROOT** directory to work. (If you don't have the file, we'll create it — see "IF YOU DO NOT HAVE A CONFIG.SYS FILE..." below.)

    If you *do* have the **CONFIG.SYS** file, we'll either add or modify the **BUFFERS** and **FILES** statements. The file may contain other statements important for running other programs or devices, so be careful not to lose what's already there. Let's view the file's contents.

Type:　　`TYPE CONFIG.SYS (RETURN)`

    After your **TYPE** command displays the **CONFIG.SYS** file, you may see the following two lines:

`FILES=22`

`BUFFERS=32`　　　(or more)

    These numbers represent minimum values for peak performance. **FILES** and **BUFFERS** instruct the computer to set aside some RAM to improve disk performance; **22** and **32** are recommended averages. However, you may get better results with different numbers.

    Let's now review an example showing you how to modify an existing file. First, use the DOS **COPY** command to make a safety copy:

Type:　　`COPY CONFIG.SYS CONFIG.SAV` 　(RETURN) (.SAV = SAVE)

Rule 3: Never edit a file without a backup or safety file.

Type: EDLIN CONFIG.SYS

Response: End of input file

Type: L (RETURN)   (**L** = **List**, to view the file.)

If the **BUFFERS** and **FILES** commands exist, and you want to change the numbers,

Type: 2   (RETURN)   (Or line number of **BUFFERS** to be changed.)

Typical Response: 2:*BUFFERS=10
                         2:*

Type: BUFFERS=32 (RETURN)

Response: *

Type: 3   (RETURN)   (Or line number of **FILES** to be changed.)

Typical Response: 3:*FILES=5
                         3:*

Type:

FILES=22 (RETURN)

Response: *

Type: E (RETURN)

Response: C:\>

If the **BUFFERS** and/or **FILES** statements are missing, then **INSERT** them. From your EDLIN ***** prompt:

Type: I   (RETURN)   (If **FILES** or **BUFFERS** are *not* in the file.)

Response: 1:*

Add the lines with **I** (Insert or Input). You can add the lines at a specific line number by starting with the line number. For example, to add a line at line **3**, type **3I**. The current line **3** will be pushed down to line **4** and you can continue to add lines, pushing the original line **3** further down the ladder. To finish,

Type: ^C   (Exit the Input mode.)

Response: *

Type: L   (RETURN)   (To list your work and view errors.)

If you made a mistake, enter the line number and correct it. Otherwise,

Type: E   (RETURN)   (**E** = End)

IF YOU DO *NOT* HAVE A CONFIG.SYS FILE IN YOUR ROOT DIRECTORY....

Type: EDLIN CONFIG.SYS   (RETURN)

Response: New file

Type: I   (RETURN)   (I = Input)

Response: 1:*

Type: FILES=22   (RETURN)

Response: 2:*

Type: BUFFERS=32   (RETURN)

Response: 3:*

Type: ^C   (CTRL-C)

Response: *

Type: L   (RETURN)   (To list your work and view mistakes.)

Type: E   (RETURN)   (E = End)

Response: C:\>

ANOTHER KIND OF CAD

The only time DOS looks at **CONFIG.SYS** is during boot-up, so you'll perform a *warm boot*, or "**CAD**" the system.

Tip: In this case, **CAD** stands for **CTRL-ALT-DEL**. When these keys are pressed simultaneously, the system will reboot. This is preferable to turning the CPU **off** and **on** (although sometimes **off-and-on** is the only method that works when a lockup occurs).

Change to your **ACAD** directory and boot AutoCAD. You should notice at least a 20 percent increase in speed if you did not previously have a **CONFIG.SYS** file with **FILES** and **BUFFERS**. (Speed improvement is less obvious if you increased the values of an existing **CONFIG.SYS** file.)

If you'd like to restore your old **CONFIG.SYS** file, remember that you made a safety copy, **CONFIG.SAV**. First, delete the current file:

Type: DEL CONFIG.SYS   (RETURN)

Then rename your safety:

Type: REN CONFIG.SAV CONFIG.SYS   (RETURN)

Now you're back to square one. In addition to the safety copy you intentionally created, EDLIN automatically created a backup file, **CONFIG.BAK**. AutoCAD also does this with your drawing, giving you lots of insurance against losing valuable data.

IMPROVED PROMPT — MANAGING THE HARD DISK WITH DIRECTORIES

To improve CAD productivity, you must master hard-disk management. You must manage the data (drawings) and know where files and programs are located.

At first, every user is overwhelmed by the hard disk; after all, you can't see inside it. You store a tremendous number of drawings on the hard disk; if all the files are in one directory (usually the **ROOT** or top directory), it becomes unmanageable.

DOS allows you to segregate your drawings and other data in different directories, like different file drawers. Although DOS doesn't automatically indicate what file drawer you're in, your new prompt does.

In Chapter One and at the beginning of this chapter, you were asked to alter your prompt with **PROMPT = PG**. **$P** causes the DOS **PATH** to be displayed, showing you both the current directory and how you got there (i.e., path). **$G** places "`>`" at the end. (You could have some fun with **PROMPT = HURRY UP – I'M WAITING PG!**)

Rather than retype your improved prompt every day, you can activate it on boot-up through the **AUTOEXEC.BAT** file.

Just as it does with **CONFIG.SYS**, DOS always looks for this file – a DOS **BATCH** file – in the **ROOT** directory on start-up.

Much like AutoCAD macros, a DOS **BATCH** file allows you to group many instructions together and execute them with one "pseudo" command. All **BATCH** files have the extension of **.BAT** (short for **batch**), but to execute them, don't type in the **.BAT** extension. (The same is true for **.EXE** and **.COM** files.)

Let's look for **AUTOEXEC.BAT**. Because it has to be in the **ROOT** directory, be sure you're in the **ROOT** directory.

Type: `CD\>`

Type: `DIR AUTOEXEC.BAT (RETURN)`

Response: `AUTOEXEC BAT   30  7-02-86  5:53am`

(If it's not there, you'll get a **File not found** message. Proceed to "**IF YOU DO** *NOT* **HAVE AN AUTOEXEC.BAT FILE**," where you'll create one as you did **CONFIG.SYS**.)

If you found your **AUTOEXEC.BAT** file, let's take a look.

Type: `TYPE AUTOEXEC.BAT`

This is how a typical **AUTOEXEC.BAT** file might read:

```
ECHO OFF
CLS
DATE
TIME
PATH C:\;C:\ACAD;C:\UTIL;C:\WP;C:\DOS
CHKDSK C:
```

```
SET LISPHEAP=39000
SET LISPSTACK=5000
SET ACADFREERAM=24
SET ACADEXMEM=1400
```

ECHO OFF means that commands aren't *echoed* to the screen, so you won't see the execution of commands that follow **ECHO OFF**. (There are also **ECHO ON** and **ECHO TEXT** where **TEXT** displays words for you to review.) **CLS** is **CL**ear **S**creen (used in Chapter One).

DATE and **TIME** prompt you for the correct date and time. If your computer has an internal clock, you normally hit (**RETURN**) to accept the current date and time.

PATH tells DOS to look for executable files in the listed directories. This allows you to be in one directory and run programs in another. For example, you could run AutoCAD from within a sub-directory called **JOB1**.

CHKDSK checks for lost disk space or other irregularities. In order to fix any of these problems, you must use **CHKDSK/F**. This should never be placed in the **AUTOEXEC.BAT** file, because there are some errors that are fatal to your disk and files if they're "fixed." Only "Lost Clusters" should be "fixed" routinely. But, by placing **CHKDSK** without **/F** in the **AUTOEXEC.BAT** file, you'll be informed of any disk irregularities that might exist.

The last three lines allocate memory for AutoCAD. They should be added if you have Version 2.18 or higher and intend to use AutoLISP. **lispheap** and **lispstack** can add up to a maximum of 45,000 bytes. **Acadfreeram = 24** controls the I/O page space. If this statement is left out, the low default value results in the **out of RAM** statement, which "bombs" your drawing session. **Acadexmem** is optional and sets up the use of extra memory above 1 Mbyte. See AutoCAD's *Installation Guide*, Performance section. So let's add our improved prompt at line **3**. From **C:\>**,

Type: EDLIN AUTOEXEC.BAT   (RETURN)

Type: 3I   (RETURN)   (Begin to Insert lines at line **3**.)

Response: 3:*

Type: PROMPT=PG (RETURN)

Type: SET LISPHEAP=39000   (RETURN)

Type: SET LISPSTACK=5000   (RETURN)

Type: SET ACADFREERAM=24   (RETURN)

Type: ^C   (CTRL-C)

Type: L   (RETURN)   (List file to check yourself.)

Type: E   (RETURN)   (End.)

IF YOU DO *NOT* HAVE AN AUTOEXEC.BAT FILE...

Type: EDLIN AUTOEXEC.BAT   (RETURN)

Response: New file

Type: I (RETURN)   (Begin to Insert lines at line **1**.)

Response: 1:*

Type: ECHO OFF   (RETURN)

Type: DATE   (RETURN)

Type: TIME   (RETURN)

Type: PROMPT=PG   (RETURN)

Type: SET LISPHEAP=39000   (RETURN)

Type: SET LISPSTACK=5000 (RETURN)

Type: SET ACADFREERAM=24   (RETURN)

Type: ^C   (CTRL-C)

Type: L   (RETURN)   **(List file to check yourself.)**

Type: E   (RETURN)   **(End)**

Reboot your system (**CTRL-ALT-DEL**) and see the new prompt. To give it a full test, let's make some directories.

Type: MD PROJECT1   (RETURN)   (**M**ake **D**irectory **PROJECT1**.)

Type: CD PROJECT1   (RETURN)   (**C**hange **D**irectory to **PROJECT1**, one level down.)

Response: C:\PROJECT1>

Type: MD ELECTR   (RETURN)   (**M**ake sub**d**irectory **ELECTR**ical.)

Type: CD ELECTR   (RETURN)   (Move another level down.)

Response: C:\PROJECT1\ELECTR>

Type: CD .. (RETURN)   (The .. places you back
                                     one directory.)

Response: C:\PROJECT1>

Type: CD .. (RETURN)   (Like **CD**, this places you in the
                              ROOT directory. You should never
                              be lost again. Directories are ideal
                              for categorizing drafting disciplines
                              and projects.)

WHEN IS A TREE NOT A TREE?

Remember the DOS **TREE** command from Chapter One?
Where did they get a name like that? Imagine that the
ROOT directory is the trunk. There might be a big branch
like the AutoCAD directory, then a secondary branch for
the project and, finally, a smaller branch for the discipline
within the project. On that branch are leaves which represent the files and drawings.

If you were an ant on the ground trying to tell a buddy
how to get to a leaf, you would describe a path much as
you would direct a lost motorist. In DOS, that path can actually be used as part of the filename. Here's how it looks:

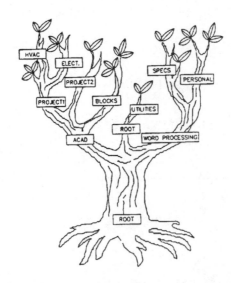

Now let's use a **BATCH** file to switch directories more quickly.

Type: EDLIN E.BAT   (RETURN)   (Opens a new file.)

Type: I   (RETURN)   (Input)

Type: CD\PROJECT1\ELECTR   (RETURN)

Type: ^C   (CTRL-C)

Type: E (RETURN)   (End, saving **E.BAT**.)

At the DOS prompt **C:\ >**,

Type: E   (RETURN)

Response: C:\PROJECT1\ELECTR>

CD** takes you back to the **ROOT directory, and **E (.bat)** takes you back into the **\PROJECT1\ELECTR** subdirectory. Try it a couple of times.

Now let's quickly learn how to remove unwanted directories. From **C:\ >**,

Type: RD \PROJECT1\ELECTR   (RETURN) **(Remove Directory)**

Type: RD \PROJECT1   (RETURN)

Another advantage of using sub-directories to manage your hard disk is that, unlike the **ROOT** directory, sub-directories can have an unlimited number of files.

Tip: Limit your sub-directories to two or three levels deep. You'll save time in the long run. Use **BATCH** files to automatically switch directories, or even boot AutoCAD.

Your **BATCH** files should have one- or two-character names, such as **EL.BAT** for electrical.

Typical ways to use directories: Set up a separate directory for each customer, each discipline (electrical, mechanical, etc.), each month, a series of drawing numbers, each CAD user.

You can use DOS path names in AutoCAD. Imagine the following scenario: You're in the **\PROJECT1\ELECTR** directory and you need an electrical symbol stored in a sub-directory called **ELEC-SYM**, off the **ACAD** directory. You could use the AutoCAD **INSERT** command like this:

Command: `INSERT    (RETURN)`

`Block name (or ?): \ACAD\ELEC-SYM\outlet`

So, not only can you run AutoCAD from any directory, but you can **INSERT** any part of any other drawing from any sub-directory on any disk!

Tip: Put these path names in your menus so you never have to type them in.

If you like the idea of directories, but have everything jumbled up in the **ROOT** directory, you may want to move AutoCAD and drawings to their own directories. To do this with AutoCAD systems files, make a directory **(MD)**, **COPY** all the files to it, then **DEL**ete unwanted files. The following is a typical sequence, from **C:\ >**,

Type: `MD ACAD    (RETURN)`

Type: `COPY *.* \ACAD`

Response: `A lot of files will be copied.`

Type: `CD ACAD    (RETURN)`

Type: `DEL *.DWG  (RETURN)`   **(DEL**ete **d**rawings.)

Type: DEL *.BAK (RETURN)   **(DELete back-up files.)**

   Note: In this scenario, be sure to save **ACAD.DWG**, the prototype drawing.
   Then **DEL**ete the **.COM** files that were transferred from the operating system into the new directory (except **EDLIN.COM** and **TREE.COM**); then **DEL**ete any other non-AutoCAD files or programs.
   When you're sure AutoCAD is working from your new **ACAD** directory, change to the **ROOT** directory and **DEL**ete the duplicate AutoCAD files.

Another method involves reloading AutoCAD into the **ACAD** directory from your diskettes. You may want to create a directory called **\ACAD\DEMO** to hold AutoCAD demonstration drawings such as **NOZZLE**. You can follow this same method to move your drawing files to their directories.

Tip: Because you don't need the AutoCAD driver files on your hard disk after configuration, you can **DEL *.DRV** safely. If you change hardware frequently, you can put driver files in a **DRIVER** sub-directory.

   You should know that **BATCH** files are used by many third-party developers to "chain" application programs to AutoCAD. To gain insight into how these applications work, list out the ***.BAT** files **(DIR)** and then use the **TYPE** command to view their contents.

MAKING HARD COPIES OF DIRECTORIES

How do you know what's on a diskette? Usually you put it into the drive and type **DIR A:**, right? Wouldn't it be nice to have a slip of paper listing all of the files on your diskette or in a directory on your hard disk? No problem with a DOS pipe. A what?
   DOS naturally directs the output of the directory command to the screen, from which it's gone forever with a

CLS. However, you can redirect, or *pipe*, the output to a text file or printer. Turn on your printer.

Type: DIR > LPT1 (RETURN)   (The directory is piped to the printer attached to the first line printer port on your computer.)

Type: DIR > JUNK.TXT (RETURN) (The directory is piped to a text file on your hard disk.)

You might even type **DIR PROJ1*.DWG > LPT1** to send out a directory of specific drawings to the printer.

Tip: If you send the directory out to a text file, use the **IMPORT.LSP** routine in The AutoCAD Productivity Library to "zap" the directory (or any text file) to a drawing.

DOS stores the drawings in the order they were created, not alphabetically. You can use a DOS filter to sort them correctly.

Type: DIR ¦SORT>LPT1   (RETURN)

Pipes and filters also work with the **TYPE** and **COPY** commands. To print out the AutoCAD **HATCH** file, for instance, load the printer with tractor feed paper and

Type: TYPE ACAD.PAT>LPT1   (RETURN)

When customizing, you'll frequently need to print out your programs and menu code:

Type: TYPE MY1ST.MNU > LPT1 (RETURN)

PATH—RUNNING AUTOCAD FROM ANYWHERE

In the interest of better drawing management, wouldn't it be better to change into the directory holding the drawings for a particular project, run AutoCAD from within that directory (even though no AutoCAD files are present) and have all your drawings automatically placed in the directory without having to think about it? It's a great way to organize your data.

If you've been losing drawings, DOS's **PATH** command is the key to solving this vexing problem. **PATH** tells DOS to look in other directories for executable files/programs (**.BAT**, **.EXE** and **.COM** only) when they aren't located in the present directory. Below is a typical **PATH** statement.

```
PATH C:\;C:\DOS;C:\ACAD;C:\UTIL;C:\WP
```

Different directories are separated with a semicolon (;). This statement tells DOS, "If you can't find the command you're looking for in the current directory, then first try the **ROOT** directory (**C:\ >**). If you don't find it there, then try **DOS**, **ACAD**, **UTIL**, then **WP**."

In the path statement, the **C:\ACAD;** allows you to run AutoCAD from any directory. (Of course, you must substitute your AutoCAD directory name, or **C:\ >** if AutoCAD is in the **ROOT**.)

From the **ROOT** directory and DOS prompt, **C:\ >**,

Type: Path C:\ACAD (RETURN)   (Be sure to use your name
                                                                           for ACAD or \ for **ROOT**.)

Response: C:\>

Type: MD TEMP   (RETURN)   (Make a **TEMP**orary Directory.)

Type: CD TEMP   (RETURN)   (Change to the **TEMP**orary Directory.)

Response: C:\TEMP>

Type: ACAD   (RETURN)   (Run AutoCAD from within the **TEMP** directory.)

While in AutoCAD, begin a drawing called **TEST**. Draw a couple of lines and circles. **End** the drawing and **exit** AutoCAD.
From the DOS prompt, **C:\TEMP >**,

Type: DIR   (RETURN)

This is approximately what you should see:

```
Volume in drive C has no label
Directory of C:\TEMP
.   <DIR>
..  <DIR>
TEST   DWG   141  6-16-86   7:42a
3 File(s) 22654976 bytes free
C:\TEMP>
```

TEST.DWG was placed automatically in the current directory. The . and .. are the invisible directory files for the subdirectory.
Note: If this command doesn't work, make sure you have the proper name for the AutoCAD directory. When it works, add it to the **AUTOEXEC.BAT** file using EDLIN, so it will be automatically executed on start-up.

Type: CD\   (RETURN)   (Return to the **ROOT** directory.)

Response: C:\>

Type: DEL \TEMP*.*   (RETURN) (**DEL**etes all files from **TEMP** directory.)

Response: Are you sure? (Y/N)

Type: Y   (RETURN)   (**DEL**etes all files from **TEMP**.)

Type: RD TEMP   (RETURN)   (**R**emoves **TEMP D**irectory.)

Note: If AutoCAD has been exited by a power outage or during a lockup, some "hidden" files may be left behind. AutoCAD uses these files during operation, then automatically deletes them. You can't remove a directory unless it's empty of files and other sub-directories.

If you suspect hidden files, you must find them before you can delete them. A trick is to go into the "stubborn" directory, start a drawing, then quit and exit AutoCAD properly. This will not help if hidden files were created by another program. See Appendix D for suggested software.

IF YOU DO *NOT* HAVE A PATH COMMAND IN AUTOEXEC.BAT...

Type: EDLIN AUTOEXEC.BAT   (RETURN)

Type: 3I   (RETURN)   (You'll insert the **PATH** at line **3**.)

Response: 3:*

Type: PATH C:\;C:\DOS;C:\ACAD (RETURN) (Use your name
                                             or the AutoCAD
                                             directory.)

Type: CTRL-C

Type: E

Response: C:\>

Reboot the system (**CTRL-ALT-DEL**). You should now be able to run DOS commands and AutoCAD from any directory.

CREATING BACKUP FILES

AutoCAD creates a backup file (**fname.BAK**) every time you open an existing drawing and **END** it. Maintaining these **.BAK** files, which are rarely needed safety files, actually doubles the amount of disk space required. They tend to quickly accumulate from not only AutoCAD but EDLIN and other programs as well. You'll want to purge your hard disk of these usually unnecessary files.

But, before you delete, or *purge*, these files, let's explore their usefulness.

Assume you lost a drawing. Enter the following command for the sake of illustration:

Type: DIR *.BAK (RETURN)   (A listing of all backup files.)

Is there a backup copy of your lost drawing (for our purposes, any drawing that's had its extension changed from **.DWG** to **.BAK**)? A drawing with a **.BAK** extension probably isn't the most recent version, but, as an example, we'll recover it anyway.

AutoCAD won't open any drawing that doesn't have a **.DWG** extension. Therefore, you must rename the backup file to a name with a **.DWG** extension.

To illustrate, pick a backup file of your choice — one that you know was a drawing — and rename it. (Don't be thrown by the abstract names we used — substitute an actual file name.)

Type: REN FNAME.BAK NEWNAME.DWG (RETURN)

Type: DIR NEWNAME.DWG (RETURN)   (Prove the file was
                                                        renamed.)

Let's try it. Boct AutoCAD and call up **NEWNAME.DWG**.
With good hard-disk management and frequent **BACK-
UPS** to a floppy, **.BAK** files just clutter the disk.

Now it's time to **DEL**ete all of the backup files and free
up some storage.

Type: DEL *.BAK   (RETURN)

Type: DEL *.$*   (RETURN)   **(DEL**ete AutoCAD tem-
                                           porary files)

You should change to your other directories and delete
the **.BAK** files. If you have files named **JUNK**, **TRASH**,
PLAY, **TEST**, **TEMP**, etc., you should delete them as well.
This should be a routine procedure.

Tip: Use names like **JUNKxxx (.dwg)** or **TEMPxxx** for any
drawings to be deleted en masse. Cleanup is easy. Type
DEL JUNK*.*, etc. Or make a **BATCH** file called
CLEAN.BAT, with the following statements:

```
DEL *.BAK
DEL TEMP*.*
DEL JUNK*.*
DEL *.$*
DEL *.CHK
```

Rule 4: Before using the **DEL** command with wild cards
(*), make sure valuable data has been copied to a floppy.

Because DOS through 3.3 doesn't prompt you when it's
deleting a file, it can be dangerous using wild cards if you
aren't sure what's being deleted. If you use **DIR** with the
same wild-card sequence, you can see what will be
deleted when you use **DEL**.

MORE HARD-DISK CLEANUP — CHKDSK/F

Note: If you're a new AutoCAD user who has not yet cluttered your hard disk, or you have a smooth-running hard

disk, you can read this section without executing the commands. However, sooner or later you'll want this information, so you may want to earmark these pages.

When you lose a drawing, how much productivity do you lose? Or fail to gain? Hours!

Imagine this situation: You've checked your hard disk with the **DIR** command. It shows **4 Mbytes free**—a lot of free storage. So you boot up AutoCAD and begin drawing. However, you've forgotten to **SAVE** your drawing for the last three hours. You **HATCH** an area and up pops AutoCAD's famous **disk full** error! You've just lost three hours of work. How can this be?

Rule 2: (worth repeating) **SAVE** your drawing often! **SAVE** whenever you're not willing to redraw something. Keep a floppy marked **SAFETY** in your disk drive and **COPY** to it as well.

While in an AutoCAD drawing, you should copy to a floppy. An example from the **Command:** prompt:

Type: SHELL (RETURN)

Response: DOS Command

Type: COPY DWGNAME.DWG A: (RETURN)

Now, back to the first problem, the mysterious **disk full**. As you use your hard disk over time, you add and delete data. If you delete a 20K file and replace it with a 19K file, DOS may not be able to re-use that 1K "hole." It becomes a *lost cluster*.

In time, your disk may contain hundreds of lost clusters, which appear as free space but are unusable. However, you can recover those lost clusters.

Type: CHKDSK   (RETURN)   **(Check Disk.)**

Response: Errors found, F parameter not specified.

                     Corrections will not be written to disk.

```
5 lost clusters found in 5 chains.
Convert lost chains to files (Y/N)? y
33462272 bytes total disk space
110592 bytes in 14 hidden files
51200 bytes in 14 directories
10676224 bytes in 858 user files
10240 bytes would be in
5 recovered files
22614016 bytes available on disk
655360 bytes total memory
460848 bytes free
C:\>
```

The **Check Disk** command is so useful, you may want to include it in your **AUTOEXEC.BAT** file. It's important to use the /F option only after verifying that "lost clusters" is the only error; otherwise the lost clusters won't be recovered (as in the above example).

Type: CHKDSK/F   (RETURN)   **(F = Fix.)**

Response: 5 lost clusters found in 5 chains.
Convert lost chains to files (Y/N)? y

Type: Y   (RETURN)

Response: 33462272 bytes total disk space
110592 bytes in 14 hidden files
51200 bytes in 14 directories
10682368 bytes in 859 user files

```
10240 bytes in 5 recovered files
22624246 bytes available on disk
655360 bytes total memory
460848 bytes free
C:\>
```

Now the clusters have been recovered. DOS actually puts them in files named **FILE0000.CHK** through **FILE9999.CHK**. Unless you're a sophisticated programmer, these files aren't important. Let's delete them:

Type: `DEL *.CHK (RETURN)`

The mysterious **disk full** error has been solved, giving you more free space on your hard disk!

RESTORING YOUR FRAGMENTED HARD DISK

Your what? Bet you didn't know you had one. Again, if you're a new AutoCAD user and have a smooth-running hard disk, you should read this section without executing the commands. Sooner or later you'll need this information, so you may want to earmark these pages.

Does your disk seem tired and slow? If you've done all of the above in hopes of retrieving that peppy hard disk that came with your machine, with no such luck, let's revitalize it.

There's a reason why your disk slows down over time. When the disk is freshly formatted and you copy a new file from a floppy, it resides on one physical spot on the disk. When you create a drawing, it too occupies one uninterrupted spot, or "*contiguous sectors*," in computer jargon.

As you add and delete files from your disk, free spaces that are too small to hold one file develop on the disk. DOS utilizes these spaces by dividing your files into pieces.

When DOS runs out of space in a location, it places directions at the end of the sector as to where to find the next piece of the file. After a few months, your files are divided and scattered all over the disk. The read/write heads of your hard disk then must skip all over the disk to find the pieces. This is hardly efficient, and only gets worse.

Many operating systems have a command called **SQUEEZE**, or **CRUNCH**, which rearranges your files. DOS has no such command.

Here are techniques for compacting your disk:

1. **COPY** all your files to floppies, **FORMAT** the hard disk and **reload** the files.

A. **Type:** Format A: (RETURN)

Respond to the prompts and format 30 360K floppies for every 10 Mbytes of data on your hard disk.

B. Use either the DOS **COPY** command or **BACKUP** to move your files to the floppy diskettes.

When using the DOS **COPY** command, **COPY** all your files to the floppies. Be sure to **COPY** files in all sub-directories. When you're sure all your files and drawings are safely stored on floppies (or some other media), then:

C. Be brave—place the DOS system diskette in the **A:** drive and,

Type: A:FORMAT C:/S   (RETURN)   (Format the hard drive and copy over the operating system.)

You'll be given a second chance, but you'd better be sure. If you change your mind and quickly turn off the machine, you may not have done any damage. When you format the hard disk, all data will be lost.

D. After the **FORMAT**, which may take about 15 minutes, **COPY** all of the DOS commands back into the hard disk, make new sub-directories and **COPY** all of your files into them. This is called "rebuilding the hard disk." All your files are now "contiguous" and no longer in pieces.

Note: If you used **BACKUP**, then you must use **RE-STORE**.

Formatting the hard disk has one big advantage: it searches for physical defects on the hard disk surface and prevents DOS from using those areas. If any defects have developed, formatting may save you trouble with lost data down the road. Thus it is a good practice to format the hard drive at least once a year.

2.　If you have a tape backup system with a file-by-file capability, make a backup to tape. Format the hard disk, as in the previous example. Reload the tape system programs onto the hard disk or execute them from floppy. Perform a file-by-file restoration.

　　We highly recommend tape backup. In recent years, tapes have improved in both performance — dramatically — and affordability.

3.　Inexpensive software exists that will compact your disk without a backup and format procedure. The files are moved around on the hard disk until they're "contiguous" and the free space is also contiguous.

　　You first must perform the **CHKDSK/F** command, which doesn't have the advantage of the **FORMAT** method, but is a good deal easier and faster and should be done on a more regular basis.

THIRD-PARTY UTILITIES

Third-party utilities are indispensible tools for managing your hard disk. They help make up for the deficiencies in DOS. Some are in the public domain and can be obtained at no cost, while others cost a sum that is nominal relative to their functionality. Here are some available functions:

- *Text editors* that are much easier than EDLIN

- *Disk compaction*

- *Graphic representation* of the directories on your disk

‒ *Disk testing*, which shows problems that would result in lost data

‒ *Unerase*, which unerases a file that you deleted by accident

‒ *Move*, which combines the **COPY** and **DEL**ete commands

‒ *System information*, which lists the hardware on your system

‒ *File searching*, which finds that lost file in the obscure directory

‒ *Directory sorting*, which reorganizes the directory listings by any sorting method you choose

‒ *Format recovery*, which recovers an accidentally formatted hard disk

For more functions, see Appendix D.

SUMMARY

You've now tuned up your computer by learning:

1. Revision of **BUFFER** and **FILES** in the **CONFIG.SYS** file, resulting in a 20 percent speed improvement.

2. A fancy new DOS prompt (**PG**) that keeps you informed of what sub-directory you're in and facilitates the use of sub-directories and good hard-disk management (less loss of data and meaningful grouping of data/drawings).

3. A **PATH** command that allows you to run AutoCAD from within any directory, again promoting good hard-disk management.

4. A way to free space by deleting unused backup (**.bak**) files.

5. Recovery of free but unusable space with the **CHKDSK/F** command, recovering lost clusters.

6. Disk compaction, to piece together your fragmented files.

An occasional tune-up will keep your computer running on all cylinders and at peak productivity.

DOS—A Closer Look

IN THIS CHAPTER

Let's further explore the hard disk to examine AutoCAD files and their structure. Then we'll make a simple modification to AutoCAD's standard menu, setting the stage for even more time-saving techniques.

EXPLORING AUTOCAD'S FILES

When arriving in a new city, some people like to drive around for several hours with no particular plan. If a street looks interesting, they explore it. If a park has a statue with a historical plaque, they get out and read it. They like to find a high place to scan the entire cityscape. Wrong turns and backtracking don't faze them. Their sense of adventure helps them develop a "feel" for the city and become comfortable in it.

The hard disk is our city and the AutoCAD sub-directory a large, interesting suburb—almost a city in itself. Let's "drive around" using:

CD	**Change Directory**
DIR	List the files
PROMPT	Show current location
TREE	Show the directories
TYPE	Display the data in the files

To get started, first **exit** to the DOS level (**C:\ >** or **C >**) if you haven't used the **PROMPT** command from the previous work. If your prompt doesn't display the DOS path, let's enter it now:

Type:　PROMPT=PG (RETURN)　　**($P** displays the path and current directory and **$G** displays the *greater than* sign.)

Now let's change to your AutoCAD directory, where you should see the path.

Type:　CD\ACAD (RETURN)　　(Enter the AutoCAD directory.)

Response:　C:\ACAD>　　(The AutoCAD directory.)

To view the files in your current directory,

Type:　DIR/P (RETURN)　　(**DIR**ectory with a **P**ause.)

Browse through the entire directory. Often you'll see files named **READ.ME** or **README.DOC** or **PRINT.ME**. These are ASCII files that contain interesting nuggets of information about the latest software release or last-minute changes that didn't make it into the *User Reference* manual.

To review the contents of the file, use the **TYPE** command:

Type:　TYPE README.DOC　(RETURN) (AutoCAD's "update" file.)

If it's not on your system, you'll find it on the original AutoCAD diskettes.

Note: If you don't want to view the entire file, press **CTRL-C**, which will cancel the command, stop the scrolling and return you to the DOS prompt. This is a typical file; yours may be different.

Response: AutoCAD

12-03-87

Version 2.52 18 for IBM PC-FAMILY

README.DOC

This file contains the following corrections and additions to the AutoCAD Installation Guide--User Guide Supplement:

AutoLISP

Shell Command Usage

Kurta Series One Digitizers

Pencept PENPAD

C. Itoh Plotter Support

Strobe Plotter Support

HIDDENxxx Layers

Plotting Drawings Created by AutoCAD 2.15

AutoCAD Plotter Pen Optimization

Calcomp 1043 ROM

Kurta Series III Tablets

Variables and Expressions Type Function

Quadram Quadport-AT Serial Port

Printronix Model 4160

Texas Instruments Omni 800

AutoLISP

AutoCAD version 2.52 supports AutoLISP for ADE3 and TRAINING packages. AutoLISP is an implementation of the LISP programming language embedded within AutoCAD. It is an extension of the "Variables and Expressions" feature.

AutoLISP is contained in the ACADL.OVL file on the EXE disk. (If you have an ADE3 or TRAINING package.) Installation of AutoCAD is the same as on previous releases.

AutoLISP may be required to run some "third party" applications. Ask the applications developers for specific requirements.

SHELL command users please note!

etc.

Now, that could be some useful information! But it went by too fast. To pause the screen, hold down the **CTRL** key and press **Num Lock** simultaneously. To restart the scrolling, tap any other key.

Let's look at *executable* files or programs: the **.COM** files, **.EXE** files and **.BAT** files.

Type: `DIR *.COM (RETURN)`

Type: `DIR *.EXE (RETURN)`

Type: `DIR *.BAT (RETURN)`

If you see an interesting **.BAT** file, use the **TYPE** command to display it. If you want a hard copy of what you see on the screen, use **SHIFT Prt Sc (Print Screen)** to send it to a printer, or use a **CTRL-P** to send it to a printer while it displays on the screen. Another **CTRL-P** deactivates this feature.

A TRICK WITH THE FUNCTION KEYS

At the DOS prompt, enter a new command, such as **DIR** or **TYPE**, or any line of text and (**RETURN**). (**CTRL-C** will stop the execution of the command.) Hit the **F3** key. The last line you typed was repeated. Hit (**RETURN**) to reenter the command. Now use the **F1** key to bring it in one letter at a time.

These keys also can save a lot of time in EDLIN. To experiment, let's enter the following commands without any floppy disks in either drive **A:** or **B:**, realizing you'll get an **Abort, Retry, Ignore** error:

Type: `COPY *.BAT A: (RETURN)`   (**COPY** all **.BAT** files to **A:**)

Now, imagine you've put the floppy in the **B:** drive and you want to reenter the command line with **A:** changed to

B:. Because you just received the **Abort, Retry, Ignore** error,

Type: A   (For Abort.)

Type: F3   (The line reappears, **COPY *.BAT A:**)

    Use the backspace or left arrow key twice to remove **A:**, then type **B:**, correcting your mistake.

    For the sake of argument, let's change the line to read:

COPY A:*.BAT B: (The addition of **A:**)

    Use **F1** to reenter the command line, character by character, to the point of entering the **A:**. Now hit the **Ins** (**Ins**ert) key on the number pad. Everything typed in now will be inserted into the line. Type **A:**, then hit **F3**. The line has been modified. Now let's restore it to:

COPY *.BAT B: (Delete **A:**)

    Use **F1** to reenter characters up to (not including) **A:**. Hit the **Del** (**Del**ete) key on the number pad twice, then **F3** to complete the line. Voila! Repaired.

    The **F1**, **F3**, **Ins** and **Del** keys work the same way in EDLIN, allowing you to change a spelling error in the midst of a line without having to rekey the whole thing. Experiment further with these commands so you can better predict their actions. Properly used, they're a real productivity enhancement.

ON TO AUTOCAD ... CHARGE!

Use the DOS **TREE** command to list the directories on your hard drive. From **C:\ >**,

Type: TREE (RETURN)   (You'll see an ACAD type directory and possibly sub-directories where drawings may be stored.)

Type: CD ACAD (RETURN) (Change to the **ACAD** directory. The name and path of your directory may be different. Use the name reported by **TREE** command.)

Your AutoCAD files may be in your **ROOT** directory. No matter where they are, to view them,

Type: DIR ACAD*.* (RETURN)

Below is what you'd see using Release 9:

```
Volume in drive C is VOLUME 1
Directory of  C:\ACAD9
ACAD     DWG      2282      10-24-87      11:18p
ACAD     EXE    202624       9-18-87       6:08p
ACAD     HDX      1804       9-15-87       7:46p
ACAD     HLP     93170       9-15-87       7:45p
ACAD     LIN       600       2-26-85      10:45p
ACAD1    MID       164       9-17-87      12:35p
ACAD2    MID       169       9-17-87      12:40p
ACAD3    MID       174       9-17-87      12:47p
ACAD4    MID       170       9-18-87       6:24p
ACAD     MNU     33289      11-12-87      10:17a
ACAD     MNX     58377       9-18-87       5:23p
ACAD     OVL    260570       9-23-87       8:53a
ACAD0    OVL     74378       9-17-87      10:10a
ACAD2    OVL     91818       9-17-87      10:10a
ACAD3    OVL    196538       9-17-87      10:10a
ACADDG   OVL      2109      11-10-87      11:42a
ACADDS   OVL     19128      11-12-87       3:04p
ACADL    OVL     74272       9-17-87       9:40a
ACADM    OVL      6546       9-17-87      10:19a
ACADPL   OVL       274      11-10-87      11:42a
```

ACADPP	OVL	274	11-10-87	11:42a
ACADVS	OVL	8381	9-17-87	9:13a
ACAD	PAT	5120	11-01-83	10:47p
ACAD	PGP	809	10-24-87	8:51p
ACAD	SLB	107082	9-02-87	1:55p
ACAD	CFG	1312	11-15-87	11:17a

26 File(s)   18909184 bytes free

Your files may come up in a different order. The **DATE** and **TIME** listings are easy to recognize. The other number indicates the size of the file. DOS omits the period separating the name and extension. **ACAD BAK** should be read as **ACAD.BAK**.

These files total approximately 1,250,000 bytes in Release 9, not counting all the font files! In Release 10, they total more than 1.5 million bytes. You have to respect the programming effort involved in producing such a large body of code.

The big file at the top, **ACAD.EXE**, is the main control program for AutoCAD, which loads itself into **RAM** and presents you with the **MAIN** menu.

The **OVERLAY** files (indicated by **OVL** in the second column) contain commands such as **CIRCLE**, **MIRROR**, etc. The AutoCAD program is too big to fit in memory at one time, so commands are *paged in* to memory in *overlays*, then *paged out* to make room for other commands.

Just for the fun of it, use the **TYPE** command to list the contents of the AutoLISP overlay.

Type: TYPE ACADL.OVL (RETURN) (AutoCAD's AutoLISP
                             overlay.)

Strange? Beeping? That signals a binary machine language file like your drawing files — the compiled, or assembled, form of AutoCAD's computer language. **ACAD3.OVL** refers to **ADE3**. **ACADPL.OVL** contains commands for plotting.

Let's look at the line file containing specifications for broken lines.

Type: TYPE ACAD.LIN (RETURN)

Response: *DASHED,__ __ __ __ __ __ __ __ __ __ __ __ __ __ __
A,.5,-.25
*HIDDEN,_ _ _ _ _ _ _ _ _ _ _ _ _ _ _ _ _ _ _
A,.25,-.125
*CENTER,____ _ ____ _ ____ _ ____ _ ___ _ ____ _ ___
A,1.25,-.25,.25,-.25
*PHANTOM,_____ _ _ _____ _ _ ____ _ _ ___
A,1.25,-.25,.25,-.25,.25,-.25
*DOT,...
A,0,-.25
*DASHDOT,__ . __ . __ . __ . __ . __ . __ . __ .
A,.5,-.25,0,-.25
*BORDER,__ __ . __ __ . __ __ . __ __ . __ __
A,.5,-.25,.5,-.25,0,-.25
*DIVIDE,__ . . __ . . __ . . __ . . __ . . __ __
A,.5,-.25,0,-.25,0,-.25

Surprise! It's just an ASCII file with a name and description for each linetype, and *pen-up* and *pen-down* values. The **HATCH** patterns appear in much the same manner.

AutoCAD's "open architecture" allows you to change these line names or values as you wish—something you'll be able to do by the time you finish this book.

Type: TYPE ACAD.PAT (RETURN)   (**PAT**tern file.)

Response: *angle,Angle steel
0, 0,0, 0,.275, .2,-.075
90, 0,0, 0,.275, .2,-.075
*ansi31,ANSI Iron, Brick, Stone
masonry

```
45, 0,0, 0,.125
*ansi32,ANSI Steel
45, 0,0, 0,.375
45, .176776695,0, 0,.375
```
etc.

This file contains AutoCAD's **HATCH** descriptions. Soon, you'll be able to revise this file or add your own **HATCH** patterns!

Let's call up the AutoCAD **HELP** file:

Type:　　TYPE ACAD.HLP　(RETURN)

(Hit **CTRL-C** if you want to **CANCEL**.)

Response:　　AutoCAD Command List (+n=ADE-n feature, etc.)

APERTURE +2	BREAK +1	DIM/DIM1 +1	END	HIDE +3
ARC	CHAMFER +1	DIST	ERASE	ID
AREA	CHANGE	DIVIDE +3	EXPLODE +3	IGESIN +3

etc.

This file contains more than 3,000 lines of text which you easily can modify to create **HELP** for any new command you invent. A companion file, **ACAD.HDX**, is the HELP INDEX, which allows AutoCAD to find **HELP** faster. Although it is an ASCII file, it's automatically created by AutoCAD, so you don't have to look at it.

If you have an **ACAD.PGP** file (**ADE3**), it might look like this:

Type:　　TYPE ACAD.PGP (RETURN)　(AutoCAD's **PIG PEN** file.)

```
CATALOG,DIR /W,24000,*Files: ,0
DEL,DEL,24000,File to delete: ,0
```

```
DIR,DIR,24000,File specification: ,0
EDIT,EDLIN,40000,File to edit: ,0
SHELL,,125000,*DOS Command: ,0
TYPE,TYPE,24000,File to list: ,0
```

This is also a user-definable ASCII file that allows you to use external commands while in a drawing. You can use DOS commands, word processors, BASIC programs and the like. Many third-party developers use this feature extensively. Using **SHELL** type commands saves a tremendous amount of time; this subject will be covered in a later chapter.

If you're trying to develop a menu, you can use the **SHELL** feature to "pop out" to EDLIN, make the changes, reload the menu and test it—all without leaving your drawing. Note that the fourth line allows you to type **EDIT** from the drawing editor and address EDLIN. For editing long menu files, you may wish to increase the memory set-aside to **100000** or more. This capability is a true productivity gem (see Appendix D).

If you have an **AutoLISP** file,

Type: TYPE ACAD.LSP (RETURN)   (This file automatically
                                                   loads AutoLISP functions.)

Response: (Defun c:IMPORT ()
               (Setq fname (Getstring "ENTER THE ASCII TEXT FILE NAME: "))
               (Setq thgt (Getreal "ENTER THE TEXT HEIGHT: "))
               (Setq lspace (Getreal "ENTER THE LINE SPACING: "))
               (Setq just (Getstring "ENTER THE JUSTIFICATION, LCR: "))
               etc. (Your file may be different.)

Other miscellaneous files are of little concern here. The **.MID** files form a **Master ID** and should never be modified. The **.CFG** file is your configuration file.

A CHANGE FOR ACAD.MNU

Now let's look through **ACAD.MNU**, AutoCAD's standard "out-of-the-box" menu. Because this file is long, be ready to **CTRL-Num Lock** to start and stop the display.

Note: Since Version 2.5, the menu files are compiled into binary code each time they're modified and loaded. The file extension for the compiled version is **.MNX** (just as shape files are **.SHX**). You may have only the compiled version of the **ACAD** menu on your hard disk. If this is the case, you can find it in the **SOURCE** sub-directory on one of the original support disks.

Type: TYPE ACAD.MNU (RETURN)

(Hit **CTRL-C** if you want to **CANCEL**.)

Response for Release 10:

```
***BUTTONS
;
$pl=*
^c^c
^B
^O
^G
^D
^E
^T
***AUX1
;
$pl=*
^C^C
^B
^O
^G
^D
^E
^T
***POP1
```

```
[Tools]
[OSNAP]^C^C$pl= $pl=* OSNAP \
CENter
ENDpoint
```

etc.

```
***SCREEN
**S
[AutoCAD]^C^C$S=X $S=S $P1=POP1 $P3=POP3
[* * * *]$S=OSNAPB
[SETUP]^C^C^P(progn(prompt "Loading setup . . . ")
  (load "setup"))
^P$S=X $S=UNITS

[BLOCKS]$S=X $S=BL
[DIM:]$S=X $S=DIM^C^CDIM
[DISPLAY]$S=X $S=DS
[DRAW]$S=X $S=DR
[EDIT]$S=X $S=ED
[INQUIRY]$S=X $S=INQ
[LAYER:]$S=X $S=LAYER ^C^CLAYER
[SETTINGS]$S=X $S=SET
[PLOT]$S=X $S=PLOT
[UCS:}$S=X $S=UC1 ^C^CUCS
[UTILITY]$S=X $S=UT
```

etc.

To copy it from the DOS prompt, **C:\ACAD >**,

Type: COPY A:\SOURCE\ACAD.MNU   (RETURN)

Do you see anything recognizable? Of course! How about:

```
[AutoCAD]^C^C$S=X $S=S $P1=POP1 $P3=POP3
[* * * *]$S=OSNAPB
[SETUP]^C^C^P(progn(prompt "Loading setup...  ")
(load "setup"))
```

Let's use EDLIN, and with a simple modification, create a new headline. First, make a safety copy of the existing menu.
From the DOS prompt **C:\ACAD >**,

Type: COPY ACAD.MNU ACAD.SAV (RETURN)

Response: C:\ACAD>

Type: EDLIN ACAD.MNU (RETURN)

Type: 1,9999L (RETURN) **(List lines 1 through 9999, the whole file, and note the line number of [AutoCAD].)**

Use **^ S** or **^ NumLock** to start and stop the display. In Release 10, you'll find the line near **431**. In Release 9 it's near **225**. In earlier versions, it's near the top and may be named **ROOT** rather than AutoCAD. Once you find the line, type **^ C** to stop the listing.

Type: # (RETURN)   **(# = Line number of [AutoCAD].)**

Response: 431: * [AutoCAD]   (AutoCAD, etc.)
431: *

Type: [M A I N]F3 (RETURN)   **(Function 3)**

Type: 425L (RETURN)   **(List the lines starting at line 431.)**

To view more of the file, enter the range of line numbers you'd like to view. **22,42L** will show you the lines between **22** and **42**. **1,9999L** will generally list out the entire file.

Type: 22,42L (RETURN)

Type: 1,9999L (RETURN)

When you've finished exploring,

Type: E (RETURN)   **(End and save the new modification.)**

Response: C:\ACAD>

Boot AutoCAD, start a drawing and see the modification you've made to AutoCAD's standard menu. Do you like **MAIN** more than **AutoCAD**? If so, leave it there as a permanent improvement. You may want to go back and change *** * * *** to **OB-SNAP**. If you didn't like the change, change it back: from the DOS prompt, **C:\ACAD >**,

Type: DEL ACAD.MNU (RETURN)

Type: REN ACAD.SAV ACAD.MNU (RETURN)   (Restore a back-up file.)

Or you can copy the **ACAD.SAV** file.

SUMMARY

You've now explored the "city" called AutoCAD, by poking around in its files. You also modified AutoCAD's standard menu. Now that you've changed it a little, you'll go on to change it a lot in the following chapters!

This book is based on the premise that Autodesk furnishes its standard menu only as a temporary aid so you can use the software straight out of the box. The folks at

Autodesk never intended it to be permanent — that's why they've given us so many tools for revising it!

Throughout this chapter, you've continued to sharpen your DOS skills. Each successive chapter will heighten your productivity with AutoCAD.

If you understand everything in this chapter, terrific! But if you still feel a little bewildered, that's only natural. You'll begin to feel more at ease as you continue to work with DOS and EDLIN.

Gradually, we'll assume you've become familiar with DOS, EDLIN or your own text editor, but we'll continue to remind you of DOS and EDLIN commands with step-by-step guidance. Now, let's go straight to the heart of AutoCAD customization.

Creating and Editing Macros

IN THIS CHAPTER

The first three chapters gave you step-by-step instructions for creating a simple, two-command menu. You then learned how to "tune up" your system for maximum performance. Finally, you explored the **ACAD.MNU**.

All the while, you were learning some important DOS tools to be used in this and later chapters. We'll continue to refer to the DOS prompts discussed in Chapter One, such as **C:\ACAD >**, which displays the directory path.

We'll merge some simple macros from The AutoCAD Productivity Library into "blank spots" on the first "page" of your **ACAD.MNU** screen menu. By the end of this chapter, you'll be able to use the fruits of your labor to pick macros of your choice from The AutoCAD Productivity Library and insert them into other "holes" in the **ACAD.MNU**.

Exploring and understanding the existing **ACAD.MNU**, which anyone can access, is the easiest way to learn how to organize your own menu.

By moving your most useful commands "up front," you'll begin to employ a concept that will evolve into the Reduced Instruction Set Command menu (**RISC** menu) in Chapter Five and pull-down menus in Chapter Seven.

You'll then be on your way to understanding customization and unlocking your creative potential with AutoCAD. You'll also create some simple macros you can use immediately to reduce drawing time and make your work easier.

THE AUTOCAD MAIN SCREEN MENU

The first menu page shown is called the **ROOT** or **MAIN** menu, and all other submenus branch out from there. The **ROOT** menu only allows you to pick another menu. However, a few available slots, or blank spots, can be filled with your own commands and macros so you can get to work immediately on start-up.

The following **ROOT** section from **ACAD.MNU**, Release 10, starts at line **431** after the pull-down and icon sections. Note how it appears on the screen menu during a drawing. When you call it up using EDLIN, you'll see a correspondence between what's on the screen and how the menu file is constructed.

Remember, you may have only the compiled file on your hard disk. If so, load it from the **SOURCE** directory on one of your original diskettes (see previous chapter).

From the DOS command prompt, **C:\ACAD >**,

Type:　　EDLIN ACAD.MNU (RETURN)

Response:　　End of input file

　　　　　　*

Type:　　1,431L (RETURN)　　(List lines **1** through **431**)

Response:
```
***SCREEN
**S
[AutoCAD]^C^C$S=X $S=S $P1=POP1 $P3=POP3
[ * * * * ]$S=OSNAPB
[Setup]^C^C^P(progn(prompt "Loading setup...    ")
(load setup"))
^P$S=X $S=UNITS

[BLOCKS]$S=X $S=BL
[DIM:]$S=X $S=DIM ^C^CDIM
[DISPLAY]$S=X $S=DS
```

```
[DRAW]$S=X $S=DR
[EDIT]$S=X $S=ED
[INQUIRY]$S=X $S=INQ
[LAYER:]$S=X $S=LAYER ^C^CLAYER
[SETTINGS]$S=X $S=SET
[PLOT]$S=X $S=PLOT
[UCS:]$S=X $S=UCS1 ^C^CUCS
[UTILITY]$S=X $S=UT
```

2

```
[3D]$S=X $S=3D
[ASHADE]^C^C^P(progn(setq m:err *error*) (prin1)) (defun *error*
(msg) (princ msg)+
(setq  *error*  m:err m:err nil) (princ)) (cond ((null
C:SCENE) (vmon)+
(if (/=nil (findfile "ashade.lsp")) (progn (terpri);+
(prompt "Please wait... Loading ashade. ") +
(load "ashade")(menucmd "S=X") (menucmd "S=ASHADE") +
(setq *error* m:err m:err nil)) (progn (terpri);+
(prompt "The file 'Ashade.lsp' was not found in your
current search directories.")+
(terpri) (prompt "Check your AutoShade Manual for
installation instructions.");+
(setq *error* m:err m:err nil) (princ))))+
(T  (setq  *error*  m:err  m:err nil) +
(menucmd  "S=X") (menucmd "S=ASHADE") (princ))) ^P
```

3

```
[SAVE:] ^C^CSAVE
```

4

Let's now examine the **ACAD.MNU** more closely. In the above example, the numbers on the right are the book's notation to identify spaces you can use for macros. These numbers don't actually appear on the **ACAD.MNU**. Blank line **4** (or more) may be available on some monitors but in general only 20 selections are available.

During the **1,431L** command, you scrolled other portions of **ACAD.MNU**. Those lines relate to the buttons on your mouse or digitizer cursor, auxiliary input devices, pull-down menus and icon menus.

To browse, use the **List** again but use ^**S** to stop and start the display. The screen menu system (as opposed to buttons, tablet or pull-downs) starts at the line ***SCREEN**. The three asterisks tell AutoCAD this is the start of a menu for a particular device, such as a tablet, cursor or CRT.

A LOOK AT ACAD SCREEN SUBMENUS

AutoCAD's menu system consists of nothing more than a group of sub-menus that reference one another. The **ROOT** sub-menu starts at ****S** and ends just before ****X 3**. The two asterisks in ****S** tell AutoCAD that all following lines, up to another submenu (****X 3**), belong to submenu S.

X 3 begins a submenu that contains only the bottom three lines seen on the screen. This was done to avoid typing the same three lines on every submenu. Because the other menus are shorter by these three lines, they merely overlay the ****X 3 menu. The **3** in ****X 3** causes the menu to start on the third line down, leaving both **[AutoCAD]** and **[* * *]** active on screen.

Because sub-menu **S** is second in line after ***SCREEN**, it's the first menu you see on the screen during a drawing. Of course, the lines aren't preceded with a double or triple asterisk, because they're menu and submenu titles.

Analyzing the first working line, **[BLOCKS]$S = X $S = BL**, you see the **BLOCKS** title. Obviously, the left and right brackets tell AutoCAD that anything contained within them should appear on the screen as a command title. (**Note:** For screen menus, only the first eight characters of a title will appear on the screen.)

Commands immediately follow the right bracket. In this case, commands activate submenus titled **X** and the **BLOCK** submenu. The dollar sign designates a submenu; **S** indicates a Screen menu. (**T** is a Tablet menu and **B** indicates a Button submenu. Thus, a screen menu pick could change a tablet area or the selections on your mouse or digitizer puck.)

Before you modify **ACAD.MNU**, you should feel safe and confident that you can recover from any mistake and get back to square one—without calling your AutoCAD dealer at 2 a.m! (Of course, you can always reload the AutoCAD menu from your AutoCAD support disk.)

So let's copy the **ACAD.MNU** file to **ACAD.SAV** and to a floppy. First, **Q**uit the current EDLIN session. At EDLIN's * prompt,

Type: Q (RETURN)

Response: Abort edit (Y/N)?

Type: Y (RETURN)

Response: C:\ACAD>

Now make a safety copy on your hard disk and a formatted floppy.

Type: COPY ACAD.MNU ACAD.SAV (RETURN)   (hard disk)

Type: COPY ACAD.MNU A:ACAD.MNU (RETURN)   (floppy)

To reopen the menu, from the DOS command prompt **C:\ACAD >**,

Type: EDLIN ACAD.MNU (RETURN) Beginners, please see important note below.[1]

---

[1]You'll now begin to modify your AutoCAD menu. If, during this process, you make errors that you find difficult to correct, you may want to start afresh with the "real" AutoCAD menu. To start over from this point,
    Type: DEL ACAD.MNU
    Type: COPY ACAD.SAV ACAD.MNU

```
End of input file
*
```

Type: 431,453L (RETURN)   (List lines **431** through **453**.)

This brings up the menu section shown above. Note the line number for the first blank line. Consolidate the current menu selections at the top by deleting the blank lines. Then you'll have free room at the bottom of the sub-menu for other goodies. To delete blank line **1**,

Type: 437D (RETURN)   (Where the line to be **Deleted** is **437**; your line number may be different.)

List the menu again to see the changes.

Type: 431L (RETURN)

Note that the lines have moved up, and the next blank line to delete has a new number. Delete blank line **2**. Be sure to **LIST** each time so that you use the correct line number.

Now, to add a macro! The second macro in The AutoCAD Productivity Library is "Simple Entry of a Single Command." Let's put the **LINE** and **CIRCLE** commands in the first two blank lines below **[ASHADE:]**. Note that **[ASHADE:]** occupies three lines as one macro by use of the + sign at the end of lines **1** and **2**.

Note: Throughout the book, macro titles appear in lower-case letters to distinguish them from normal AutoCAD commands.

Remember that to enter a ⌃C, you must use two keys: **SHIFT-6** and **C**.

Type: 459 (RETURN)   (The line number of the first blank line.)

Response: 459:*   (Indicates a blank line.)
              459:*

Type: [line]^C^CLINE; (RETURN)

Response: *

Release 9 or later users may include an asterisk preceding the macro to make it repeat. Generally, this is recommended. The **LINE** and **CIRCLE** commands would then read:

[line]*^C^CLINE; and [circle]*^C^CCIRCLE;

Because you just used the only blank line, you now must **INSERT** the next menu line between the **LINE** commands, then **SAVE**.

Type: 460I (RETURN)

Response: 460:*

This "pushes down" the existing line **460**.

Type: [circle]^C^CCIRCLE; (RETURN)

Response: 461:*

Type: ^C   (Exit insert mode and return to command mode.)

Response: *

Type: E (RETURN)   **(End the EDLIN session.)**

Response:

C:\ACAD>

LET'S TRY IT

Boot AutoCAD. Your screen should look like this:

```
AutoCAD
* * * *
SETUP
BLOCKS
DIM
DISPLAY
DRAW
EDIT
INQUIRY
LAYER
SETTINGS
PLOT
UCS
UTILITY
3D
ASHADE
line
circle
SAVE
```

If your menu is different, it might be that your prototype drawing remembers a different one (see Chapter 10). Just type the **MENU** command from the **Command:** prompt and respond with **ACAD**.

Let's test your additions to the **ROOT** menu. Although **LINE** and **CIRCLE** are simple commands, it's easy to misspell a command or omit a bracket. Now comes a process integral to any menu development, known as ...

DEBUGGING

Making mistakes is the price one pays for trying something new. Tracking down these mistakes can be a challenge leading up to a moment of exhilaration when you shout "EUREKA! IT WORKS!!"

"Debugging" is a trial-and-error cycle of testing, correction and retesting. You may have to repeat the cycle several times. If one of your macros isn't working properly, **QUIT** your drawing, **EXIT** AutoCAD and return to the DOS prompt.

For learning purposes, let's assume that when you were in the drawing, the **CIRCLE** command looked like this:

```
circle^
```

Aside from looking bad, it doesn't work. Not to worry—it's a common problem and easy to correct. (If you have a different problem, you must also return to EDLIN as shown in the hypothetical example below. If your menu works well, you can skip this example. However, earmark this page, because you'll eventually want to refer to it.)

From the DOS prompt **C:\ACAD >**,

Type: \EDLIN ACAD.MNU (RETURN)

Response: End of input file

                *

Type: 431,453L (RETURN)

Response: a screen listing of the ACAD menu.

Review the macros, looking for a missing [or], or a ^ that's out of place, or a misspelling. You have two problems: a missing right bracket and a misspelled word. Because the bracket was omitted, AutoCAD thought the whole line—not just the word "circle"—was the screen title. From EDLIN, type in the faulty line number.

Type: 460 (RETURN)

Response: 460:*[circle^C^Ccircle;
               460:*

Type: [circle]^C^Ccircle; (RETURN)

Response: *

Type: E (RETURN)   (End the EDLIN session, saving
                                   the changes.)

Response: C:\ACAD>

Boot AutoCAD, enter a drawing and test your repairs. While you're at it, test all the macros again, because often you'll fix one "bug" only to create another in a macro that previously worked.

Rule 5: Test your work in small increments or modules; otherwise, the debugging process can be difficult.

Tip: Make a one-command menu to test a macro. Then, when everything is working well, copy it into the **ACAD.MNU** or the menu in which you're working.

Tip: Set up your text editor in the **ACAD.PGP** file so that you can create and debug your menus without exiting AutoCAD (see Appendix D).

Most editors, including EDLIN, allow you to "insert" or merge a macro into another menu, just as AutoCAD allows you to **INSERT** one drawing into another. A typical EDLIN example works like this (only an example, don't actually type it):

Type: 461TRECTANGL.MCR (RETURN)   **(T** = Transfer)

This means: starting at line **461,** Transfer into the current file the contents of a file named **RECTANGL.MCR.**

LET'S ADD AUTOLISP

Although simple, **LINE** and **CIRCLE** are true macros because each combines four functions into one. The ***,** if used, causes the whole macro to repeat until cancelled. The ^C^C is a double cancel that allows you to jump from the middle of one command to another. You then have the command itself and the **;,** which causes a **(RETURN)** to be executed automatically.

Regardless of your software version, always look for ways to combine actions in a macro. The simplest macros are often your biggest time-savers.

Now, let's fill in the last two available slots with macros from The AutoCAD Productivity Library (including an AutoLISP routine) providing menu selections for **Rectangle** and **ZOOM WINDOW** (Macro 22).

Note: We now assume that you know the EDLIN and DOS commands used to this point. For example, when you're asked to **LIST** the first **34** lines of **ACAD.MNU** using EDLIN, you should know to do the following and take mental note of what's on the screen:

*1,34L (RETURN)

Unless we're showing you something new, this chapter will be the last time we use **Type:** and **Response:**. By now you may have realized that EDLIN isn't the most efficient, easy-to-use editor; you may have learned another. And you'll be much more productive at development and debugging if you run your editor from within an AutoCAD drawing, using the **SHELL** feature.

As a matter of fact, this book was written from within an AutoCAD drawing so macros and AutoLISP routines can quickly be checked for accuracy. (For information on alternate editors and using an editor in the AutoCAD **SHELL,** see Appendix D.)

RECTANGL

From the DOS prompt **C:\ACAD>**,

Type: EDLIN ACAD.MNU (RETURN)

Type: 431,462L (RETURN)

At the first line after **[circle]** (**461** on my machine—yours may be different), insert the following lines using EDLIN. Type in the letters and numerals exactly as shown, remembering that LISP is "case-sensitive."

Type: 461I (RETURN)   (Or the first blank line)

Response: 461:*

Type:

461:*	`[rectangl]*^C^C(Setq P1 +`	(RETURN)
462:*	`(Getpoint "First Point: "));\+`	(RETURN)
463:*	`(Setq P2 (Getpoint +`	(RETURN)
464:*	`"Diagonal corner point: "));\+`	(RETURN)
465:*	`Line !P1 (List (Car P2) (Cadr P1));+`	(RETURN)
466:*	`!P2 (List (Car P1) (Cadr P2)) CL;`	(RETURN)
467:*	`[zoom-w]'zoom;w`	
468:*	CTRL-C (Terminate the insert mode.)	
*****	E (RETURN) (End the editing session.)	

Response: C:\ACAD>

LET'S TRY IT (and More Debuggin')

LISP, at last!!! You have just created a simple AutoLISP routine. Boot AutoCAD, enter a drawing, pick **rectangl** and follow the prompts. When finished, you should see a rectangle of your specified length and width on the screen.

It would be amazing if you didn't make a mistake. The three most common LISP mistakes are: 1) to omit a parenthesis, 2) to omit a quotation mark, and 3) to have "spaces" at the end of a line which AutoCAD interprets as **(RETURN)**.

If your problem is with a quotation mark or parenthesis, AutoCAD will let you know by prompting **1**, where **1** represents the number of open parentheses. To correct this while you're in a drawing, enter a right parenthesis **)**, **(RETURN)** from your keyboard. The number should decrease. If not, try a quotation mark (").

Repeat the process until your **Command:** prompt returns. Then **EXIT** AutoCAD, open up the menu file and, using EDLIN, begin counting parentheses and quotes. Add the ones missing and save your work.

It's normal to be frustrated with this debugging process. Remember, you can make a one-command menu to test complicated macros, then use the Transfer command to insert the macro into **ACAD.MNU**.

Line **467** is a **ZOOM** window. Since you'd like to use this command in the "transparent" mode, change the typical **CANCEL** to an apostrophe '. (*Transparent* means that you can zoom around while another command is active.)

RECTANGLE REVIEW

Okay, now that you've created and tested your first AutoLISP routine, let's review what you did and see how AutoLISP works. (While this book doesn't purport to be a treatise on AutoLISP, explanation of this simple example and the next will help you devise and edit your own macros. For your convenience, we've placed a condensed listing of common AutoLISP commands in Appendix C, "AutoLISP Notations.")

Assuming that your macro starts at line **461**, we'll refer to lines **461** through **468**.

Line **461**, including its continuation on Line **462**, has five actions. First is the title, **rectangl**, that appears on your screen. Then, the ***** causes the whole macro to repeat for Version 9 or later users. Next, the ^C^C cancels all previous commands.

Now, working outward from the innermost pair of parentheses, **Getpoint** (and the prompt in quotes) retrieves a specified point and gives it to AutoLISP, whether you key in coordinates or pick it from the screen. **Setq** is an AutoLISP command that assigns the point retrieved by **Getpoint** to the variable **P1**. After running **rectangl** you can type **!P1** from the **Command:** prompt to see the value of the point.

A point is a pair of numbers—the **X** and **Y** coordinates—so **P1** actually has both the **X** and **Y** values stored. At the end of the line are three characters: ;, \ and +. The semicolon is a (**RETURN**) which "submits" the statement to LISP. The backslash, \, tells the system to "pause for user input." The + continues the macro to the next line. These three characters are omitted in true AutoLISP, where functions are defined.

Just like creating an **EDIT WINDOW** in AutoCAD, a rectangle requires a diagonal corner point. Line **463**, including its continuation on line **464**, prompts you to enter this second point and sets it equal to the variable **P2**.

It's time to draw the four lines counterclockwise. The word "Line" on **465** is simply the **LINE** command. Line **465** continues on **466**. The exclamation point, !, tells AutoLISP to retrieve the contents of the variable **P1**, which happens to be a point (a pair or list of **X** and **Y** coordinates).

Working from the inside pair of parentheses, you'll see more peculiar LISP language.

AutoLISP thinks of a coordinate as a **List** of two numbers separated by a space. **car** means the left member of the list, the **X** coordinate, and **cadr** means the right member of the list, or the **Y** coordinate.

The **List** command combines the **X** and **Y** values of **P1** and **P2** to form new coordinates (or lists) for **P2** and **P3**.

In the illustration, Point A is a list made up of the **X** coordinate of **P2** and the **Y** coordinate of **P1**.

So, starting the line at **P1** (which you specify) on line **461**, we draw to Point B, which has been "fabricated" by AutoLISP. (Points A and B reference the illustration only, and are not names used in the **rectangl** macro.)

On line **466**, **!P2** is again user-specified. **Pt3** is a compilation of the **X** coordinate of **P1** and the **Y** coordinate of **P2**. The **CL** is AutoCAD's **CLOSE** command.

VARIATION ON A THEME . . . WITH AN ANGLE

Now, let's replace the rectangle with another macro that will allow you to enter a square at any angle. From the DOS prompt, **C:\ACAD>**,

Type: \EDLIN ACAD.MNU (RETURN)

Type: 431,469L (RETURN)

Then delete the rectangle lines. **(246,251D)**

Type: 461I (RETURN)   (Begin inserting new lines at the end of the **rectangl** macro.)

Response: 461:*

Type:

461:*	[square]*^C^C(Setq Pl +	(RETURN)
462:*	(Getpoint "First point: "));\+	(RETURN)
463:*	(Prompt "Enter second point: ");+	(RETURN)
464:*	Line !Pl;\;(Setq P2 +	(RETURN)
465:*	(Getvar "Lastpoint"));+	(RETURN)
466:*	(Setq D (Distance Pl P2));+	(RETURN)
467:*	(setq Ang (Angle Pl P2));+	(RETURN)

```
468:*   Line !P2 (Polar P2+              (RETURN)
469:*   (+ (/ Pi 2) ANG) D);+            (RETURN)
470:*   (Polar (Getvar "Lastpoint") +   (RETURN)
471:*   ANG (- 0 D)) !P1 C;              (RETURN)
472:*   CTRL-C   (Cancel the insert mode.)
```

Response: *

Type: E (RETURN)   (End EDLIN session, saving
                                modifications.)

Now let's try the **square** macro. Boot AutoCAD (if you're not running in **SHELL**), begin a new drawing, select the **square** option and follow the prompts. When you're finished, your drawing screen should show a square of the length and angle you specified.

This macro creates a square of any angle determined by the first side. The first two points also determine the square's size. Two points complete your input. Lines **462** and **463** are input and prompt for two points.

Also note *polar*, which deals with angles and distances—polar coordinates.

Tip: Remember that AutoLISP measures angles in radians, not degrees. 2 * Pi radians equal 360 degrees. For example, in line **469**, (+ (/ Pi 2) ANG) adds 90 degrees to the value of **ANG**.

The other tricky part of this macro is **(Getvar "Lastpoint")**. AutoCAD remembers many system variables, such as current **SNAP**, **GRID**, **LIMITS** and the **LASTPOINT** entered. This point and other system variables can be retrieved through the **GETVAR** command. During a drawing, enter **Lastpoint** with a single @ when you're prompted for a point. This is handy for drawing concentric circles and setting up relative coordinates.

A NOTE ...

... about the **square** and **rectangl** commands: Since Version 2.5, a square, which is simply a four-sided polygon, can be made with the **POLYGON** command. If you draw a lot of squares, it might be useful to either 1) create a macro that automatically implements the four-sided option of a polygon, or 2) write an AutoLISP routine that combines a four-sided polygon into a new command. Because Versions 9 and 10 have no **rectangl** command, this macro is useful as is.

AutoLISP functions can be placed in a file called **ACAD.LSP** that automatically loads when you start a drawing. Let's assume you've placed the **rectangl** routine in **ACAD.LSP**. Further, let's say you named the rectangle function **RCT**; anytime you type **RCT (RETURN)** during a drawing, you'll draw rectangles. Below is an AutoLISP version of **rectangl**:

```
(Defun C:REC ()
(Setq Pl (Getpoint "\nFirst point: "))
(Setq P2 (Getpoint "\nDiagonal corner point: "))
(Command "Line" Pl (List (Car P2) (Cadr Pl))
P2 (List (Car Pl) (Cadr P2)) "C")
)
```

The first line says, "Define a function (**Defun**), which will be an AutoCAD command (**C:**) called **REC**." The **\n** tells LISP to start a new line of text, which makes program execution more readable. Note the lines aren't continued with a + because the entire program is surrounded by a set of parentheses. (AutoLISP doesn't need the \ to pause for user input.)

Finally, AutoLISP commands are executed with the **command** command. Otherwise, the two techniques for creating and editing macros are quite similar.

DON'T STOP THERE

Square, **rectangl** and **rectangl/LISP** are variations of a mathematical rectangle. The **square** macro allows rotation; **rectangl** doesn't. A fourth variation might be a combination of these two macros that creates a rectangle at any angle. Another variation might be a rectangle with rounded corners.

Yet another variation might be to take a rectangle with rounded corners and reduce the straight part of two opposite sides to zero length, thereby producing a slot!

The point is this: our examples can be modified for your specific needs. Just look a bit beyond our instruction and analyze your work to identify repetitive tasks. Then use a little creativity to modify or combine macros, menus and AutoLISP to better suit your needs.

SUMMARY

You've begun to put your DOS tools, as well as The AutoCAD Productivity Library, to use. In addition, you now have some useful commands at your fingertips, so when you finish loading a drawing, you're ready for action — not a search through the **ACAD.MNU**.

You entered two simple AutoLISP routines (**rectangl** and **square**) and probably had to "debug" them. And you've learned a little about AutoLISP functions, which you now can begin to recognize.

Finally, we hope you're beginning to see the power of customization. We hope that your creative juices are beginning to flow. Although entering code and debugging can be painful at first, be assured that creating a macro (such as **square** or **rectangl**) is no more than a 20-minute process once you get the hang of it.

Copy the input section of one routine, add to it the mathematics of another — instant macros and increased productivity! You then have them forever, saving time with each use. New commands assigned to a menu system become new solutions. Now, on to bigger and better productivity enhancement.

Improving Your Screen Menu

IN THIS CHAPTER

In the last chapter, we filled in some blank spots on AutoCAD's **ROOT/MAIN** screen sub-menu. We'll become more scientific in this chapter and carefully analyze the position and interaction of AutoCAD's commands. You'll find out how better menu construction can save you enormous preparation and drawing time.

We'll borrow and paraphrase an industry buzzword — RISC (*Reduced Instruction Set Command*) — and show you how it applies to good menu design.

You'll develop a RISC menu that will increase your work speed considerably. You'll learn how to merge it with the existing **ACAD.MNU** to create a new high-speed system combined with the old familiar system you can always fall back on.

In this chapter, we'll assume that you now have a working knowledge of a word editor, such as EDLIN, and are able to access it while you're in an AutoCAD drawing (see Appendix D). However, when we cover new material, or feel that a small reminder is warranted, we'll return to our "tutorial" mode. For a refresher, refer to the Appendices for DOS and EDLIN commands.

Because many users don't have digitizers, we'll work with screen menus first. You can apply the techniques learned in this chapter directly to tablet menus, which are covered in Chapter Seven.

You'll see in the following examples that planning is the major difficulty in menu development. Implementation is easy.

THE MENU SYSTEMS

At the heart of customization and productivity are the powerful, user-definable menu systems pioneered by AutoCAD. You can invent hundreds of new commands with AutoLISP, but unless they're organized in a meaningful, intuitive way, a menu is of little use.

By organizing the macros, commands and AutoLISP routines from *The AutoCAD Productivity Book* (and those of your own creation), you'll create a high-productivity system for doing your work better.

AutoCAD now offers limitless possibilities for menus:

1. Each of four tablets has an unrestricted number of squares.

2. Ten pull-down menus with 20 lines each can be changed on-the-fly to organize thousands of options.

3. Button menus assign the most complex functions to a single button on your digitizer's cursor. These too can change as a command is activated.

4. Icon menus now offer a way to present limitless menu choices graphically. Sometimes words are not enough. How better to select a hatching pattern or a symbol than from a graphic image?

5. Screen menus, on the right side of your monitor, are the most commonly customized.

6. Auxiliary menus work with any wild device that may eventually be created — perhaps devices activated by speech or brain waves!

All these menus are interactive; something created on a tablet can change the screen menu, or cause an icon menu to appear. Menus can be beautifully simple or overly complex. The **ACAD.MNU** furnished with AutoCAD is now in excess of 3,000 lines long. But don't worry —

Autodesk supports all forms of menus when most users would not.

Note: Your graphics card may not support the pull-down and icon menus.

EXAMINING AUTOCAD'S STANDARD SCREEN MENU

Autodesk's John Walker once said, "We have bet our future on the intelligence of our users." In writing this book, we've made the same wager. This chapter offers a streamlined model of a high-speed menu system — one that you can and should tailor to your specific needs. We've provided the thinking tools and the foundation — now you supply the creative polish.

To better understand good menu design, let's analyze a typical drawing sequence using AutoCAD's standard menu from Release 10.

From this point on, closely examine every interactive step between you and your menu to see how you can revise it for greater efficiency.

Let's boot AutoCAD and load in an existing drawing from task **2** of the **MAIN** menu. **Menu Loading**... we're ready to begin.

Add some diagonal and horizontal (**ORTHO**) lines to the drawing, using **OBJECT SNAP** to attach them to existing line work. From the **ROOT** menu,

1. Select: DRAW

Response: DRAW menu

2. Select: LINE

Response: Command: From point:

3. Select: * * * *

Response: OBJECT SNAP menu

4. Select: ENDPOINT (object snap menu disappears.)

Response: Command: From point: Endpoint

5.   Pick points to create several lines.

6.   Note that you must use two "picks" each time you wish to use **OBJECT SNAP**.

Now, while you draw lines, use **ORTHO** to **SNAP** the lines vertically or horizontally. Alas, there's no **ORTHO** command on the **LINE** menu, so look for it. Aha! Not to be found. It used to be in the **MODES** menu which is no longer in existence. However, it seems logical to have it right there in the line menu.

Hit **F8** on the keyboard and go back to drawing lines.

7. Select: DRAW

Response: DRAW menu

8. Select: LINE

Response: LINE menu

9. Select: CONT

Response: Continues the line from where you stopped.

10. Select: * * * *

Response: OBJECT SNAP menu

11. Select: NEArest

Response: You lose the OBJECT SNAP menu.

12.   Hit **ENTER**

Response: LINE command terminated.

Suppose you drew the last three lines by mistake. An **UNDO** from the **Command:** prompt would erase too much. It would be handy to erase them in reverse order, in the way the backspace on a keyboard works. **ERASE LAST** would do it. Let's count the menu selects or picks.

13. Select: EDIT

Response: EDIT menu

14. Select: ERASE

Response: ERASE menu

15. Select: LAST option

Response: One item is selected but is not erased.

16.   Reach over to the keyboard to hit **RETURN**

Response: Entity erased.

17. Select: ERASE

Response: ERASE

18. Select: LAST option

Response: One item is selected but is not erased.

19.   Reach over to the keyboard to hit **RETURN**

Response: Entity erased.

20. Select: ERASE

Response: ERASE

21. Select: LAST option

Response: One item is selected but is not erased.

22.　　　　　　Reach over to the keyboard to hit **RETURN**

Response:　　Entity erased

Isn't it surprising to see how many steps are required just to draw a few lines? For example, it took nine selects or picks to simply **ERASE** the last three objects. Shouldn't there be a **RETURN** on the screen menu to let you terminate the **ERASE** command without reaching for the keyboard? Is there a practical way to reduce this **ERASE** sequence to only three picks and triple the speed of this operation? Sure! In a minute we'll modify **ACAD.MNU** to speed your work.

SCREEN MENUS—AN OVERVIEW

Screen menus can present only 20 commands and macros at one time. Some monitors only accommodate 21. AutoCAD now has more than 122 commands listed in **HELP**, with an average of perhaps five options for each command.

In addition, while executing a command, you may want to select from 12 types of **OBJECT SNAP**, plus **ORTHO**, **GRID**, **SNAP** and 12 object selection possibilities, not to mention all of the **SETVAR** variables and dimensioning variables. (122 x 5 + 12 + 12)/20 (items per screen) = 32 menu screens!

The average user cannot possibly interact effectively with this staggering number of commands and options. This may explain why (1) a "plain vanilla, out-of-the-box" menu may not work optimally for you, and (2) why so many AutoCAD operators are great one-handed typists. Do you remember the good old days when your major drafting decision was choosing whether to use a hard or soft lead pencil?

It's important to remember that with a screen or tablet menu, you must learn not only the commands, but their location in the menu. For example, when you want to erase the last entity in the drawing, you think **ERASE L** as one thought, not **CANCEL**, **EDIT** menu, **ERASE** option, **LAST** sub-option and **RETURN**.

This additional layer of thought can be minimized if not eliminated altogether. CAD should be a transparent process, allowing you to think only of drawing and design and nearly forget that you're using a CAD system to accomplish the task. In other words, a menu should be intuitive. AutoCAD's menu customization features make that easy.

LOGIC VS. FREQUENCY

To manage more than 630 commands and options, you can develop a key word *system* that will lead you from one menu page to another, in much the same way the word **DRAW** on the **ROOT** menu calls up the **DRAW** sub-menu for entering **LINES**, **CIRCLES** and **TEXT**. Thus, **LINE** appears as an option and you can call up the **LINE** menu, where * * * * (**OBJECT SNAP**—who knows why **OSNAP** doesn't appear in the title) appears as an option. You then can access **OBJECT SNAP** commands, and so on.

This is known as a menu *hierarchy*, not unlike the hierarchy of DOS directories and sub-directories discussed in earlier chapters.

The hierarchy of the AutoCAD standard menu is strictly logical and alphabetical. It groups commands dealing with blocks in the **BLOCK** menu. The **DRAW**ing entity commands are in the **DRAW** menu. The **INSERT** command is both a **BLOCK** operation and a **DRAW**ing entity command, so it appears in both menus. Display functions such as **ZOOM** and **PAN** are in the **DISPLAY** menu, and so on.

Regardless of how frequently you might need a command, the required "picks" access different branches in AutoCAD's standard menu tree function in a consistent, logical manner.

You can think of **DRAW\LINE* * * *** as a sort of DOS path through directories. The AutoCAD standard menu allows you to take shortcuts to the **ROOT** menu (like **CD** in DOS), to the **PREVIOUS** menu (**CD..** in DOS) or to other frequently used menus. However, these paths may not be best for you, and AutoCAD has the built-in tools to change them to suit your needs.

ON TO THE WORKING DETAILS

Let's use the above premises to improve your standard **ACAD.MNU**. First, you'll modify the **ACAD.MNU** to speed the process of drawing lines. Later in the chapter, you'll go on to discuss and build an entire menu system based on the RISC methodology.

Below is the **LINE** submenu as it appears in **ACAD.MNU**—at about line **927**. Let's revise it to make it work better. From the EDLIN prompt *

Type: 927L (RETURN)   (The **927** Line number assumes the additions you made in Chapter Four. This will be approximately Line 625 in Release 9.)

Response: 927:***LINE 3

928: [LINE:]^C^CLINE

929:

930: [continue]^C^CLINE;;

931: close

932: undo

etc.

Let's briefly examine submenus and how they're invoked. ****LINE** is the title of this submenu. (The first asterisk at line 927 belongs to **EDLIN**, showing you the last line edited.) The double asterisk, ******, tells AutoCAD this is a submenu, whereas ******* is an entire menu system, such as *****SCREEN** and *****BUTTON**. The **LINE 3** submenu is invoked from the DRAW menu (****DR**) with the statement **[LINE:]$S = X $S = LINE ^C^CLINE**.

AutoCAD is showing off some clever customization here that saves on menu size. There are actually three menus active when you see the **LINE** menu on the screen (and during most other menus as well). The **3** in the submenu title tells the **LINE** menu to start at the third line down on the screen. This leaves **[AutoCAD]** and **[* * * *]** undisturbed and active. Most of the other submenus have a similar **3** in their titles, including the **X** submenu.

$S = X calls up the **X** submenu, which has 15 blank lines down to the commands **LAST, DRAW** and **EDIT.** Next **$S = LINE** invokes the **LINE** submenu. So, submenus **S, X** and **LINE** are active at once on your screen.

Finally, **^C^CLINE** cancels any previous command and enters the **LINE** command. If five lines are used in the **LINE** menu, two in the **S** menu, and three in the **X** menu, then ten (20 minus 10) are available for customization.

Except in the first screen menu, submenus may occur anywhere.

MAKING LINES FASTER

Let's make the following modifications and additions to your **LINE** menu, using EDLIN or another text editor. Don't type yet; the line numbers are for your reference only.

```
927:***LINE 3
928: [LINE:]^C^CLINE
929: [ORTHO]^O
930: [continue]^C^CLINE;;
931: close
932: undo
933: center
934: endpoint
935: insert
936: intersec
937: midpoint
938: perpend
939: quadrant
940: tangent
941: [SNAPTOG]^B
942: [ZOOM D]'ZOOM D
```

etc.

Now all **LINE** functions are grouped together with their associated options, so the most frequently used combinations of **SNAP** and **ORTHO** can be accessed without switching to another menu. We even inserted **ZOOM** Dynamic, which (because of the apostrophe) is transparent and can by used in the middle of the **LINE** command. You might want to consider **TRIM**, **EXTEND**, **FILLET R 0** (join) and **OFFSET**, which are closely related to line work.

Rule 5: A menu should be forgiving. It should anticipate that you'll make mistakes.

LET'S TRY IT!

Boot AutoCAD and begin a new drawing. Using the menus **\DRAW\LINE**, repeat the "etch-a-sketch" example from the beginning of this chapter. Be semi-scientific about it and count your selects. You immediately should discover several time-savers.

Tip: A good operator rarely draws a freehand point. He or she uses **coordinates**, **SNAP**, **ORTHO** and **OBJECT SNAP** to maintain the accuracy of the math-model we loosely refer to as a drawing. That's why we place such importance on **OBJECT SNAP** being closely coupled with commands such as **LINE**.

The critical question is "Did we reduce the number of selects?" The answer is a resounding "Yes!"

Now go back into the **ACAD.MNU**, find the ****ERASE** sub-menu, add the following lines and try it:

```
[ERASE-L]^C^CERASE;L;;
```
(The semicolons are **RETURN**s.)

```
[ERASE-AU]*^C^CERASE;SI;AU
```
(Release 9 or later only.)

You'll really like **ERASE-AU** because it immediately erases a single entity when one is touched. If you make your first pick in an empty space, it stretches a regular window as you move to the right and a crossing window as you move to the left. Once the diagonal corner point is picked, the entities will be picked immediately.

You'll use this for 80 percent of your **ERASE** operations. Autodesk should be applauded for this one. The ***** causes the command to repeat. **SI** causes the command to erase immediately and **AU** executes the **WINDOW** option.

Tip: Minimize stylus movement whenever possible, especially on tablets, by placing the most commonly used items closest at hand. You can place the **LINE** command at the bottom of the sub-menu, resulting in less hand movement. Or, move **ERASE-AU** right under the **ERASE** sub-menu command in the **EDIT** menu. Then you can make two picks with no movement. As an additional refinement, arrange your **OSNAP** commands in order of most frequent use instead of alphabetical order.

WHAT YOU'VE LEARNED

You've just learned that you don't have to endure inefficiency. Do something about it! Three further goals of these examples (and this book) are 1) to encourage scrutiny and analysis of how you work, 2) to foster creative thinking in finding ways to be more productive with AutoCAD, and 3) to give you general concepts and techniques that can be applied in many different situations.

RISC, described below, is one such important concept— and one of the key ideas of this book.

RISC

RISC (Reduced Instruction Set Computer) is an important term in the computer industry. Let's borrow the concept and apply it to AutoCAD productivity. First, let's examine how RISC applies to computers.

For years, computer manufacturers have been adding commands at the hardware level—machine instructions to make life easier for software developers. Computer makers found it both easy and a competitive necessity to take several computer instructions and implement them in hardware — "silicon macros," if you will. New chips had more numerous and faster functions.

In the last few years, however, demand for even more speed has outpaced the ability of the chip makers to deliver faster chips at a reasonable cost.

In investigating how most software interacted with the computer, developers found that just 20 percent of the hardware commands were used 80 percent of the time!

They then discovered that if the silicon were optimized for that most-used 20 percent of instructions (while the software managed the less-used hardware commands), the net throughput of the computer jumped, even though 80 percent of the commands were now executed with software at a much slower rate. Thus the RISC concept was born!

RISC AND AUTOCAD

Do you use certain AutoCAD commands only rarely? Do you use others only two or three times per drawing session? Do you use still other commands all the time?

Right now, take a few minutes to compile a list of your most frequently used commands and their options. If you're using about 20 percent of AutoCAD's commands about 80 percent of the time, then read on.

By placing all commands in a logical order, the **ACAD** standard menu assigns equal weight to each one. For example, a machine designer has no great need for **SKETCH** and **TRACE** commands. However, **SKETCH** is frequently used for contours in civil work, while **TRACE**s are vital to printed circuit board design. Yet all these commands are listed in alphabetical order in AutoCAD's **DRAW** menu. Because AutoCAD has no way of knowing your discipline, the program by necessity is designed for the lowest common denominator!

There are two full menu pages of **DRAW** commands. **LINE**, for example, now has equal weight with **DONUT** on the first page. It takes an additional pick to access the frequently used **TEXT** command.

Similarly, if you're an architect, you don't want your macros for doors, windows and walls buried in some backwater sub-menu. Frequently used commands must be placed at your fingertips!

Let's name this concept "Reduced Instruction Set *Command*" menu (a RISC menu). Now let's assemble a small group of your most important commands, options, macros and AutoLISP routines into a menu with no more than two screen menu pages — about 40 options. They'll be the first selections on your screen. You'll then attach this to the front of your standard **ACAD.MNU** screen menu, so you easily can toggle back and forth to access your less frequently used commands.

At the top of our RISC menu you'll see **A-C-A-D**, which will return you intact to terra firma, the **ACAD.MNU**. The one notable addition to the **ACAD.MNU** will be a new selection, **R-I-S-C**, which takes you back to our high-speed "front end," without cutting you off from the past.

CREATING YOUR RISC MENU

As a working example, let's create a RISC menu for machine design, a fairly generic menu. While working through the rest of this chapter, you should translate the RISC menu to your discipline, using our recommendations as a guideline. For example, if you use the **QUICK OBJECT SNAP** option, then by all means add it to your menu in place of one of our recommended commands.

Only you know how AutoCAD works best for you. From here on, this book becomes increasingly conceptual, allowing you to make your own creative choices.

Back to work. Let's get the RISC menu working before you modify it for your applications. Below is the list of commands, options, macros and AutoLISP routines you'll use to create your RISC menu. Don't type these in for now; just review them.

	**RISC1		**RISC2
1.	A-C-A-D	1.	STRETCH
2.	COPY	2.	MIRROR
3.	MOVE	3.	MACROS

4. ERASE/ed	4. SNAP
5. REDRAW	5. GRID
6. PAN	6. PEDIT
7. ZOOM	7. POINT
8. **SAVE**	8. SHELL
9. LAYER	9. INQY/DIST
10. INSERT	10. HATCH
11. TEXT.125	11. POLYGON
12. ARC-SCE	12. ARRAY
13. CIRCLE	13. UNDO
14. OFFSET	14. EXTEND
15. PLINE	15. TRIM
16. LINE	16. BREAK
17. UCS	17. CHANGE
18. DVIEW	18. DIM
19. VPORTS	19. FILLET
20. RISC2	20. RISC1

On the first **RISC** menu page, we place commands in a bottom-up order of importance. Because **RISC2** commands aren't used as frequently as **RISC1** commands, they're organized more loosely. When you become more familiar with the menus, reorganize them as you see fit.

If you don't have Release 10, DVIEW, UCS and VPORTS should be replaced by other frequently used commands.

Note line **3** of the **RISC2** menu, **MACROS**. We've created a submenu for your macros (or macros you select from the The AutoCAD Productivity Library). Because it appears just after the **RISC** submenus, you can find it easily.

With the exception of the first screen menu, you can arrange screen sub-menus in any order.

CREATING YOUR SCREEN RISC.MNU

Because of the length of the full menu, we show full code for only the first two menus. (Besides, it's time to leave most of it up to you.) For other submenus, we show and discuss important macros and concepts. The full **RISC** menu is available on *The AutoCAD Productivity Diskette*.

Before creating your **RISC** menu, copy **ACAD.MNU** to **RISC.MNU** (C:\ > COPY ACAD.MNU RISC.MNU).

Note: To differentiate **RISC** submenus, preface **RISC** menu titles with an **R**. Thus, the ****LINE** submenu will appear ****RLINE**. This also will speed your search for RISC menu items when revising or debugging.

For example, in EDLIN you can access the RISC **TEXT** submenu (**RTEXT**) by typing **1,9999S**RTEXT**, where **S** means search. Remember to match upper and lower cases.

Beginning at the line right after *****SCREEN** (line **431** in Release 10), type the two **RISC** menus (the Insert mode in EDLIN):

```
***SCREEN
```

Begin here:
```
***RISC1
[   A-C-A-D ]$S=S
[       COPY]$S=RCopy ^C^CCopy
[       MOVE]$S=RMOVE ^C^CMove
[   ERASE/ed]$S=RErase *^C^CErase;Si;Au
[    REDRAW]'Redraw
[        PAN]'Pan
[       ZOOM]$S=RZoom 'Zoom;D
[   **SAVE**]^C^CSave
[      LAYER]$S=RLayer ^C^CLayer
[     INSERT]$S=RInsert1 ^C^CInsert
[   TEXT.125]$S=RText ^C^CText;\0.125;\
[        ARC]$S=RArc *^C^CArc;
[   CIRCLE R]$S=RCircle *^C^CCircle
[     OFFSET]$S=ROffset *^C^COffset
[      PLINE]$S=RPline ^C^CPline
[       LINE]$S=RLine *^C^CLine
[        UCS]$S=RUcs ^C^CUcs
[      DVIEW]$S=RDview ^C^CDview
[     VPORTS]$S=RVports ^C^CVports
[      RISC2]$S=RISC2
```

```
**RISC2
[ STRETCH]^C^CStretch;C
[  MIRROR]$S=RMirror ^C^CMirror
[  MACROS]$S=RMacros
[    SNAP]$S=RSnap ^C^CSnap
[    GRID]$S=RGrid ^C^CGrid
[   PEDIT]$S=RPline ^C^CPedit
[   POINT]$S=RPoint *^C^CPoint
[   SHELL]$S=RShell
[INQY/DIS]$S=RInquiry *^C^CDist
[   HATCH]$S=RHatch ^C^CLayer;S;6;;Hatch
[ POLYGON]$S=RPolygon *^C^CPolygon
[   ARRAY] $S=RArray ^C^CArray
[    UNDO]$S=RUndo
[  EXTEND]*^C^CExtend
[    TRIM]*^C^CTrim
[   BREAK]$S=RBREAK *^C^CBreak
[  CHANGE]$S=RChange *^C^CChange
[     DIM]$S=RDim ^C^CDim
[  FILLET]$S=RFillet *^C^CFillet
[   RISC1]$S=RISC1
```

Note: After a statement that switches menus (such as $S = GRID), you must add a space, not a semicolon.

Note the use of an asterisk to make commands repeat. If you want to use the AutoLISP program, use the following syntax:

```
[RECTANGL]^C^C(IF (NOT C:R);+
(LOAD "C:/ACAD/R"));MULTIPLE;R;
```

This menu statement uses an AutoLISP **if** statement to check whether **R.LSP** has been loaded. If not, then it loads it from the **C:\ACAD >** directory. Note the forward slash in the directory path. You may use \\ or /, but not a single backslash, which signifies a control character. Note the use of a new command, **MULTIPLE**, which like * causes a command to repeat. The * must begin the line. In this case an asterisk will cause AutoLISP to begin "looping." Sometimes one works better than the other.

RISC SUBMENUS

The above are two main **RISC** menus that attach directly to AutoCAD's **MAIN** menu (**ACAD.MNU**). Below are submenus invoked by selections in the two **RISC** menus.

Be sure to place this line on each submenu:

```
[RISC1]$S=RISC1
```

Without it, you can't get back to, or out of, the submenu!

Finally, just as in the **LINE** submenu we discussed earlier in this chapter, place common **OBJECT SNAPS** and commonly related commands in every submenu where useful (such as **CIRCLE**, **PLINE**, etc.).

Macros

You may enter your own macros or use The AutoCAD Productivity Library to enter your preferred macros. Use the **rectangl** example to load **LISP** (see Chapter Four).

```
**RMACROS
[MY LISP]^C^C(IF (NOT C:MYLISP)
(LOAD "C:/ACAD/MYLISP"));MULTIPLE;MYLISP;
etc.
```

Lines

This menu should be approximately the same as the one you created earlier in this chapter.

```
**RLINE
  etc.
```

Polylines

Polylines have assumed a major role since Version 2.5.
You can **SKETCH** with them (**SETVAR SKPOLY**). In
Release 9 or later, you can use **PEDIT** to turn them into
splines. You'll want to place **PLINE** on your first RISC
menu (**RISC1**).

By combining **ACAD.MNU** submenus you can reduce
the **PLINE** options from five submenus to three.

```
**RPLINE
[PLINE:]^C^CPline
[ARC:]Arc $S=RPArc
etc.

**RPARC
[ANGLE:]A $S=RPArcang
[CENTER:]CE $S=RPArcang
etc.

**RPARCANG
[CENTER]C Drag $S=
[RADIUS]R \$S=
etc.
```

Circles

You may want to place **ELLIPSE**, **3D-CIRC.LSP** (from the
library), **POLYGON**, **BREAK** and **OBJECT SNAPS** in the
circle submenu.

```
**RCIRCLE
etc.
```

Arcs

There are a lot of **ARC** options! You may want to omit
rarely used options, such as **CHORD**, which can be
invoked easily with a one-letter keystroke, so that you have
room for some **OBJECT SNAPS**.

```
**RARC
```
etc.

Text

Many speed improvements in our **RISC** submenus result from combining the command and its option on a single line. For example, if you enter **right-justified** text, change your mind and want **centered** text, you need only reselect the desired option. This is part of our "single pick" philosophy.

The **ACAD.MNU** forces you to cancel your current command, reselect the **TEXT** command, then select the **centered** option. Your **RISC** menu gives a three-to-one improvement!

You should also combine the **QTEXT** and **STYLE** menus into the **RSTYLE** menu with several predefined styles. Text fonts don't have to be typed in; you now can even obtain a listing of available fonts. Most of the **STYLE** options return you to the previous menu with the **$S =** .

Because our most common text is 1/8" high, that's also the default option. We always put our annotation on **layer 4**; as you pick **TEXT**, you're automatically placed on that layer. You may change to any layer you wish.

Consult The AutoCAD Productivity Library for **TEXT**-related AutoLISP routines. For example, Macro No. 42, **TSZ.LSP**, globally changes **TEXT** heights.

Here are the complete **TEXT** menus as an example. Note the use of related commands, such as **MOVE**.

```
**RTEXT
[QTEXT ON]^C^CQText;On $S=RStyle
[STYLE:]^CStyle $S=RStyle
[ERASE-L]^C^CErase;L;;
midpoint
nearest
insert
center
intersec
```

```
endpoint
[MOVE]^C^CMove
[TEXT-SZ]^C^C(IF (NOT C:TSZ);+
(LOAD "C:/ACAD/TSZ"));MULTIPLE;TSZ;
[SPELL]^C^CChange;\;;;;;;
[ORTHO]^O
[NEW LINE];
[TEXT-S]^C^CText;S;
[TEXT-A]^C^CLayer;S;4;;Text;A;
[TEXT-R]^C^CLayer;S;4;;Text;R;
[TEXT-C]^C^CLayer;S;4;;Text;C;
[TEXT-L]^C^CLayer;S;4;;Text;
[TEXT.125]$S=RText ^C^CLayer;S;4;;Text;\0.125;\
[RISC1]$S=RISC1

**RSTYLE
[QTEXT OF]^C^CQText;Of $S=
[CREATE]^C^CStyle
[STYLE:]^C^CStyle
[LISTING]^C^CStyle;?
[FONTS ?]^C^CDir;*.SHX
standard
simplex
vertical
complex
italic
[ACTIVATE]
[ITALIC]^C^CText;S;Italic;^C$S=
[VERTICAL]^C^CText;S;Vertical;^C$S=
[SIMPLEX]^C^CText;S;Simplex;^C$S=
[COMPLEX]^C^CText;S;Complex;^C$S=
[STANDARD]^C^CText;S;Standard;^C$S=
[STYLE 1]^C^CText;S;1;^C$S=
[STYLE 2]^C^CText;S;2;^C$S=
[STYLE 3]^C^CText;S;3;^C$S=
[LASTMENU]$S=
```

Symbol Insertion

Screen menus offer many ways to insert symbols. With only eight characters to uniquely describe each symbol and the average operator using more than 100 symbols, it quickly becomes difficult to give rarely used symbols meaningful names.

The following generic symbol names (when coupled with a wall chart or other hard-copy scheme to associate symbol and name) offer a way of standardizing the interface for all users. (Note that tablets enable you to access the visual symbol directly from the tablet's surface.)

We hope our names are obvious:

HDWR = Hardware,
ELEC = Electrical and
HYDR = Hydraulic.

Tip: Most text editors allow you to perform a global replacement if you want to change sub-menu names. For example, you might want to change all **HDWR** symbols to **PIPE** symbols. In EDLIN, we would use the *replace text* option:

```
1,999RHDWR^ZPIPE    (RETURN)
```

Finally, we've placed **BLOCK** and **WBLOCK** on these menus because of their close relationship to symbols.

Three types of symbols are used on a drawing:

1. Symbols inserted at full scale that should not be scaled. A 36 x 36 shower stall is always 36 x 36.

2. Architectural schematic symbols that must be scaled in relation to the drawing scale (because you would use the same on the plastic template regardless of the scale).

3. Symbols that must be scaled every time. Consider creating a hex head bolt that is 1 inch across the flats. When you scale it, it becomes every bolt ever made!

Below are examples of how you might handle each of the three examples:

```
[36x36swr]*^C^CInsert;36x36swr;\1;1;;
[outletl]*^C^CInsert;Outletl\;(getvar "dimscale");;;
[hexhd]^C^CInsert;hexhd
```

If you want to know the size of the symbol, you could have the macro **BREAK** a line to the proper length. For example, in a piping schematic, you could draw the straight lines, then insert valve symbols into the line work—at angles, if you wish. Here's a simple example:

```
[syml]*^C^C(setq pt (getpoint "Insertion Point: "));\+
break !pt @1,0;+
insert;syml;!pt;1;1;0
```

To try it, draw some horizontal lines and make a square symbol, **SYM1**, a 1"x1" box like this:

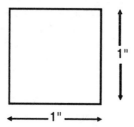

```
**RINSERT1
[BLOCK]^C^CBlock
[WBLOCK]^C^CWBlock
[HDWR001]^C^CInsert;HDWR001;Drag
etc.


[--MORE--]$S=RInsert2
[ELECT]$S=RInsert3
[HYDR]$S=RInsert4
[RISC1]$S=RISC1
```

```
**RINSERT2
[HDWR015]^C^CInsert;HDWR015;Drag
etc.


[LASTMENU]$S=RInsert1
[ELECT]$S=RInsert3
[HYDR]$S=RInsert4
[RISC1]$S=RISC1

**RINSERT3
[ELEC001]^C^CInsert;ELEC001;Drag
etc.


[HDWR]$S=RInsert1
[HYDR]$S=RInsert4
[RISC1]$S=RISC1
**RINSERT4
[HYDR001]^C^CInsert;HYDR001;Drag
etc.
```

Offset

OFFSET is a wonderful way to draw — sloppy and fast. Just throw up a few lines, then **OFFSET** them with little care for their length and whether they mate. Finally, **TRIM**, **EX-TEND**, **BREAK** and **JOIN** (**FILLET R = 0**) to clean it all up.

If you're an architect, you may want to put your most common wall sizes on this menu.

```
**ROFFSET
[OFFSET-D]^C^COffset
[OFFSET-T]^C^COffset;T
1"
4 5/8"
etc.
```

Undo

This function works so well that it might be considered one of the major reasons to purchase AutoCAD. An operator should be working so fast and concentrating so hard on the design that one out of ten moves is a mistake! What? Encouragement to make mistakes? Yes. If you aren't making lots of mistakes, you're going too slowly and thinking too long about each operation! AutoCAD is very tolerant. With the **UNDO** command you can recover instantly.

```
**UNDO
[U]U
[UNDO]^C^CUndo
[SET-MARK]^C^CUndo;Mark
[UNDO-GRP]^C^CUndo;G
etc.
```

Layers

Layers with long names are fine, but you can enter numbers much faster. As with symbol insertion, a wall chart with layer assignments is useful.

Architects who use many layers probably will prefer numbers. For example, in the **300** series used for **electrical**, you can turn off all electrical layers just by typing **3***.

When layers have been set up, the main activity is switching between them. Of course, you can put these layers in **ACAD.DWG** (prototype drawing), so you won't have to reset them.

You can even build layer-switching into some commands. For example, hatching can be placed on a certain layer, such as **6**, so you never have to think about it. Similarly, we've put the options on a separate sub-menu and included related commands, such as **LINETYPE** and **RENAME**.

You may want to include an AutoLISP routine for deleting all entities on a layer. (See Macro 36 in the Productivity Library.)

```
**RLAYER
[1]^C^CLayer;S;1;;$S=
[2]^C^CLayer;S;2;;$S=
etc.


[OPTIONS]$S=RLayer2
[RISC1]$S=RISC1

**RLAYER2
[NEW]^C^CLayer;N
[SET]^C^CLayer;S;\;
[COLOR]^C^CLayer;C
etc.
```

Zooms, Pan, Views and Slides

You can make the most commonly used display features, particularly **VIEWS** and **SLIDES**, much easier to use. Now you just have to remember numbers—a real time-saver.

Also, **[ZOOM-VS]** will display the drawing **EXTENTS** without a double **REGEN**. If drawing **EXTENTS** have been changed by drawing an entity outside **EXTENTS**, then use the standard **ZOOM-E**.

```
**RZOOM
[MSLIDE2]^C^CMSlide;2
[MSLIDE1]^C^CMSlide;1
[VSLIDE2]^C^CVSlide;2
[VSLIDE1]^C^CVSlide;1
[REGEN]^C^CRegen
[MAKE-V2]^C^CView;W;V2;W
[MAKE-V1]^C^CView;W;V1;W
[RESTR-V2]^C^CView;R;V2
[RESTR-V1]^C^CView;R;V1
[PAN]^C^CPan
[ZOOM]^C^CZoom
[   .3X]^C^CZoom;0.3X
```

```
[   .75X]^C^CZoom;0.75X
[ZOOM-E]^C^CZoom;E
[ZOOM-VS]^C^CZoom;W;(Getvar "VSMIN");(Getvar "VSMAX")
[ZOOM-P]^C^CZoom;P
[ZOOM-A]^C^CZoom;A
[ZOOM-W]^C^CZoom;W
[VPORTS]^C^CVPORTS
[RISC1]$S=RISC1
```

Erase and Edits

Since there are more empty spots on this submenu than
ERASE options, you might take the opportunity to fill them
with other handy editing commands. The **FILTER** (Macro
51) would be a natural. Also remember the **ERASE;SI;AU**
options in Release 9, and place your most common erase
option right under the **ERASE** selection in the **RISC1**
menu, line **6**. An **ENTER** square might be appropriate, so
that you can avoid reaching for the keyboard when you
want to end the selection process. Here's how:


```
[ENTER];
```

Simple!!


```
**RERASE
```
etc.

Break

BREAK-1P will split a line in two parts, requiring you to
enter one point. **BREAK-2P** is the standard **BREAK** command and requires two user points. **BREAK-3P** requires 3
points: a point to select the object and two more to indicate the break points. Include **OBJECT SNAPS** and **TRIM**
in this one.

```
  **RBREAK
[BREAK-1P]^C^CBreak;\@0,0
[BREAK-2P]^C^CBreak
[BREAK-3P]^C^CBreak;\F
etc.
```

Moving

Have you ever moved or copied something in your draw-ing, only to have it zapped into outer space because you hit an extra (**RETURN**) at the wrong moment? You had better put **U** for **UNDO** in this sub-menu. The **SI** and **AU** options work well for this command. You also may want to include **ORTHO**.

```
  **RMOVE
[MOVE]*^C^CMOVE;SI;AU
[ORTHO]^O
etc.
```

Copies

The **COPY** command is like **MOVE**. Be sure to have a pick for the multiple option of **COPY**.

```
  **RCOPY
[COPY-AU]^C^CCopy;SI;AU
[MULTI]m
etc.
```

Arrays

Creating rectangular and circular patterns is a common task. However, putting a rectangular pattern on an angle involves setting the **SNAP ANGLE** to a new angle. You may want to include forms of the **SNAP** command on this submenu.

Note: Although we've been recommending that you use an asterisk to repeat most commands, the asterisk should not be used with **ARRAY**s, which are not repeated often. It's important to consider these subtle differences.

Fight every extra CAD motion. In some cases the repeated command causes the extra action of a **CANCEL**. You must weigh the benefits against the occasional extra **CANCEL**.

Below is a handy macro for circular **ARRAY**s. Let's say you want to put 13 objects on a circular **ARRAY**. When AutoCAD prompts you for **Angle between items:**, you might have to use your calculator. The **calc ang** macro automatically performs this calculation. You can create other macros that do all sorts of common calculations and conversions, such as changing civil units to architectural.

```
**RARRAY
[ARRAY]^C^CArray;SI;AU
[calc ang]^C^C(Setq P1 +
(Getreal "Enter the number of items"));\+
(Setq P1 (Rtos (/ 360.0 P1) 2 4))
[ROTATED]^C^CSnap;R
```

Mirrors

You can **MIRROR** an **OBJECT** to nearly any angle, so why not include a few standard angles in this sub-menu so that you don't have to type them? Notice that because the **MIRROR** command asks for two points, the **[45-deg]** is followed by a polar coordinate at 45 degrees.

Because you'll usually want to mirror around 90 degree increments, put **ORTHO** in this menu. Finally, you can **MIRROR** text or have it "right reading," by using the transparent **'setvar** command. If you have a definite preference for right-reading text, call up the **ACAD.DWG** prototype drawing, set the mirrored text right reading, and then save it.

```
**RMIRROR
[MIRROR]^C^CMirror;SI;AU
[ORTHO]^O
[MIRRTXT]'setvar;mirrtext;1
[RITE-TXT]'setvar;mirrtext;0
[45-deg]@1-
etc.
```

Dimensioning

There are so many dimensioning options that it's impossible to summarize them all in this chapter. We suggest that you call up prototype drawings (usually blank drawings with layers and preset variables). Then set the dimension variables and units and save them. This can save space in your menus.

Productivity Tip: Set up your dimension to be correct at 1 = 1 scale. Then use **DIMSCALE** to correct for different scales, yet maintain the correct proportions when plotted out. In an integrated system of customization, the **DIMSCALE** variable can be accessed to scale everything in the drawing, including symbol insertions.

```
**RDIM
etc.
```

```
**RVAR 1
etc.
```

Snaps

Apply the "single pick" philosophy to this submenu by including the snap increments most commonly used in your business.

    Note: You can change the **SNAP** increment while drawing a line, however, using **setvar**, you must turn **SNAP** on as a separated function. Look closely at how this can be done. (The $S = returns to the previous menu.)

```
**RSNAP
[1/8]'Setvar;SnapUnit;0.125,0.125;$S=
[1/4]'Setvar;SnapUnit;0.25,0.25;$S=
etc.


[Snap on]'Setvar;SnapMode;1
[Snap off]'Setvar;SnapMode;0
```

Grids

Because most people **SNAP** to a fourth or a half of the **GRID** setting, there should be fewer **GRID** than **SNAP** settings. You may be surprised that we advise the inclusion of **LIMITS** in this menu. Why? The **LIMITS** command controls the area where **GRID** is located.

Like **SNAP**, **GRID**s can be changed transparently with the **SETVAR** command.

Note two unusual steps in the macros for setting up the screen size (**[17 x 11]**.....):

1) We draw a line larger than the desired screen;

2) Then we **ZOOM EXTENTS** and **ERASE LAST**.

In the first line, we set a new grid. However, the grid doesn't appear or change except after a **REDRAW**. All happens transparently.

```
**RGRID
[.100]'Setvar;GridUnit;.100,.100;'Redraw;$S=
[ 1/4 ]'Setvar;GridUnit;.25,.25;'Redraw;$S=
[grid-on]'Setvar;Gridmode;1;'Redraw
[grid-off]'Setvar;Gridmode;0;'Redraw
[ LIMITS]^C^CLimits
[17 X 11]^C^CLimits;-1,-1:18,12; +
Line;-1,-1; 18,12;;+
Zoom;E;Erase;L;;
[   SNAP]$S=RSnap ^C^CSnap
[ E-UNITS]^C^CUnits 2 4 2 2 Graphscr
[ A-UNITS]^C^CUnits 4 16 2 2 Graphscr
etc.
```

SHELL, the ACAD.PGP file

Most people don't realize the great value of AutoCAD's ability to **EXIT** to the operating system. Now that you're more familiar with DOS, you'll begin to see the possibilities.

For example, with **SHELL**, you can use DOS's copy command without leaving your drawing. Also, you can access EDLIN while you're in a drawing, make an ASCII word processing file, then pull it into your drawing with an AutoLISP routine (with the added ability of controlling the vertical line spacing and making quick revisions). See Macro 45 ("Import").

Using a text editor from **SHELL** is also great for long bills of materials or notes and specifications.

You can even run BASIC programs that create drawings in the form of **SCRIPT** files or **DXF** files, which then can be executed into the current drawing (great for a family of parts).

Tip: You can cut menu design and AutoLISP development time in half if you shell out to a word processor to make your modifications without leaving your drawing. If you're working on a menu, use the **MENU** command to reload it. If you're in AutoLISP, type **(load fname)** to reload an AutoLISP function.

Remember, the **ACAD.PGP** file that controls the **SHELL** feature is simply an ASCII file that AutoCAD reads once during boot-up. You can add your own AutoCAD commands by following the existing line patterns.

To access EDLIN from a drawing, add this line to the **ACAD.PGP (Pig Pen)** file:

```
EDLIN,C:\DOS\EDLIN,100000,File to edit: ,0
```

Note that you can specify the path to the directory, possibly the DOS directory, where **EDLIN.COM** is located, so that you only need one copy on your disk.

Using **SHELL** and your knowledge of DOS, you can create a simple online database. For example, if you need information on drill sizes, you can call up a size listing.

Just use the DOS **TYPE** command in the **PGP** file to type out an ASCII file listing drill sizes. You can do the same for fraction-to-decimal conversions, screw thread data, anything! We've included some of these commands in this submenu.

```
**RSHELL
[SHELL]^C^CShell
[DIR]^C^CDir
[EDLIN]^C^CEdlin
[CONVER]^C^CConver
[FLHSCREW]^C^CFlhscrew
[DRILL]^C^CDrill
[FRACS]^C^CFracs
[PIPETHD]^C^CPipethd
etc.
```

These are some typical **ACAD.PGP** entries:

```
FRACS,TYPE \ACAD\FRACS,50000,,0
NUT,TYPE \ACAD\NUT,50000,,0
PIPETHD,TYPE \ACAD\PIPETHD,50000,,0
```

Inquiry

CAD creates both a mathematical description of your drawing and a database of other text information, either text itself or attributes. Although you usually think of CAD as a drafting tool, your exquisite inked drawings are only by-products of the mathematical models created on the screen.

Thus, you can expect more from your CAD drawings, such as the computation of accurate areas and distances, or the number of screws that appear in a given drawing or view.

The **INQUIRY** section is an important resource for checking and maintaining the accuracy of your work.

Entity access and selection set filters in AutoLISP allow you to total the number of screws, two-by-fours, lines or any drawing entity. You easily can develop routines to total the length of 1/2" pipe, amount of conduit and so on.

You can place such macros in the **INQUIRY** submenu. See The AutoCAD Productivity Library for **FILTER.LSP** (Macro 51).

Tip: To measure a large, complex area, use **OBJECT SNAP** to draw a continuous **POLYLINE** over its perimeter, including curves. Or convert the existing line work to a **POLYLINE**. Then use the **AREA** command to get the area. If you're in facilities management, you may put these **POLYLINES**, representing rooms, on a unique layer. To move walls, **STRETCH** the corresponding **POLYLINE**. With a modification to the **FILTER.LSP** routine, you can quickly retotal the areas.

In the **INQUIRY** submenu, you may want to include **SNAPs**, and even **PLINE**.

```
**RINQUIRY
[  AREA]^C^CArea
[LIST]^C^CList
[DIST]^C^CDist
etc.
```

Hatching

Hatching normally is done on a separate layer, which can be frozen to improve display times. To prevent you from having to remember switching layers, you can build this process into the **HATCH** macro on this sub-menu. In the macro below, the **LAYER** command preceding **HATCH** automatically places you on **LAYER 6**. After hatching, you must reset to another layer.

You'd hardly expect to find **PLINE** on this menu, would you? But as any experienced user knows, hatching is difficult. You first must create the perfect "bottle" to contain the hatching—otherwise stray lines are inevitable.

What better way to create the perfect bottle than by tracing over the area with a **POLYLINE**? With **PLINE**, **OBJECT SNAP** and a little practice, you now can trace over any irregular boundary containing arcs and lines, then **HATCH LAST**!

EXPLODE is handy, too. Hatching comes in as a block. If you want to correct a few errant lines, just **EXPLODE** your hatching, then use **TRIM**.

```
**RHATCH
[HATCH]^C^CLayer;S;6;;Hatch
[MAGNESUM]ansi37
[ALUMINUM]ansi38
[LINES]line
[PEDIT]^C^CPedit
[PLINE]^C^CPline
[TRIM]^C^CTrim
[EXTEND]^C^CExtend
etc.
```

Fillets and Chamfers

Place your most common **FILLET** options on the menu for a single pick. If you normally perform multiple fillets (e.g., when constructing plates), modify the menu lines for automatic fillet repetition.

Example: `[FIL 1/16]^C^CMultiple Fillet;R;0.0625`

The **JOIN** selection is a fillet with a zero radius, which creates a sharp corner.

```
**RFILLET
[FIL 1/8]^C^CMultiple;Fillet;R;0.125;;
[FIL 3/16]^C^CMultiple;Fillet;R;0.1875;;
[JOIN]^C^CMultiple;Fillet;R;0;;
etc.
```

```
**RCHAMFER
[CHF 1/16]^C^CChamfer;D;0.0625;;;
etc.
```

Change

When created as a macro, **CHANGE** is somewhat inflexible in the selection process, which may cause some **CHANGE** commands to "bomb out." For example, if you define your **TEXT** height with the **STYLE** command, the **CHNG-TXT** macro has the wrong number of **RETURN**s. To make it work for that type of text, remove one semicolon (;).

With entity access in AutoLISP, many **CHANGE** functions work better as AutoLISP routines. For example, Macro 42 in The AutoCAD Productivity Library is an AutoLISP routine that changes **TEXT** height regardless of how the text was created.

[EXTEND2] appears in this sub-menu because it is a variant of the **CHANGE** command. **CHANGE** is often used to lengthen a line, but when the line is at an angle, maintaining the angle is difficult. **[EXTEND]** will not change the line angle.

```
**RCHANGE
[EXTEND]^C^C+
(Setq P1 (Osnap (Getpoint "Touch line") "End"));\+
(Setq P2 (Osnap P1 ""Mid"));+
(Setq A (Angle P2 P1));+
(Setq P3 +
(Getdist P1 "Enter extension distance: "));\+
(Setq P4 (Polar P1 A P3));+
Change;!P2;;!P4
[CHNG-TXT]^C^CChange;\;;;;;;
[ CHANGE]^C^CChange
etc.
```

You might want to add **CHPROP** for 3D change properties in Release 10.

Point

Does the **POINT** command deserve its own sub-menu? A good question! Perhaps it's not needed in older versions, but beginning with Version 2.5, AutoCAD offers a number of choices for the point style (such as **CROSS**, **CIRCLE** and **BOX**). In addition, you can control the point size relative to screen size.

On this sub-menu you may include a cross and an arrowhead, which are just AutoCAD blocks.

Let's consider an interesting use for the cross. First, for ease of scaling, make it 1" x 1". Now, imagine you have a very large part that you need to dimension end-to-end. At each end you have several entities that make it impossible to use **OBJECT SNAP** and be certain of locking onto the right choice.

Now, **ZOOM WINDOW** around one end. Place a cross exactly where you want it. **SCALE** it to a ridiculously large size and **ROTATE** it 45 degrees. Then **ZOOM** the other end and do the same. **ZOOM** to see the full object. Now dimension to the insert points of the crosses and **ERASE** them. This method certainly saves a lot of eye strain! Of course, you could use a transparent **ZOOM** to avoid this.

```
**RPOINT
[ARROWHD]^C^CInsert;Ahd
[CROSS]^C^CInsert;Cross
[POINT]^C^CPoint
etc.
```

Because it's always easier to modify an existing menu than to enter one in "from scratch," we encourage you to obtain *The AutoCAD Productivity Diskette*, so that you can immediately benefit from these time-saving ideas.

SUMMARY

You really got serious about AutoCAD productivity in this chapter!

First, you did some scientific thinking about how you interact with AutoCAD. You analyzed how many selects it took to draw lines. Surprised by the number of menu interactions, you said, "That's not good enough," and created an enhanced **LINE** submenu for **ACAD.MNU** that significantly improved interaction and saved you time.

You asked the question, "Do I use 20 percent of the AutoCAD commands 80 percent of the time?" Then, armed with the knowledge that you can alter your AutoCAD environment to meet your needs, you began striving for even greater enhancements through the **RISC** menu.

Intended primarily as an instructional tool, **RISC** embodies most of the concepts and techniques outlined in this book, including:

1. Reducing menu interaction to a bare minimum;

2. Making your interactions intuitive, so all necessary options appear as needed without additional selections;

3. Continually analyzing how you interact with AutoCAD to accomplish a task, then making a macro or AutoLISP routine that requires as little interaction as possible;

4. Limiting your "fast" menus to the 20 percent of commands and options that you use 80 percent of the time, and typing the rest or accessing them from the **ACAD.MNU**;

5. Creating a **RISC** menu for each discipline (sometimes for each project) to ensure peak productivity.

As item 4 implies, the **RISC** menu doesn't cut you off from the past, but acts as a high-productivity "front end" to AutoCAD's standard menu.

Because each business has different needs, our **RISC** menu probably isn't your best **RISC** menu. Analysis and creativity are the keys to attaining higher productivity.

You've discovered it takes some thought to sort out the "customization" puzzle. You probably also discovered the task requires careful planning and a good deal of keyboarding. Remember, creating and debugging new menus and macros is a one-time project. At the end of the rainbow is a quantum leap in productivity that more than justifies your efforts.

Designing and Creating Tablet Menus

IN THIS CHAPTER

Every graphics tablet has its pros and cons, proponents and detractors. Some users' opinions are based on economics — a tablet costs three to seven times more than a mouse. Let's explore why they're well worth the price.

We'll show you how all the commands and macros from the previous chapter can easily be activated from the tablet surface. To help you increase your productivity, a small sample menu overlay is included that can be copied from the book.

In addition, we'll analyze the organization of a typical tablet menu and comment on some of its "ergonomic" factors, including button menus.

Finally we'll discuss the steps involved in creating your own tablet overlay and menu software.

WHY A TABLET AND OVERLAY?

Think of any mini- or mainframe CAD system. Can you imagine one without a digitizer as the primary input device? Would it have a user-definable tablet overlay? Most large CAD systems have digitizers and user-definable tablet menus. There must be a reason for that.

With screen menus or pull-downs, your command organization is fragmented into discrete units of 20 options — even fewer, when you consider that one, two or three spaces are required at the bottom of each submenu just to return you to the top menus or **lastmenu**.

Because each screen submenu is a discrete unit, you have to put common options, like **OBJECT SNAP**, on each one. (You can put **OBJECT SNAP** in a menu by itself, but that requires two additional selects for every use.) In the **RISC** menu, the **endpoint** option occurs 17 times. On a tablet, **endpoint** requires only one placement.

Tablet menus are simpler to create and organize than screen menus. They're also an important learning tool that can dramatically reduce training time for new AutoCAD users in three important ways:

1. An overlay is like a smorgasbord — everything is laid out for you to see. Unlike screen menus, tablets give easy access to commands and macros, allowing users to quickly choose the best option without having to ponder all the possibilities.

2. While searching the tablet for a way to accomplish a drafting task, a new user will spot icons and words that actually suggest the task. Thus, he/she will be encouraged to experiment.

A new user has the same problems as a person learning the English language. All of the words are in the dictionary, but it's hard to find the correct spelling of "physics" if you don't know that "ph" sounds like "f." In fact, AutoCAD's screen menu system is built like a dictionary — in alphabetical order.

In addition, valuable but less frequently used options, such as * for symbol insertion, can be included on the overlay for easy reference. Although it's well documented in the *User Reference* manual, how many of us missed * the first time around?

3. The tablet works the way you work, allowing direct, immediate access to commands as you think of them. In a screen menu, you first must find the menu that holds the command — a disruptive and time-consuming thought process.

Because you can make each menu selection cancel the previous command, the tablet allows you to change your mind instantly and without penalty. (Screen menus may require three selects to find a desired command—and two additional selects if you change your mind!)

By using a tablet and a good overlay, users can realize a 50 percent improvement in learning, as well as a 25 percent increase in productivity over other input devices.

For example, a mouse is a relative device—you must pick it up and "stroke" it on the table. As an "absolute" device, a tablet offers one-to-one correspondence between your hand and the cursor, which is both faster and more natural.

As you know, one of the primary goals of *The AutoCAD Productivity Book* is to reduce every invoked action to a single "pick," making the process of CAD so transparent you can concentrate on design and drafting. A tablet with an overlay is the only practical input device that can realize that goal. Without a table or an overlay, you're missing a lot of productivity.... Read on!

ERGONOMICS OF TABLET DESIGN

Before you get your hands dirty creating a tablet, let's consider some ergonomic basics of tablet design. Take an imaginary 11" x 11" digitizer and divide it into 1/2" squares. If you subtract a hundred squares from the middle for a cursor movement area, 384 options remain at your fingertips, waiting for you to insert AutoCAD commands and functions. However, with so many options, how do you find each command quickly?

Have you ever looked at the instrument panel of an airplane and asked how the pilot could keep track of so many gauges? It's simple—instruments are organized with the most important ones closest at hand. In addition, instruments and gauges have different visual characteristics—such as size and color—that register subconsciously for easy reference.

While it's handy to have all instruments, switches and controls nearby, only 20 percent require constant monitoring. The pilot can take an extra second to spot the other

80 percent that aren't as crucial. Beginning to sound familiar?

The same principles hold for a well-constructed tablet menu. By placing your most commonly used commands closest, and by using simple mnemonic devices such as color and symbols, a digitizer with a good overlay can be more productive than any other input device.

If you use many symbols in your work, a digitizer can be even more productive because an *icon*, or small drawing, can be created for each symbol and placed on the overlay. What you see is what you get. It's much faster to locate the symbol visually than to memorize cryptic names.

A typical overlay for an 11" x 17" tablet can hold more than 300 user-desirable symbol icons. In addition, overlays (or the symbol part of the overlay) can be exchanged quickly when you move from one discipline or project to another.

TABLET AREAS AND AUTOCAD

Tablets and overlays can interface with AutoCAD in many ways. For example, you can toggle between your tablet and screen menu or turn off your screen menu altogether and work strictly from the tablet. You also may use your tablet in conjunction with a multi-button puck.

The tablet areas can be placed independently anywhere on your digitizer surface as long as they're aligned vertically and horizontally (normally they touch but they don't have to). Below are some common configurations.

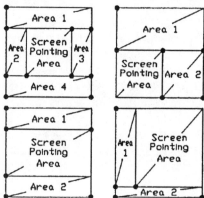

The heavy dots on the upper left, lower left and upper right of each tablet area are used to identify the tablet area to AutoCAD. You give the points to AutoCAD during configuration, which then "knows" where to find that tablet area.

Of course, you can place tablet overlays onto large digitizers as well. Below is a picutre of a typical configuration. Notice that the menu areas aren't even connected.

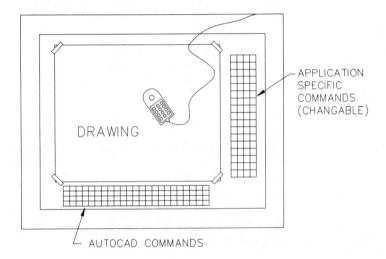

APPLICATION SPECIFIC COMMANDS (CHANGABLE)

DRAWING

AUTOCAD COMMANDS

Also note, one of the areas is labeled "AUTOCAD COMMANDS" and the other is labeled "APPLICATION SPECIFIC COMMANDS." That's because if you digitize a floor plan one day and a map the next, you may need two different menus with different symbols. If you keep most of your menus constant and just change one section specific to the discipline in which you're working, then you have less to learn—and less to tape down.

This same principle holds true for small digitizers. In fact, the upper portion of the tablet menu that comes with AutoCAD is meant to be customized. You may want to create several sections that you can slip under the AutoCAD overlay for customization, such as a 3D menu for Release 10 or a piping menu.

AutoCAD also needs to know the number of squares you want. Just like the **ARRAY** command, it asks for the row and columns. AutoCAD software then divides the area into rectangles to which numbers are assigned.

Each configuration has its pros and cons. But before you can evaluate which best suits your needs, you must know how to evaluate, design and produce a tablet overlay. Let's focus on that now.

EVALUATING A TABLET MENU

Learning to analyze an existing tablet menu will help you choose a tablet overlay system or develop your own. Let's call it an overlay "system" because it's generally composed of four parts designed to work together and increase your productivity.

The first part, the physical overlay, should be evaluated using the following criteria:

1. Are your most needed commands included on the surface?

2. Does it work with screen menus?

3. Are the most commonly used commands accessible with a single pick?

4. Is the layout easy to follow?

5. Do colors or other visual aids help you find often-used commands?

6. Is the overlay designed for right- or left-handed use?

7. Are areas designated for user customization?

8. Can you look at each box and determine its function?

9. Is the overlay made of durable material?

10. Will the overlay fit your digitizer?

11. Is it aesthetically pleasing?

Software is the second part of the system. A critical issue is encryption — can you modify the software? Beginning with Version 2.5, AutoCAD compiles the menu for very fast loading (similar to compilation of shape files). The menu files are converted from **.MNU** files to **.MNX** files.

Be sure you get the source code, the **.MNU** file. One thing is certain — you'll want to make at least a minor modification someday. Here are other important considerations:

1. Has the software been upgraded to the current version of AutoCAD?

2. Does it require 640K or a hard disk?

3. What are other users' experiences?

4. Is the software bug-free? If not, what is the vendor's return policy?

5. Is the documentation clearly presented?

6. Does the documentation show how to modify the software?

7. Are macros and AutoLISP routines well prompted? Are the prompts similar to AutoCAD's?

8. How well do the macros and LISP anticipate your needs? Are they "intuitive"?

9. When you examine the code, is the software concisely written?

10. How many beneficial macros and AutoLISP routines are included? How many have been omitted? Can you add the rest?

11. What is the philosophy of user interaction: Single pick? Screen menus? Layer management? Symbol management?

12. How is drawing scale handled? Are certain symbols automatically scaled?

13. What notable conveniences have been included, such as a calculator, special **SHELL** commands, bill of materials, etc.?

14. Is the software integrated with other programs? How smoothly does information pass between one program and another, and between programs and AutoCAD?

15. Has the vendor demonstrated commitment to updates when AutoCAD upgrades?

Once you've evaluated the physical overlay and software, it's time to examine the third system component: application software. This is the software that runs outside AutoCAD yet works with the overlay as a system. Such a system might be a package for civil engineers that calculates contours and "downloads" them to AutoCAD. Another might be NC machining.

You must be the judge of the program's technical merit for your application. Here are a few questions to consider:

1. Can AutoCAD "speak" in the terminology of your business?

2. Does the command structure differ from AutoCAD's? Does it matter?

3. Are you constantly aware that you're using two programs? (Imagine the mistakes you'd make because of wrong commands if you used two different word processors.)

The final component of the tablet overlay system is the symbol library. This consideration is generally less important for three reasons: 1) AutoCAD makes it quick and easy to create a symbol library; 2) Most vendor-supplied symbols are usable but not exactly what you want — so you end up redrawing them; 3) Our familiar 20/80 rule — 20 percent of the symbols are used 80 percent of the time — yet you may be paying equally for each symbol.

Symbols become an issue when there's little room for them on the overlay, or when you're not allowed to modify symbols that work rigidly with application software.

Here are other considerations:

1. How many symbols have been included?

2. How many can you use?

3. Has associated attribute information been included?

4. Are the attribute information requests reasonable or do they require too many prompts?

5. Have they been designed for use with **GRID** and **SNAP**?

6. Is it easy to join symbols to lines for schematics?

7. Are parametric symbols provided? These are useful when a single macro or AutoLISP routine covers the range of sizes and options. (Doors and windows are the most commonly misused symbols—an AutoLISP routine often works better.)

8. Does the overlay provide enough space for your own customization and special symbols?

9. Are symbols easy to read or chosen from cryptic screen names?

10. Are symbols well documented? Do they include size and insertion point?

A WORD OF CAUTION

Don't even consider encrypted menus! There will always be some important improvements that could be made. It is understandable that AutoLISP routines are encrypted, but not menus. Be sure that applications and menus you purchase at least take advantage of the most recent version of AutoCAD. This indicates a company's commitment to timely updates.

If you modify a purchased menu there are negatives:

1. Every time your application is upgraded, you must upgrade your modifications to integrate them into the new version.

2. If you alter the menu software, don't expect free support from the people who generated the application.

USING A TABLET OVERLAY

Before designing your own tablet menu, you might want to consider purchasing a good, low-cost generic tablet menu, knowing you'll eventually modify or abandon it. Even if you intend to make your own, it's much easier to start with an existing base.

In addition, you'll learn faster and get an idea of what you want from a menu. Be sure to get the source code for the overlay so you can explore and modify it. Most overlay artwork comes from making an AutoCAD drawing. If you purchase that AutoCAD drawing file, you'll save hours of work.

In selecting a tablet overlay, first decide whether to look at one created specifically for your business or a generic menu that you can adapt to your methods of drafting and design. In designing your own, closely examine others.

For example, even the best architectural menu overlays may not be entirely suitable for an individual architectural office. Choose the best for you, get a feel for its strengths and weaknesses, then create your own menu from your newly gained perspective.

DESIGNING YOUR OWN TABLET MENU

A digitizer does only one thing: It sends its **x,y** coordinates to the computer. AutoCAD software, after tablet configuration, evaluates each coordinate received to determine which menu "box" the pointing device is indicating. When that occurs, it then correlates that box with the menu software you've created and executes your commands.

AutoCAD supports five areas on your tablet: four areas for commands and the fifth for screen pointing. Although you must specify the screen pointing area, you can choose between 0 and 4 tablet areas. The **TABLET** command, **CFG** option, controls the tablet configuration.

By specifying a combination of tablet menu size, row and columns, the actual "pick" boxes on the overlay can be any size rectangle. In addition, you sometimes may want to use two or more squares together to provide room for a word description, a symbol or visual emphasis.

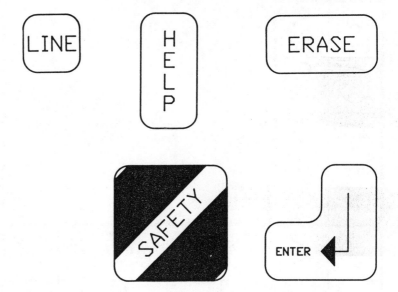

If that isn't enough flexibility, you can even toggle a menu area instantly between two different sets of commands, just like the screen submenus. This can give you two or more functions for every tablet menu box. In the next section, you'll see how it works.

YOUR FIRST TABLET MENU

To clarify our discussion, we've illustrated a simple tablet below. To get your feet wet, you can reproduce this menu overlay and enter in the lines of commands. You also can add the button menu from the end of this chapter.

ERASE	OOPS	COPY	MOVE	ARRAY	MIRROR	CHANGE	FILLET
LINE	PLINE						LAYER / LIST
⊙	⊙						LIMITS / HATCH
◯	◯						SAVE / DIM
◠	INSERT						END / DIST
TEXT	SKETCH						TOGGLE
END	MID	INTER	PAN	RDRAW	ZM-W	ZM-P	ZM-E / GRID
CEN	QUAD	TAN	NEAR	ORTHO	SNAP	PLOT	QUIT / SNAP

Key the following into an ASCII file called **MY1STTAB.MNU**:

```
***TABLET1
[T1-1]*^C^CERASE;SI;AU
[T1-2]^C^COOPS
[T1-3]*^C^CCOPY;SI;AU
```

```
[T1-4]*^C^CMOVE;SI;AU
[T1-5]^C^CARRAY;SI;AU
[T1-6]^C^CMIRROR;SI;AU
[T1-7]^C^CCHANGE
[T1-8]^C^CFILLET;R;\;;MULTIPLE;FILLET
***TABLET2
[T2-1]*^C^CLINE
[T2-2]*^C^CPLINE
[T2-3]*^C^CCIRCLE
[T2-4]*^C^CCIRCLE;\D
[T2-5]*^C^CCIRCLE;2P
[T2-6]*^C^CCIRCLE;3P
[T2-7]*^C^CARC
[T2-8]^C^CINSERT
[T2-9]*^C^CTEXT
[T2-10]^C^CSKETCH
***TABLET3
**T31
[T3-1]^C^CLAYER
[T3-2]^C^CLIMITS
[T3-3]^C^CSAVE
[T3-4]^C^CEND
$T3=T32
[T3-5]^C^CZOOM;E
[T3-6]^C^CQUIT
**T32
[T3-1]^C^CLIST
[T3-2]^C^CHATCH
[T3-3]^C^CDIM
[T3-4]^C^CDIST
$T3=T31
[T3-5]^C^CGRID
[T3-6]^C^CSNAP
***TABLET4
[T4-1]END
```

```
[T4-2]MID
[T4-3]INTER
[T4-4]'PAN
[T4-5]'REDRAW
[T4-6]'ZOOM;W
[T4-7]'ZOOM;P
[T4-8]CEN
[T4-9]QUAD
[T4-10]TAN
[T4-11]NEAR
[T4-12]^O
[T4-13]^B
[T4-14]^C^CPLOT
```

Can you use the lines of code from the **RISC** menu in Chapter Five? Yes—and without change. However, you need not enter the titles enclosed in brackets (although they don't hurt). The titles are an easy way to find tablet squares.

To create tablet menus, you have to change your thinking from vertical to horizontal. Tablet menus are organized horizontally with box numbers increasing from left to right. From the right end, they start back at the left end, next row down, and continue.

LET'S TRY IT!

After keying in the above, copy the overlay from the book and tape it to the digitizer. Register it with the **TABLET** command, **CFG** option. Then use the **MENU** command to activate **MY1STTAB** (.mnu).

Tablet area **1** is a single row across the top, containing edit commands. Tablet area **2** has two columns on the left side and contains drawing entity commands. Tablet area **3** is a single column with a submenu toggle so that each box can perform two functions with the use of submenus; it is devoted to utility commands. Tablet area **4** is two rows across the bottom.

Note the difference in pattern between areas **2** and **4**. One is two columns wide; the other is two rows deep — an application of left-to-right ordering.

CREATING YOUR TABLET OVERLAY

The first step is to plan. Make a list of your needed commands, macros and AutoLISP routines. How many symbols do you need? How many overlay boxes? Estimate the number of squares needed. Do you want to interact with or turn off menu screens? What size digitizer do you have?

Next, plan out the tablet areas and make a blank drawing of the menu. Sketch it first, make revisions, then make an AutoCAD drawing of the overlay. Plot out two copies at 1.5X to 2X normal size and number each box sequentially in small type.

Now, write in the commands and symbols on these working prints. Keep an electric eraser nearby. Don't use any software until this stage is complete.

When a good overlay design emerges from the creative fog, transfer your pencil doodles to AutoCAD using a copy of the blank menu drawing, but don't invest much time in icons, fancy headings or art.

Because you'll continue to have new ideas and refinements, don't "fix" the overlay design until the last minute. Below is an idea of how you might spend your time in developing a menu:

Plan and overlay	40%
Create software	25%
Rework and debug	20%
Teach others to use	5%
Rework and debug	10%

Finally, write the overlay menu software, as described earlier in this chapter. Then, using AutoCAD, transcribe your penciled overlay to a drawing and plot it out full scale for testing. At this point, invest as little time as possible in the drawing.

Tip: Although command titles we used in screen menus aren't required in tablet menus, you can use them anyway. It's handy to place the box number in brackets to identify the beginning and end of macros. By using your text editor's search function, you easily can go directly to a box number for debugging. For example, to find box **T1-23**, using EDLIN,

Type: 1,999S[T1-23]   (RETURN)   (**S** means Search.)

Work with your menu as a production drawing tool for at least a week. Make a couple of copies and have co-workers use it. Don't make a lot of changes yet. Take notes, pencil in changes and correct software bugs.

When all the comments are in, go to work on major changes. This is the time to make an investment in the overlay artwork. Plot the overlay again, do more tests and note comments for aesthetic improvement.

PRODUCING YOUR OVERLAY

To make a really professional overlay, plot the artwork 1.5X to 2X, then photographically reduce it to working size. Remember, the line weight will be reduced too, so use a large pen.

For small quantities, color overlays and printing may be too expensive, so you may want to plot color borders around logical groupings. A large color copier can make reproductions.

For protection, the overlay can be laminated or you can lay a piece of acetate on top of the paper.

Another technique involves creating a mirror image of your overlay before plotting (**MIRROR** the text). You then plot the overlay on the back on mylar. Place the mylar ink-side down on your digitizer to protect the inked surface.

A NOTE ON BUTTON MENUS

Buttons are the keys on a mouse or digitizer cursor. Because only digitizer cursors have up to 16 buttons, we've chosen to place the discussion of button menus in this chapter.

As with any other menu, you can assign any task, no matter how complex, to a single button (except the first button—always the "pick" or "select" button—which may be button **#0** or the leftmost button or the button at the top of a diamond pattern; there's no way to reassign it, although there should be).

However, simple, often-used commands such as **(RETURN)**, **LINE**, **REDRAW**, **OSNAP** and **toggles** are best assigned to the buttons.

Below are some typical button assignments:

```
***BUTTONS
;
^CREDRAW
^C
^B
^O
^G
^D
^E
^T
```

To explain, the "pick button" is assumed at the top of the list. If your "pick" button is **#1**, your button section will start at button **#2**. In order, the first button is a **;** or **(RETURN)**, then **REDRAW**, **CANCEL**, **SNAP** toggle, **ORTHO** toggle, **GRID** toggle, **Coordinate Display** toggle, **Isometric Cursor** toggle, **TABLET ON/OFF**.

If you have only three buttons, the rest will be ignored. If you have 12 buttons, you'll want to add several functions.

One addition might be the **LINE** command. With button menus, a special feature allows you to enter not only the command with a button but also the first point (i.e., the location of the cursor).

While this appears to be true "single pick" philosophy at work, it doesn't allow interactive **OBJECT SNAP**. If you're devising a menu for schematic drawing, where a **GRID** and **SNAP** increments remain set, this may be handy. Merely add a single \ to the command:

Example: ^C^CLine;\

THE AUTOCAD STANDARD MENU

AutoCAD now provides a standard menu free with each AutoCAD system. This menu provides virtually all of the AutoCAD commands in three of the four available menu areas. Although it may not be laid out in the best manner, it's organized by large function groups and provides a high proficiency increase in productivity over screen menus.

Needless to say, the standard AutoCAD menu can be modified with very little trouble. But even though you might consider this menu structure less than optimum, it does have one overriding feature to it. It is standard.

What this means to you is that it has become the standard menu structure of a lot of special program menus. Just as the QWERTY keyboard is the standard for most typewriters and computers, the AutoCAD tablet overlay is quickly becoming a standard. Once it's learned, an individual can feel equally at home on most AutoCAD workstations that use this menu. And even though QWERTY is considered to be less efficient than other keyboard layouts for the typewriter, it will probably never be replaced because too many people have learned to use it efficiently.

As time goes by and the AutoCAD system evolves, we must accept these standards and learn to enhance and modify the menu while working within the structure.

First, while maintaining the basic commands on the tablet menu, feel free to modify their underlying meanings. For example you might find it more efficient to change each of the **OBJECT SNAP** commands to **OBJECT SNAP MODE** commands using **(setvar)**. For example,

```
(setvar "osmode" 1)
```

will permanently set the **OBJECT SNAP** to end point until the next **OBJECT SNAP** is chosen. A general **ERASE** command might be specialized. These are simple modifications that can be made without customizing the menu beyond the recognition of others you may have working on your system.

The real customization will come using tablet menu area number one. The AutoCAD tablet is divided into four menu areas. Areas two, three and four are reserved for the standard tablet. This leaves area one, an area at the top of the tablet menu, capable of holding two to three hundred blocks. This is where your special macros and parts should be placed. If most of the software vendors will recognize this menu structure, not only will everyone feel comfortable with the main menu structure, but you'll be able to slip your own underlays into any menu software program and feel right at home.

SUMMARY

Tablet menus present commands in a smorgasbord fashion, saving you the trouble of hunting through screen menus. They result in faster learning and experimentation, leading to a level of increased productivity that more than justifies the expense of a digitizer.

Yet, no matter how well they're designed, you'll want to customize the overlay and software. In this chapter, you analyzed, conceptualized and designed, then made your own decisions.

Surveys of users' groups show that 95 percent of users never modify their menus. Therefore, they accept a programmer's solution. What does a programmer know about your business?

However, you may be too busy to develop your own system. It's not bad to start with someone else's menu and modify it. Consider this: if it takes you a week to create (or modify) a menu system, what percentage of time is that in relation to the amount of time you'll use it? What's a week of development compared to three years of use? Remember, only menus that are not encrypted are worth your consideration. Check to see when it was last revised. A menu should take advantage of AutoCAD's latest version.

A good menu, customized for your business, can save you an hour of work every day. A week's effort in creating a menu would pay for itself in 40 working days and make life a lot easier, not to mention creating faster turnaround of sales proposals and other drawings.

Customization is worth the effort and, like a big puzzle, it's fun. Meet the challenge!

AutoCAD's Advanced User Interface

IN THIS CHAPTER

Since Release 9, Autodesk has introduced four new on-screen menu interfaces:
- menu bars
- pull-down menus
- icon menus
- dialogue boxes

Let's discuss the pros and cons of each and then show you how to program them. You'll also learn how to improve the **ACAD.MNU**.

SHADES OF AutoSKETCH

AutoSKETCH, the inexpensive package for the casual user, showed where Autodesk was headed with its more expensive software. Because no one can afford to support and train for a CAD package in this price range, AutoSKETCH had to be easy to learn and use.

The menus from AutoSKETCH have found their way into AutoCAD. These menu options, called the Advanced User Interface (AUI), form the basis of a consistent user interface that is now a part of all Autodesk products, such as AutoSKETCH, AutoSHADE and AutoFLIX.

This interface style was first incorporated on the Apple LISA and Macintosh. Because Apple forced all software developers to adhere to the same user interface, Apple has become known for being easy to use and learn. All programs operate in a similar manner, so it's easy to switch between them.

This type of interface is now part of many other programs, such as Microsoft Windows and GEM Windows user interface.

Although the new interface options aren't necessarily better for the "power user," they *are* consistent, easier for the novice—and they can be bypassed, at least in Autodesk products. However, in most circumstances, a good tablet menu is still best. Let's explore some of the pros and cons of AutoCAD's advanced user interface.

POSITIVE FEATURES

1. All three types of menus disappear after you've made your selection. In addition, they require no precious space on your screen.

2. Icon menus graphically show hatch patterns, symbols and the like, so that you don't have to remember their names.

3. The dialogue boxes simplify complex commands, such as **LAYER**, with lots of options.

4. Dialogue box commands work transparently, extending the range of transparent options.

5. These new options lend themselves well to customization or application development.

6. With pull-down menus, you can view commands much faster than paging through 20 screen menu commands at a time.

7. The new menu options are easier for the novice to learn.

8. You can use 70-plus characters in the pull-down menus to provide a better description of the function.

9. The options allow a "heads up" display. In other words, you can keep your eyes glued to the screen for better concentration. Some people swear by this approach.

However, it may be more tiresome than introducing a little head and eye movement.

NOT-SO-POSITIVE FEATURES

1. The menus require a "pick" — an extra step. It takes two picks to execute a command, and you can't race along the top searching for a desired command.

2. The dialogue boxes currently cannot be customized.

3. The dialogue boxes don't display enough information. For example, the **LAYER** dialogue box, activated by **DDLMODES**, shows only five layers at a time. A **page down** "button" shows the next five layers — very tedious for an architect with 50 layers. On an EGA monitor, with tighter organization, 15 or more layers could easily be displayed.

4. Layers and attributes aren't numbered within dialogue boxes. They should be numbered so you can tell where you are when you page down and up.

5. **ATTRIBUTE EDIT** and **INSERT** dialogue blocks don't show the block name or whether an attribute is **Constant**, **Invisible** or **Preset**. Neither do they show all the attributes (all should be shown even if they can't be edited).

6. You must click an **OK** button to close a dialogue box, when the space bar or (**RETURN**) would work more efficiently, in some cases.

7. The size, number and placement of icon menus can't be controlled. The icon menus should be like menu squares on a tablet, where you can control variables.

8. Why is there a small box to the side of the icon for selection? Why not point to the icon itself and click?

9. You can't display variables in the menus. It would be handy, for example, to see the current value of the **DIMSCALE** or **MIRRTEXT** when you're dimensioning, without having to execute the command. (Fight every pick that takes time from real work!)

The title for this section, "**NOT-SO-POSITIVE FEA-TURES**," was carefully chosen. Like anything new, the AUI isn't perfect. I've included this section to illustrate the kind of thought that leads to development of time-saving macros.

Autodesk has always been driven by its users. You can help the AutoCAD community, and Autodesk as well, by not accepting the status quo. Put your ideas in writing and send them to Autodesk and the AutoCAD users' magazines!

Just imagine, for example, a dialogue box interface with AutoLISP. For a custom application, a dialogue box would show all the current defaults and allow you to change only a few numbers, rather than stepping through a long series of sequential questions. Then you'd hit the **EXECUTE** button. How often do you have to restart an AutoLISP program because of a typo?

Aside from these minor suggestions, the new Advanced User Interface deserves applause. Let's explore how to make it work best for you.

HOW TO USE PULL-DOWN MENUS

To get started let's first look at the **DRAW (***POP2)** section from the **ACAD.MNU**, Release 10. Ten pull-down menus are allowed across the top of the menu bar (which overwrites the status line). Like tablet menus, sections are preceded by ******* and numbered **1** through **10**. They're similar to screen menus in that the word(s) surrounded by brackets appear as titles in the pull-down.

Note that the first line is the title that appears in the menu bar when you first move the cursor into the status line region.

```
***POP2
[Draw]
[Line]*^C^C$S=X $s=line line
[Arc]*^C^C$S=X $s=poparc arc
[Circle]*^C^C$S=X $s=popcircl circle
[Polyline]*^C^C$S=X $s=pline pline
```

```
[3D Polyline]*^C^C$S=X $S=3dpoly 3dpoly
[Insert]^C^Csetvar attdia 1 $S=X  $s=insert insert
[Dtext]*^C^C$S=X $s=Dtext Dtext
[Hatch...]^C^C$i=hatch1 $i=*
[3D Construction...]$i=3dobjects $i=*
```

For example, when you select **Line** in the above menu code, it updates the side-screen menu with both the **X** menu (**$S=X**, the top three lines) and the **LINE** menu (**$s=line**). This is highly flexible. The opposite is also true. You could pick a square on a tablet overlay and have a menu pull-down, or have icons appear. You can even have AutoLISP programs activate the menus.

Notice that the **Hatch** line uses icons. **$i=hatch1** activates **hatch1** as the current icon menu. **$i=*** displays or *pulls* the menu.

Also, in the **Insert** line, there's a new variable, **attdia**. When **attdia** is set to **1**, a dialogue box will appear to help you enter attributes. It shows multiple attributes and allows you to accept all defaults at once or randomly modify only the ones that you want to revise. This is much better than stepping through a long list of questions as in previous versions of AutoCAD. So, using several attributes with a block is faster with the dialogue box.

Tip: To edit a block with multiple attributes, use **DDATTE** (which uses a similar dialogue box to show all attributes at one time), and edit the attributes randomly.

WORKING WITH PULL-DOWN MENUS

Menu Bar

The menu bar appears across the top of the screen—where the status line normally would be—only when you move the cursor into that region. Up to ten menu items may appear in the bar. Each menu item is limited to 14 characters.

However, because you're limited to 80 characters across the display, you can only use five items of 14 characters each. Each item is separated by two blank spaces plus one blank space on either end of the bar. So if you want to place all ten items in the menu bar, you must limit yourself to an average of six characters per item.

The first line in a pull-down menu appears in the menu bar. A command on the first line won't work. The first line only pulls down the menu.

The Submenus

The main pull-down menu headings are of the form *****POPX**, where **X** is a number from 1 through 10. There can be any number of submenus in the pull-down system, headed with ****XXXXXXX**, where **X** represents any unique alphanumeric name. One consequence is that a single submenu can be shared between screen, pull-down and even tablet menus! Try adding these lines to the **ACAD.MNU**, under **POP2 (DRAW)**:

```
[DRAW 1]$p2=dr $p2=*
[DRAW 2]$p2=dr2 $p2=*
```

You just used a pull-down menu to call up AutoCAD's draw menus, intended as screen menus. To restore the **Draw** pull-down, use the **MENU** command to reload it. See how you can call a screen menu into the pull-downs?

Important Note: Blank lines aren't allowed in pull-down menus. All lines after a blank line are ignored. If there are no commands after the pull-down title, or if there's a blank line immediately after the title line, you won't be able to highlight the item in the menu bar.

Also, pull-downs support the **start at line** provision of screen menus. For example, a submenu title for a screen menu of ****DR 3** would start the screen menu on the third line down, skipping over the first two lines (leaving the **X** menu intact). The same is true for pull-downs. Because the first line is the menu bar title, using a submenu title of the form ****XXX 2** would leave the menu bar title the same.

This small point could lead to some clever menu interaction.

Twenty items plus a menu bar title are allowed in a pull-down submenu. The length of the item title (not the pull-down title of 14 characters) can include up to 78 characters in **POP1**. Thus, you can describe functions. As you move to the right, you're permitted fewer characters. In **POP10** you'd have just a few.

Tip: As a development strategy, place commands that could benefit from explanation in the first pull-downs.

Menu Development Philosophy

Remember the principle of **RISC** (Reduced Instruction Set Command menu) in Chapter Five? Let's apply it to Autodesk's implementation of pull-downs in the **ACAD.MNU**.

Pick the **DRAW** pull-down and then select **CIRCLE**. What if you want a 2-point circle? You must select that from the side menu. What if you want to turn off the side menu and recover the precious screen area? When picking the option from the side screen, you make three picks before you can do any real work! Why not put the most common options in the **DRAW** menu? You probably could use 20 percent of the commands 80 percent of the time — our familiar 20/80 rule.

There's now no reason why you should continue to use the side menu. Here's one way to modify **POP2** for more efficient operation:

```
***POP2
[Draw]
[Line]*^C^Cline
[Line-Cont]^C^Cline;;
[Arc-3 point]*^C^Carc
[Arc-Continue]^C^Carc;;
[Arc-Start, Cen, End]*^C^Carc;\c;
[Circle-Radius]*^C^Ccircle
```

```
[Circle-Diameter]*^C^Ccircle;2p
[Circle-3 point]*^C^Ccircle;3p
[Circle-Tangent, Tangent, Radius]*^C^Ccircle;ttr
[Polyline]*^C^Cpline
[Polygon]*^C^Cpolygon
[Rectangle]^C^C(IF (NOT C:R) (LOAD "C:/ACAD/R")) +
MULTIPLE R;
[Insert]^C^Csetvar;attdia;1;insert
[Text-Left]*^C^Ctext
[Text-Right]*^C^Ctext;r
[Text-Center]*^C^Ctext;c
[Text-Left 1/8 0d]*^C^Ctext;\0.125;0
[Hatch-Lines]^C^Clayer;m;6;hatch;line
[Hatch-Steel]^C^Chatch;m;6;steel
[Hatch]^C^C$i=hatch1 $i=*
```

Note the use of fully described commands, like **Circle-3 point**. This can really accelerate learning!

Note: For **rectangle** to work, there must be an **R.LSP** routine in a DOS subdirectory, **ACAD**. For the AutoLISP code, see Chapter Four or The AutoCAD Productivity Library. Also note that **HATCH**ing is automatically placed on **LAYER 6**.

Here's another idea that's even more "RISCy." Because the AutoCAD pull-down menus use only seven of the ten pull-downs, why not use the **RISC1** and **RISC2** menus from Chapter Five as the first ***POP1** and ***POP2**! Be sure to renumber the other seven as **3** through **9**, something like this:

```
***POP1
[RISC1]
etc.
***POP2
[RISC2]
etc.
```

```
***POP3
[Tools]
etc.
```

... and so on. Be sure to expand the prompts in the **RISC** menus to take advantage of the expanded character capacity.

Tip: A **CONTROL P** (^P) will suppress command echo from a menu. Alter the **rectangle** menu line from above like this and try it again:

```
[Rectangle]^C^C^P(IF (NOT C:R) (LOAD "C:/ACAD/R")) +
MULTIPLE R;
```

Or add the following two lines to a menu and note the difference in execution—the one with a ^P is much cleaner.

```
[Hello]^C^C^P(prompt "hello")
[Hello]^C^C(prompt "hello")
```

Use of Submenus

Now you'll use some submenu switching to avoid using the screen menu in **ACAD.MNU**. When you select **3D VIEW** from the **DISPLAY** pull-down, an icon screen helps you select a view. Then you must use the side menu to select a viewing height. What if you want to turn the side menu off? Here's how to make another submenu pull-down.

First, add this submenu, or modify the existing submenu in **ACAD.MNU**.

```
**EYELEVEL
[Eye Level]
[ABOVE  5]^C^Cvpoint none (strcat vp "1.5") $p4=
[       4]^C^Cvpoint none (strcat vp "0.9") $p4=
[       3]^C^Cvpoint none (strcat vp "0.6") $p4=
[       2]^C^Cvpoint none (strcat vp "0.3") $p4=
[       1]^C^Cvpoint none (strcat vp "0.1") $p4=
```

```
[GROUND 0]^C^Cvpoint none (strcat vp ".0000001") $p4=
[      -1]^C^Cvpoint none (strcat vp "-0.1") $p4=
[      -2]^C^Cvpoint none (strcat vp "-0.3") $p4=
[      -3]^C^Cvpoint none (strcat vp "-0.6") $p4=
[      -4]^C^Cvpoint none (strcat vp "-0.9") $p4=
[BELOW -5]^C^Cvpoint none (strcat vp "-1.5") $p4=
```

Next make the following modifications to the **3DVIEWS** submenu.

```
***ICON
**3DViews
[Select 3D View]
[acad(ul)]^C^C(setq vp "-1,1,")+
(princ "Enter Eye level from pull-down menu: ")+
$P4=EYELEVEL $P4=*
[acad(l)]^C^C(setq vp "-1,.0000001,")+
(princ "Enter Eye level from pull-down menu: ")+
$P4=EYELEVEL $P4=*
[acad(ll)]^C^C(setq vp "-1,-1,")+
(princ "Enter Eye level from pull-down menu: ")+
$P4=EYELEVEL $P4=*
[acad(user)]
[acad(u)]^C^C(setq vp ".0000001,1,")+
(princ "Enter Eye level from pull-down menu: ")+
$P4=EYELEVEL $P4=*
[acad(p)]^C^Cvpoint none 0,0,1 $S=X $S=3D
[acad(lo)]^C^C(setq vp ".0000001,-1,")+
(princ "Enter Eye level from pull-down menu: ")+
$P4=EYELEVEL $P4=*
[acad(user)]
[acad(ur)]^C^C(setq vp "1,1,")+
(princ "Enter Eye level from pull-down menu: ")+
$P4=EYELEVEL $P4=*
[acad(r)]^C^C(setq vp "1,.0000001,")+
```

```
(princ "Enter Eye level from pull-down menu: ");+
$P4=EYELEVEL $P4=*
[acad(lr)]^C^C(setq vp "1,-1,")+
(princ "Enter Eye level from pull-down menu: ");+
$P4=EYELEVEL $P4=*
[acad(user)]
[acad(t)]$S=X $S=3D VPOINT;;
[acad(h)]$S=X $S=HIDE
```

Here's how it works. When you pick **3D VIEW** from the **DISPLAY** pull-down, this is the command line executed:

```
[3D View]^C^C$i=3dviews $i=*
```

$i = 3dviews activates the ****3DVIEWS** submenu from the *****ICON** section and **$i = *** pops it onto the screen. Here's a single line from the modified **3DVIEWS** icon menu. Let's see what it does.

```
[acad(l)]^C^C(setq vp "-1,.0000001,")+
(princ "Enter Eye level from pop-down menu: ")+
$P4=EYELEVEL $P4=*
```

In icon menus, the text between the brackets isn't a title, but a reference to the slide library from which to draw a slide for the icon box. Here you're looking for the **L** slide from the **ACAD** slide library (**ACAD.SLB**).

Next, a variable, **vp**, is set to a text string **"-1,.0000001,"** which sets up a view on one side. Then **$P4 = EYELEVEL** sets **POP4** equal to the **EYELEVEL** menu. **$P4 = *** then pulls the menu down and you can see that the original pull-down menu has changed into the **EYELEVEL** menu.

From the **EYELEVEL** pull-down menu, you then select an eye level. Let's assume you pick the following.

```
[ABOVE 5]^C^Cvpoint none (strcat vp "1.5") $p4=
```

Here's how this line works. You enter the **VPOINT** command. Then **OBJECT SNAP** is set temporarily to **none**. The **1.5** is concatenated (added) to the end of the contents of variable **vp**, making **vp** equal to "**-1, .0000001, 1.5**". The contents of **vp** are then submitted to **VPOINT** command. Finally **P4=** resets **POP4** back to its original self. (It works!)

Note that some other lines in the **3DVIEWS** icon menu address screen menus. It is an exercise for you to give them the same treatment as above and recover the side menu for more drawing room.

ICON MENUS

Icon menus are fun. First you must build a slide library to conveniently group many slides into one file. This is done at the DOS level after you've created the slides you need, using the **SLIDELIB(.EXE)** program now provided with AutoCAD.

An icon screen can be grouped in any number up to 16. Four icons will give you four large squares. When you go to five squares, the screen will be divided into nine sections (3 x 3). When you go over nine, the screen is divided into sixteen smaller squares (4 x 4).

Let's just do a quick experiment to see how it works before you spend a lot of time on something complicated.

Tip: When exploring a new feature, always devise a simple experiment first.

First, make a series of 16 simple slides. The slides will be numbered **1** through **16**. When you make the slides, save them as **1**(.**sld**) through **16**(.**sld**). Here's how to make the slides fast:

1. Start a new drawing. Use the name **JUNK**, **PLAY**, **TRASH** or **TEST**.

2. Place the number **1** on the drawing at any size, **0 ROTATION**, using the **TEXT** command.

3. **ZOOM EXTENTS**. Then **ZOOM .9X**.

4. With **ORTHO ON**, position the numeral in the center of the screen.

5. **MSLIDE 1**.

6. Use the **CHANGE** command on the **Last** (and only) object, hit a few **RETURNS** and **CHANGE 1** to **2**.

7. Make slide **2**.

8. Repeat the process for 16 "quickie" slides.

Now you'll make an ASCII list of the slides you want in your library by using your text editor through AutoCAD's **SHELL** feature. Open a text file called **MYSLDLIB.LST** and type in the following 16 lines:

```
1
2
.
.

.
16
```

Still simple! Next, shell out to your current DOS directory. From the DOS prompt, type the following:

```
SLIDELIB MY1ST <MYSLDLIB.LST
```

In a few seconds you'll have your first slide library, named **MY1ST.SLB**. To use it, you will have to make a menu to address the slides. Let's make **POP8** as follows:

```
***POP8
[My1st Icons]
[Show Icons]$i=my1st $i=*
```

Now, under the icon section, create the following submenu.

```
***ICON
**MY1ST
[THIS IS MY FIRST ICON EXPERIMENT]
[MY1ST(1)]
[MY1ST(2)]
```

```
[MY1ST(3)]
```
.

.
```
[MY1ST(16)]^C^C^P (Prompt "You have activated
the 16th icon box.")
```

Reload the menu with the **MENU** command and try it. Note how the icons come in, just the opposite way that tablet squares are numbered. They're numbered sequentially down one row and then down the next.

Of course, you can associate any commands whatsoever with an icon, as we did on the sixteenth box.

That's all there is to icons. Again, I'd like to see them operate as tablet menu squares do. Then you could make them any size or any number and activate them directly, rather than by a small box to the side.

DIALOGUE BOXES

Dialogue boxes are a boon to new users and in some cases can help power users, as previously mentioned. Here's a list of available dialogue boxes:

1. **'DDRMODES** — changes and activates **GRIDs**, **SNAPs**, etc.

2. **'DDEMODES** — creates entity line types, colors, etc.

3. **'DDLMODES** — creates **LAYER**, colors, line types

4. **'SETVAR ATTDIA 1 INSERT** — creates a dialogue box for attribute entry

5. **DDATTE** — uses a dialogue box for editing attributes

6. **DDUCS** — uses a dialogue box for UCS selection.

1 through **4** are transparent, extending the available **TRANSPARENT** command. Use them in your menus.

SUMMARY

A new user interface for the world's most popular CAD program is an exciting event, particularly when the first release adds so much capability!

Autodesk is certainly improving its software in the right direction. With its consistency with other Autodesk programs and ease of learning, AUI will make AutoCAD even more popular.

Yet, thank goodness, despite a clever new menu scheme, Autodesk hasn't forsaken the power user and existing application software that depend on other menu systems. Autodesk is saying, in effect, "Use our products in a way that is best for your business, in a way that best suits your level of expertise."

The Menu Compiler— The First Step

Beginning with Release 10, the **ACAD.MNU** file is now more than 3,000 lines long, mainly due to embedded AutoLISP code within the menu itself. Although there aren't any restrictions on the menu's size, you probably shouldn't use it for large or extensive macros. That would drastically increase the size of the menu—and the functions you write won't be accessible from the keyboard, only from where you placed them in the menu structure.

It's best to write most of your major functions as AutoLISP programs to be placed in the **ACAD.LSP** file, then accessed through the menu structure. That way, you can execute them not only from the screen menu, the pull-downs and the tablet, but also from the keyboard. This lets you take advantage of abbreviated keyboard macros, which speed access to these commands and thus increase your productivity.

All the same, AutoCAD's menu is large and cumbersome. Finding the exact place in the menu structure that corresponds to the tablet block for each entry can be time consuming. Also, having to type codes required by the menu over and over, such as **NEWLINE**, can be a chore.

All is not lost. The bonus disk holds a file called the **Menu Compiler**. The name is a little misleading—it doesn't compile your menu to a **.MNX** file; this is still handled automatically when you enter the AutoCAD drawing editor. The **Menu Compiler** isn't required to modify your menu structure. You can still revise your menus using the many techniques explained throughout this book.

The purpose of the **Menu Compiler** is to help you modify your menus and to make life a little easier. It's not hard to use, and if the source file is properly maintained, **Menu Compiler** can really help when you want to rearrange your menu structure.

IS IT A MENU MAKER?

Before you learn how the **Menu Compiler** works, let's make clear what it's going to do by showing you what it won't do. When you read the sparse documentation in the **MC.DOC** file on the bonus disk, your first impression is that the **Compiler** is a menu maker. If you're looking for a user-friendly program that will guide you through the menu maze and let you effortlessly design your own menu structure, then you're in for a disappointment. But the **Menu Compiler** *can* keep you from having to manually correlate the menu with the tablet, or rearrange and insert the right macros on the right lines. We applaud Autodesk for taking this first step in the right direction and encourage them to further improve the program.

WHERE IS IT AND HOW DOES IT WORK?

The **Menu Compiler** is found on the bonus disk with Release 10.

Three **Menu Compiler** files are on this bonus disk: **MC.EXE, MC.DOC** and **ACAD.MND. MC.DOC** is the total documentation of the **Menu Compiler**. The first thing you should do is copy the **MC.DOC** file to your printer so that you'll have a hard copy of the documentation. To do this, log on to the same drive and directory as the file.

Type: `COPY MC.DOC  LPT1: (RETURN)`

This will dump the documentation to your printer. Because this is an ASCII file, you can also load it into your favorite word processing program as a DOS TEXT file and print it through the word processor.

The second file on the bonus disk is **ACAD.MND**, a sample file that shows you how to prepare and use the **ACAD.MNU** file as a source for the **Menu Compiler**. The **Menu Compiler** will read in an existing noncompiled menu file, process it to see if you've used any of its features, and output a ready-to-use **.MNU** file. The original source menu input file cannot have the extension **.MNU**. Its extension must be **.MND**.

If you renamed the **ACAD.MNU** file to **ACAD.MND** and ran it through the **Menu Compiler**, it would produce an unchanged **ACAD.MNU** file. On the other hand, if you modify the renamed **ACAD.MND** file using the features of the **Menu Compiler**, the **Compiler** will process those changes and incorporate them into the newly created **ACAD.MNU** file, ready for AutoCAD to use.

The final file on the bonus disk is **MC.EXE**. This is the **Menu Compiler** itself. The syntax for the **Menu Compiler** is:

```
MC filename -switch
```

MC is the program. **Filename** is any valid AutoCAD menu file. This file must have the extension **.MND**, but don't use the extension when you run the program. The switch is one of three options available to the program:

-D	List all the macros used in the source file.
-I	List the entire source code of the file.
-M	Disable the macro translation feature of the **Menu Compiler**.

The switch is optional and isn't required during the compiling process. An example of the normal syntax of the **Menu Compiler** is:

```
MC ACAD (RETURN)
```

This will compile the existing **ACAD.MND** source menu file to **ACAD.MNU**, executing the added features you used. If an **ACAD.MNU** file already exists, it will be destroyed and replaced by the new file. Therefore, it's very important that you back up the existing **.MNU** files to floppy disk so that you don't accidentally destroy one.

WHAT DOES IT DO?

The **Menu Compiler** has two main features. First, it can place the same macro throughout the menu structure with a single command; second, it lets you use variables within your macro commands. The documentation for the **Menu Compiler** calls these variables "macros," but that can be confusing. It's better to call **Menu Compiler** macros "variables," since that's what they really are.

These variables are the easiest part of the **Menu Compiler** to understand. They're a powerful feature that lets you condense very long strings into shorter variable names. For example, suppose that a certain sequence is used in several commands, such as

```
$S=X
```

**X is the screen menu area that produces:

```
[__LAST__]

[  DRAW  ]

[  EDIT  ]
```

You can define this sequence to a variable, **{A}**. The variable must be enclosed in {} and you use either upper or lower case. To define **{A}** to this sequence, you would input:

```
{A}=$S=X
```

You might also want to define the ^**C** and ^**P** sequence to **{B}**:

```
{B}=^C^C^P
```

Thus, suppose within the menu structure you need to use the following:

```
[RISC1]^C^C^P$S=X $RIS=RISC1
```

Instead of having to write this out every time, you'll simply use the variable and input:

`[RISC1]{B}{A}$RIS=RISC1`

The documentation for the **Menu Compiler** says that these variables can also be used *recursively*. This means that you can use one within another. If you define:

`{c}=[RISC1]{B}{A}$RIS=RISC1`

notice how you can then use the newly defined variables **{A}** and **{B}** within the variable **{C}**.

Therefore, when you use **{c}** it would produce:

`[RISC1]^C^C^P$S=X $RIS=RISC1`

This can be a real time-saver from the many repetitive codes required in the AutoCAD menu structure.

The second feature of the **Menu Compiler** handles multiple line insertions. This is useful because you don't have to find a specific line with a word processor in order to insert your macro. You can define which blocks on your tablet go with which line numbers. Then all you have to do is give each macro a line number, in any order.

The **Menu Compiler** will place each macro in the proper position within the menu. This makes maintaining the menu structure a snap. If you ever want to rearrange or change your menu structure, just change specific user-specified block numbers or the macros beside those numbers and let the **Menu Compiler** do the work for you.

A corollary to this feature is that you can indicate multiple block numbers for a single macro — you don't have to find specific lines in this huge menu with EDLIN or your word processor. Second, you don't have to type in the same macro over and over.

An example of this, used on the standard AutoCAD menu, is the **REDRAW** command. Next to the screen area of the tablet menu is a long vertical bar labeled **REDRAW**. You can pick anywhere on this vertical bar and redraw your screen. Unfortunately, the AutoCAD menu system sees the bar as single, individual blocks on the defined tablet. Therefore, you need to place the ^C^C'REDRAW macro in each block down the vertical path of the tablet bar.

For example, if you wanted the ^C^C'REDRAW macro to be on blocks 11, 22, 33, 44, 55, 66, 77, 88 and 99, then you could use the following syntax (to be placed at the beginning of the menu):

```
<11,22,33,44,55,66,77,88,99>'REDRAW
```

and ^C^C'REDRAW would be automatically placed on each of those nine lines when it was processed by the **Menu Compiler**.

WHICH LINE IS WHICH?

This is one of the biggest problems with the AutoCAD menu system. Line numbers *per se* have no meaning in the menu structure. EDLIN provides line numbers to help you find your way around within a file, but most word processors do not. And to make matters worse, these line numbers not only change from AutoCAD release to AutoCAD release, but become totally worthless when you begin modifying and adding to your new menu.

We use line numbers in this book only to refer you to the approximate location of any given menu structure. Your actual line numbers may differ depending on your version of the menu. There's a better way to find your way around within the menu, but it takes a little preparation on your part.

As you'll remember, each menu section begins with ** or ***. For example, a section might be **FILTERS, ***SCREEN, ***POP1, ***TABLET1 or ***TABLET2— and you can create your own sections.

Within those sections, you can number the lines for use with the **Menu Compiler**. But you must follow certain rules or you'll risk losing some of your lines.

An example of numbering is in the **ACAD.MND** file on the **Menu Compiler** bonus disk. A lot of the work has already been done for you by numbering each line in the first section of the tablet menu. Look at a side-by-side example of part of the original **ACAD.MNU** file and the prepared **ACAD.MND** file for **TABLET1**.

```
ACAD.MNU                    ACAD.MND

[A-1]                       <1>[A-1]
[A-2]                       <2>[A-2]
[A-3]                       <3>[A-3]
[A-4]                       <4>[A-4]
[A-5]                       <5>[A-5]
etc...                      etc...


[B-1]                       <26>[B-1]
[B-2]                       <27>[B-2]
[B-3]                       <28>[B-3]
[B-4]                       <29>[B-4]
[B-5]                       <30>[B-5]
etc...                      etc...
```

Notice that all of the lines under *****TABLET1** have been labeled numerically in preparation for the **Menu Compiler**. This is the key to using the **Menu Compiler** correctly. You must label *all* of the lines within any single section. The advantage, however, is that you don't have to label them in any specific order. The **Menu Compiler** will later rearrange them correctly.

Be sure that you don't have even one blank line in the section that isn't numbered or a simple text line without a number. If you do, then these lines — including the blank lines — will be rearranged beginning at the first line in the section and will replace your real lines, some of which may get lost. If this happens, you'll get an error message that simple text has been mixed. You'll then need to go back into the **.MND** file and find out why.

MAKING LARGER PICK AREAS

You can also place the same information on more than one line. Look at the example under *****TABLET2** in the **ACAD.MND** file.

```
***TABLET2
<7,18,29,40,51,62,67,68,69,70>;
<71,72,73,81,84,92,95>;
<11,22,33,44,55,66,77,88,99>'REDRAW
<1>{B} $S=HIDE
<2>{B} $S=VPOINT VPOINT;;
<3>{B} $S=ELEVTHK ^C^CELEV
<12>[VPOINT  ]^C^CVPOINT R;<<135;{B} $S=VPOINT3D
<13>[VPT rear]^C^CVPOINT R;<<90;{B} $S=VPOINT3D
<14>[VPOINT  ]^C^CVPOINT R;<<45;{B} $S=VPOINT3D
<23>[VPT left]^C^CVPOINT R;<<180;{B} $S=VPOINT3D
<24>[VPT plan]^C^CVpoint 0,0,1
<25>[VPT rigt]^C^CVPOINT R;<<0;{B} $S=VPOINT3D
<34>[VPOINT  ]^C^CVPOINT R;<<225;{B} $S=VPOINT3D
<35>[VPT frnt]^C^CVPOINT R;<<270;{B} $S=VPOINT3D
<36>[VPOINT  ]^C^CVPOINT R;<<315;{B} $S=VPOINT3D
<4,15>{B} $S=UCS1 ^C^CUCS
<5>^C^CUCS;PREV
<6>^C^CUCS;V
<16>^C^CUCS;;
<17>^C^CPLAN;W
```

As you can see, multiple lines are given simply by their line numbers. These are the relative positions they will occupy only in this section of the menu file. The line numbers don't affect the other sections of the menu in any way. Note also in this example how **{B}** is used as a variable.

WHAT'S THE BEST WAY TO USE THE MENU COMPILER?

First, define the variables you want to use throughout the menu. Particularly useful would be expressions that define other menu areas, such as **$S = RISC1**, or ones that you might use over and over. Remember, these variable definitions can go anywhere in the menu, but they only become active after they've been defined. In general, it's a good practice to put them all at the beginning of the file. Don't put them in the various sections like the line numbers.

Next, either use **ACAD.MND** or begin preparation on your own. The first menu area you'll want to modify is the *****TABLET1** section. If you use the **ACAD.MND** file, the labels for this section are already prepared for you; you won't need to find each and every line when you're ready to put in your own commands. If you place your numbers after *****TABLET1** and before the first line, then your entries will replace those that have been reserved.

Third, when adding new sections of your own, it's best to simply indicate the lines using the **Menu Compiler**. This makes it easier to edit and maintain those lines.

Finally, always maintain your **.MND** file, editing your menu each time from this file rather than from the **.MNU** file. Then simply run it through the **Menu Compiler** and the corresponding **.MNU** file will be replaced with the updated one.

WHAT ARE THE SWITCHES FOR?

You can invoke three optional switches with the **Menu Compiler**:

-D	Dump macro definition.
-I	List input.
-M	Disable macro facility.

Using **ACAD.MND** as an example, the syntax would be:

```
MC ACAD -I
```

The **-D** will give you a screen listing of all the variables (macros) in the **.MND** file. The **-I** will list the entire **.MND** file. **-M** is the most important; if you aren't using variables in the **.MND** file, but some of your lines have { or } in them, you should disable the macro facility so that the **Menu Compiler** will ignore the symbols.

You can also get a listing of your options with the **-?** switch. But you can get the same thing by typing **MC** without a file name. The **HELP** listing is simply the syntax and a list of the switches.

WHAT CAN GO WRONG?

Plenty, if you're not careful. Above all, *be sure* you have a very good backup of your **.MNU** file. The **Menu Compiler** doesn't warn you if you already have a file by that name. It simply overwrites that file with the new one after the compilation.

If you number lines in a section, be sure that all the lines are numbered, including blanks. The first unnumbered line, blank or otherwise, will make you lose lines from the beginning of the section down to that line.

Remember, though, that not all *sections* must be numbered. You can use the **Menu Compiler** in only those sections that you choose. But once you begin to use it, be sure you follow all the rules.

Line numbers outside of major ** or *** sections will not work, although the variables will work anywhere within the menu. Finally, pay attention to error messages. The only good compilation is one where there are no messages whatsoever; you must solve any error messages or warnings before you use the resulting menu.

WHAT ABOUT THE FUTURE?

Much of AutoCAD's productivity and ease of use center around customizing the menu structure. The **Menu Compiler** is a small start in that direction.

As you can see, learning the ins and outs of Release 10's new menu structure can be time-consuming. In the previous chapters, you learned the rules and requirements of menu structure. But the 3000-plus lines of source code in the standard menu contain a lot of embedded AutoLISP routines and other interrelated code that you shouldn't touch. The best way to increase your productivity is to develop a shell within this massive structure where you can move around freely while still maintaining the original AutoCAD "out-of-the-box" menu. That will make it easily accessible to you or to others unfamiliar with your modifications.

What we ultimately need is a user-friendly menu maker that will spare the user the frustration of counting lines and maintaining the menu structure. Whether it's developed by Autodesk or a third-party developer, it would enhance productivity a great deal.

Automating Your Drawings

IN THIS CHAPTER

If AutoCAD helps you earn a living, this chapter is for you. Although one of the shorter chapters, it's the most important in terms of productivity. We outline techniques for automating your drawings that can reduce hours (even days) of work to minutes. Productivity gains of 20 to 1 are common.

You'll learn which kinds of drawings and procedures can be automated successfully. You'll go beyond the drafting department to consider the benefits of integrating your CAD database with other operations and departments.

Finally, you'll create an automated drawing example to serve both as an AutoLISP tutorial and a conceptual tool for further exploration and productivity.

THE POWER OF AUTOCAD

AutoCAD's power never ceases to amaze me. Before AutoCAD, systems capable of automation cost an average of $100,000 per seat. With AutoCAD's powerful new tools, that price has dropped by 90 percent—to about $10,000! With Releases 9 and 10, AutoCAD became even faster and more powerful, further increasing cost-efficiency.

Even in earlier versions of AutoCAD you could write a program in BASIC that would prompt you for a few design parameters, then perform the calculations and create an AutoCAD script file (an ASCII file). You then would enter a drawing, play the script and watch your drawing be created without intervention. After the automated drawing was created, you could use AutoCAD's interactive environment to improve it.

AutoCAD's interactive ability to modify graphics must be stressed. Applications that move directly from program to plotter are never satisfactory—they all require some human intervention.

Many developers now write the programming they are familiar with, then input the results to AutoCAD, using AutoCAD as a graphics post-processor. Including interactive graphics in their programs would be costly and difficult; just think of all of the devices AutoCAD supports. Now it's easy: you program the application and AutoCAD does the rest.

AutoCAD can be a pre-processor too. Think of how easy it is to create precise geometry on the screen. Now you can send those points out to a CAM program or desktop publishing. And with the 3D capabilities of Release 10, the pre- and post-processing features will be even more important.

SCRIPT FILES

Here's one easy way to bring the output of another program into AutoCAD. Let's create and examine a simple script that makes an octagon. Using a text editor or EDLIN, create the following ASCII file, called **OCT.SCR**. (Your file must have an **.SCR** extension.)

```
PLINE
1,0
2,0
3,1
3,2
2,3
1,3
0,2
0,1
close
```

Execute this file from the AutoCAD **Command:** prompt by typing **SCRIPT**. Then respond to the prompt with **OCT** (**RETURN**). If you don't see anything, **ZOOM E**.

This isn't merely a way to make stop signs. It illustrates how you can take a series of coordinates and manipulate it to automate a drawing.

This suggests many possibilities. It's easy to have a BASIC program generate points, or a typist key a coordinate list into a file. With your editor, you place the word **PLINE** at the top, execute the file and take all the credit for the drawing. It's great for scientific data graphing.

When you draw the perimeter of a complicated building, you can use AutoCAD's **SHELL** feature to access your text editor, create a script file with coordinates, **exit**, **SHELL** back to the drawing and execute it. If you make a mistake, you can use the editor to correct the script file and reexecute. It's to drafting what paper tape is to accounting, allowing easy examination and modification of script files.

THINKING AUTOMATION

Most AutoCAD systems are purchased to speed the drawing and design process. When the CAD system arrives, many users waste their energy attempting to make the CAD drawings look just like manual drawings but with legible text! They tend to be more concerned with the drawing's looks than its information content. Humans are good at drawing curved lines and filled areas; computers are not. For example, free-form curves consume huge amounts of computer storage, and drawings take a long time to load or **ZOOM**. A good CAD user will think his or her way around such problems by approximating free-form curves with a series of arcs.

The same holds true for text. If you use more elaborate fonts (such as Simplex), you soon discover they're slow in loading, displaying and plotting. But you can think your way around the dilemma and use the **TXT** font until plot time, then substitute the fancy font at the last moment, using the **STYLE** command to redefine the text.

Developing these time-saving techniques is an important part of mastering CAD. You must rise above the mindset of manual drafting, discover what CAD does best and compromise your drawing style, using new tools to achieve greater speed and efficiency.

An important step toward breaking that mindset is to look for parts of the drawing-design process that can be automated. This requires a different thought process than the one we used to create the "utility" macros in previous chapters.

An automated parts list (Macro 34) is a good application of simple drawing automation. An AutoLISP routine can be created to ask where you want the list and the number of parts. AutoLISP then draws all line work and sequentially numbers the items.

This parts list places even text in the spaces. For use in my office, I even developed a fully automated bill of materials program (once part numbers have been assigned) that uses an external database for part information.

Another application is stairway design. An AutoLISP program can ask the floor-to-ceiling height, a beginning point and the tread depth. Wham — instant design! (And a great way to quickly explore "what-if" situations.)

Yet another form of automation involves complete, fully dimensioned working drawings, including title sheets and bills of materials.

RISING EXPECTATIONS

Until now, our suggestions for automation have remained in the drafting and design department. The following suggestions cut through departmental barriers, bringing engineering, technical illustration, manufacturing and drafting together:

1. Suppose you're engineering an I-beam to span a given distance. You know the distance and loads. You have a catalog of standard beams and their properties and a standards book that prescribes the connections at each end, including the number of bolts.

From this information, you use standard formulas to find the required section modulus of the beam (generally handled with a microcomputer or programmable calculator). You then consult your reference books for a beam with the right properties. Next, you look up the recommended end connections from the standards book. Finally, the information is scribbled, sketched and handed to a draftsman. Total time: three hours.

Using AutoLISP, you're prompted for load factors and beam length. AutoLISP does the calculations. Stored on disk is a database of beam properties and end connections. AutoLISP or a BASIC program can read the data to pick out just the right beam and its properties (such as depth, flange width and flange thickness) along with the end connections.

AutoLISP now has all the required information to make a drawing, compose a bill of materials and calculate the beam weight. An external file is created for total material. That file is "beamed" to purchasing via a local area network (LAN). Total time: ten minutes.

2. Compression spring design is a function of loading, available physical space, number of active coils, wire gauge, free length, collapsed height, type of wire, spring rate, diameter-to-length considerations, allowable stress, etc.

You vary one parameter and all others factors will change accordingly. Spring design is often a repetitive process. A computer program lets you make several attempts quickly to reach the optimum design. But with AutoCAD, you not only get the calculations, you get the drawing!

AutoLISP can help in two big ways. First, let's assume you're in the middle of a project which requires placement of a loaded spring in a restricted area. Using an AutoLISP program, you use the crosshair to position the spring and indicate the "envelope" size. After you answer a few prompts, AutoCAD draws the spring.

To the side, AutoCAD draws a table of parameters (including spring rate and stress) and illustrations of the spring collapsed and fully extended. You can then **DRAG** these images, superimposing them on your loaded spring to understand visually how they would affect your design.

If you're not pleased, you can **ERASE** or **UNDO** and try again. This is truly "design on the fly."

AutoLISP can also produce a finished drawing that can be furnished to a custom spring manufacturer. You can then **WBLOCK** the spring image to a file and **INSERT** it into your design.

SALES, BIDDING, DESIGN AND MFG— BRINGING HOME THE BACON

Suppose your company makes custom kitchen cabinets, with several different modules that can be grouped together to make counters and overheads.

The sales department lands a request for quotation, comprised of one type "A," two type "C"s, a type "X-100" sink module (including a garbage disposal), and type "A" end modules. These five modules must fit exactly along a 20-foot wall.

From the cabinet list, AutoLISP can make dimension adjustments to fit a 20-foot wall, and create a proposal drawing for the customer and a bill of materials.

The bill of materials then goes into another external program (such as a database) which contains current pricing. An accurate estimate is generated and returned to sales. Total time—one hour.

The salesperson returns a proposal to the customer the same day with a drawing. The potential customer is impressed and awards the order with a few changes.

Revisions are made and approved the next day. Manufacturing begins by using the geometry AutoLISP created for the cabinet doors, which guides the router to make the fancy trim.

The cabinets are delivered to the job site ahead of schedule. They fit exactly.

When departments can be brought together, communications improved, double entry of data eliminated and accurate bids turned out quickly with a drawing, your company gains a tremendous competitive advantage. CAD and drawing automation form the core of this process.

A SAMPLE AUTOLISP ROUTINE

Enough fantasy! Let's look at a practical AutoLISP program for the automation of base plates.

The base plate program below is a straightforward example of automated drawing, geometric construction and AutoLISP programming techniques that can be applied to any discipline.

Even if you're not a mechanical engineer, you'll want to study and use this program to understand the principles common to all automated drawing.

As you create this routine, think about how it can be adapted to your discipline. For example, an architect might have the same problem drawing a building's outside perimeter, then spacing the support columns. That can be handled automatically in the same way we space holes on the base plate.

The base plate program was written for Releases 9 and later. It uses lots of node space, so issue the following commands from the DOS prompt, if you haven't already put them in the **AUTOEXEC.BAT** file:

Type:
```
SET LISPHEAP=35000     (RETURN)

SET LISPSTACK=10000    (RETURN)

SET ACADFREERAM=24     (RETURN)
```

This increases AutoLISP's default settings, allowing you to run larger programs. You may have to remove any RAM resident programs like Sidekick or ProKey.

You'll also need the following layers and linetypes in your drawing before running **BPLATE**:

Layer #	Linetype
Layer 1	Continuous
Layer 2	Hidden
Layer 4	Continuous

The **BPLATE** routine actually was developed for an AutoCAD user who designs steel light poles. It's a good teaching example because it has all the elements of drawing automation and good programming without the fancy trigonometry.

Welded to the bottom of each pole is a base plate with center hole and bolt holes. The light pole is bolted to a concrete base through the base plate. The size, thickness and bolt spacing are determined by the bending moment produced in a strong wind.

These engineering calculations have been omitted and replaced with a different user-input section. However, you could enter the pole height, overhung load and wind loading. AutoLISP could then calculate the size and thickness of the base plate, the bolt diameter and the proper center hole. A fully dimensioned drawing is created and the part geometry is fed to a plate-burning machine.

Below is a typical base plate produced with the AutoLISP routine, called **BPLATE.LSP**:

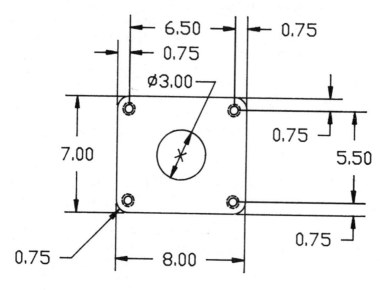

The drawing time required to perform such a task has been reduced from two "manual" hours to two "AutoCAD" minutes. If you don't have an NC burning machine, you could turn off the dimensions (**LAYER 4**) and plot out a burn template.

We've taken the liberty of generalizing **BPLATE.LSP** to show you a few AutoLISP tricks. For example, the center hole and rounded outside corners are optional, and threaded bolt holes can be specified.

Like good programmers, we've placed comment statements at the heads of program modules, identified with a semicolon (;). AutoLISP ignores anything to the right of the semicolon.

Also, this program is structured in modules for input, geometry creation and annotation. The line numbers are for your reference and aren't to be used in the program.

Note: To make life easier for beginners, indention isn't used in this book. However, as you gain AutoLISP expertise, you should use indention, which makes it easier for others to read your work.

Also, because of margin restrictions, many "logical" lines are continued on the next text line. You can modify the program by pulling these lines together, but be careful: What you see below works! Don't use the line numbers; they're for reference only. Also, don't type in the + signs that appear at the end of some lines. They indicate that the line continues on the next line.

BPLATE.LSP

```
1    ;For Releases 9 and 10
2    ;---- INITIALIZE ----------------
3    (Defun C:Bplate ()
4    (Setvar "Cmdecho" 0)
5    (If (= SIDE1 nil) (setq SIDE1 6.0))
6    (If (= SIDE2 nil) (setq SIDE2 6.0))
7    (If (= BOLTHOLE nil) (setq BOLTHOLE 1.0))
8    (If (= CHOLE nil) (setq CHOLE 3.0))
9    (If (= CRADIUS nil) (Setq CRADIUS 0.5))
10   (If (= TAPSTRING nil) (setq TAPSTRING ""))
11   (If (= INSET nil) (setq INSET CRADIUS))
12   (If (= DS nil) (setq DS 1.0))
13   ;    Deletes all.
14   (Initget "YN")
15   (Setq x (getkword  +
       "Erase previous design? Y/<N> : "))
```

```
16  (If (= (strcase x) "Y")
17  (progn
18    (Setq A (Ssget "X"))(IFA
19    (Command "Erase" A ""))
20  ))
```

Now let's examine the program. The above AutoLISP code is the initialization section. Line **3** defines a function (**defun**) to be used as an AutoCAD command, **BPLATE**. The **C:** causes the function to be treated as an AutoCAD command that can be executed just like **LINE**, **CIRCLE** or **ARC**.

Next, set up the initial default in a series of **if** statements. If you've run the program before, you may want to use the previous values, so check to see if they exist for lines **5** through **12**.

Next, you have seven lines that erase a previous design. This not only helps you explore "what ifs," but also lets you create dozens of base plates without ever leaving AutoCAD. Just save them with a different name each time. You could "crank out" dozens of plates in the short span of an hour!

The Input Section

Lines **21** through **59** are the input section, which primarily asks questions and stores your responses under variable names. Later, you can use the variable names to retrieve those values.

Often, one design will be similar to the previous design, like a family of parts, so we have gone to some trouble to remember the old value and offer it as a default if you respond to the prompt with a (**RETURN**).

Let's examine lines **22** through **25**. You'll assign the width of **SIDE1** to a temporary storage variable **x**. The width is a real number, so you'll use the **getreal** function. **Getreal** allows you to form a prompt from three separate text *strings*. You "concatenate" the three parts together, using a **strcat** function. The middle component is the **rtos** statement (real-**to-s**tring). It converts the previous value of **SIDE1** to a text value, using decimal units to three-place accuracy.

If you hit a (**RETURN**) to accept the default, **x** would be set to **nil**, and you wouldn't want to change the previous value of **SIDE1**. However if **x** is *not* nil, then we assume that you've entered a new value and set **SIDE1** equal to **x** in line **25**.

Lines **34** and **35** are a **Yes/No** function: "Do you want tapped holes?" If the answer is yes, then you need to ask for the tap specification. Because you want to remember the previous specification as a default, it takes three lines of code. To do this in an **if** statement, you must group them with a **progn** statement.

If the answer to the **Yes/No** function is no, then we just need a hole call-out. So on line **43** we convert the **BOLT-HOLE** from a real number to text and add to it the ANSI symbol for a hole (**%%c**).

```
21   ;---- INPUT SECTION -------------
22   (Setq x (Getreal
23     (Strcat "\nEnter the baseplate width "
24       (Rtos SIDE1 2 3) ": ")))
25     (If (/= x nil) (setq SIDE1 x))
26   (Setq x (Getreal
27       (Strcat "\nEnter the baseplate length "
28       (Rtos SIDE2 2 3) ": ")))
29     (If (/= x nil) (setq SIDE2 x))
30   (Setq x (Getreal
31       (strcat "\nBolt hole size"
32       (Rtos BOLTHOLE 2 3) ": ")))
33     (If (/= x nil) (setq BOLTHOLE x))
34   (Initget "Y N")
35     (Setq TAP (Getword +
         "\nAre the holes tapped <N>: "))
36     (If (= TAP "Y")
37       (progn
38         (Initget (+ 2 4))
39         (Setq x (Getstring (Strcat
```

```
40            "\nEnter tap specification"  +
                TAPSTRING ": ")))
41            (If (/= x "") (setq TAPSTRING x))))
42        (If (/= TAP "Y")
43        (Setq HOLESTRING (Strcat "%%c"  +
            (Rtos BOLTHOLE 2 3))))
44  (Setq x (Getreal (Strcat "\nCorner radius"
45            (Rtos CRADIUS 2 3) ": ")))
46            (If (/= x nil) (setq CRADIUS x))
47        (If ( BOLTHOLE CRADIUS)
48          (progn
49            (Setq x (Getreal (strcat  +
                "\nEnter bolt hole inset"
50            (Rtos INSET 2 3) ": ")))
51            (If (/= x nil) (setq INSET x)))
52          (Setq INSET CRADIUS)
53          )
54        (Setq x (Getreal (Strcat  +
            "\nCenter hole diameter"
55            (rtos CHOLE 2 3) ": ")))
56            (If (/= x nil) (setq CHOLE x))
57        (Setq x (Getreal (strcat "\nEnter the
            dimension scale"
58            (rtos DS 2 4) ": ")))
59            (If (/= x nil) (setq DS x))
```

Next, you're asked to enter the **corner radius**, and the program must make a judgment. If the corner radius, **cradius**, is less than the bolt hole diameter or **nil**, you're prompted for an inset dimension for the bolt hole (line **49**). Otherwise, use **cradius** as the inset dimension. This is a built-in engineering judgment. Thus, lines **47** through **53** are an "if-then-else" statement that prevents the holes from being too close to the edge of the plate.

At line **57** we ask for the dimension scale and set it to **DS**. This variable is used both to place the text and dimensions at a proper distance from the plate and to scale the text for a wide range of plate sizes.

Drawing Setup

Because it's best to see the geometric construction while it's being created during an automatic drawing, you want to size your viewing screen in this section. You'll also want to size the line scale for broken lines. Since you'll use **DS**, the **D**imension **S**cale variable, to space dimension lines away from the part, you'll use **DS** as a factor in setting your new drawing limits on lines **61** and **62**.

Note: We'll begin the lower left of the part at **0,0**. **Grid** and **ltscale** are also functions of **ds**.

On line **70**, **(command)** performs the function of **CTRL-C** and exits the dimensioning mode.

```
60  ;--- SET SCREEN SIZE, LIMITS, GRID, LTSCALE,  +
    ;AND DIMSCALE --
61  (Setq LOWER (List (* DS -5) (* DS -5)))
62  (Setq UPPER (List (+ (* 5 DS) SIDE1)  +
    (+ (* 5 DS)    SIDE2)))
63  (Command "Zoom" "W" LOWER UPPER)
64  (Command "Limits" LOWER UPPER)
65  (Command "Units" 2 2 2 4 "" "")
66  (Command "Grid" (* 2 DS))
67  (Command "Dim" "Dimscale" DS)
68  (Setvar "Blipmode" 0)
69  (Setvar "Ltscale" DS)
70  (Command)
```

Drawing the Outside

In drawing the outside, first you specify the four corner points. Since you didn't ask for points in the **input** section, you must construct them using the **list** function. According to AutoLISP, a point is a list with two numbers, the **x** and **y** coordinates (or three coordinates with 3D). By picking **0,0** as the lower left corner, you make your task easy. Thus **(list 0,0)** is assigned to **P1**, the first point, and so on.

Unlike menu macros, you can't use a drawing editor command directly in an AutoLISP function. The AutoLISP **command** command has to be used as shown in lines **64** through **67**. Note the "" in line **65**. A double quote is used when an extra (**RETURN**) is required.

You'll use **PLINE** to draw the outline. Rather than ending the **PLINE** back at **P1**, you'll **close** so the last corner will fillet.

Finally, you'll check to see if **cradius** is greater than **0**. If it is, then you'll **FILLET** the **POLYLINE**.

```
71  ;--------- CORNER POINTS ----------------
72  (Setq Pl (List 0 0))
73  (Setq P2 (List SIDE1 0))
74  (Setq P3 (List SIDE1 SIDE2))
75  (Setq P4 (List 0 SIDE2))

76  ;--------- DRAW OUTSIDE ----------------
77  (Command "Layer" "M" 1 "")
78  (Command "Pline" Pl P2 P3 P4 "Cl")
79  (If ( CRADIUS 0)
80  (Progn
81  (Command "Fillet" "R" CRADIUS)
82  (Command "Fillet" "P" "Last")))
```

Creating the Holes

Lines **84** through **87** determine the center points for the bolt holes. Again, knowing where **0,0** is makes life easier.

Starting at line **89**, you'll draw the bolt holes using a two-by-two **ARRAY**. Then, at line **94**, test to see if the holes should be tapped. If **yes**, then you'll switch to **LAYER 2** with broken lines, draw a single circle and repeat the **ARRAY** again.

Note in line **98** the diameter of the tap is 1/16 bigger than the bolt hole at **ds = 1**. This dimension must be a function of plotted scale; otherwise the dashed line would blend in with the bolt hole. It doesn't have to be to scale, but must indicate that the holes are to be threaded.

```
83  ;-------- HOLES --------------------------
84  (Setq Cl (List INSET INSET))
85  (Setq C2 (List (- Sidel INSET) INSET))
```

```
86  (Setq C3 (List (- SIDE1 INSET) +
    (- SIDE2 INSET)))
87  (Setq C4 (List INSET (- SIDE2 INSET)))

88  ;-------- DRAW BOLT HOLES ----------------
89  (Command "Circle" (List INSET INSET)"D" BOLTHOLE)
90  (Setq S1 (- SIDE1 (* 2 INSET)))
91  (Setq S2 (- SIDE2 (* 2 INSET)))
92  (Command "Array" "L" "" "R" 2 2 S2 S1)

93  ;------- DRAW TAPPED HOLES --------------
94  (If (= TAP "Y")
95    (Progn
96      (Command "Layer" "M" 2 "")
97      (Command "Circle" (List INSET INSET)
98        "D" (+ BOLTHOLE (/ DS 16))
99    )
100   (Setq S1 (- SIDE1 (* 2 INSET)))
101     (Setq S2 (- SIDE2 (* 2 INSET)))
102     (Command "Array" "L" "" "R" 2 2 S2 S1)))
103 ;---------- DRAW CENTER HOLE ----------------
104   (If ( CHOLE 0)
105     (progn
106       (Setq MPT (List (/ SIDE1 2) (/ SIDE2 2)))
107       (Command "Layer" "M" 1 "")
108       (Command "Circle" MPT "D" CHOLE)))
```

Because the center hole may not be needed, a test has been included at line **106**, which says, "If the variable **CHOLE** has been assigned a value, then find the midpoint and assign it to **MPT**."

Then the program returns to **LAYER 1** and draws the circle.

Generally you can perform only one action in an **if** statement. That's why the two actions have been grouped under a **progn** statement (**progn** groups a number of actions into one).

This completes the part geometry.

Dimension Points

For dimensioning, you'll need some points that weren't required for the part geometry. You might have noticed that all four bolt hole centers were constructed, but only **C1** was used and **ARRAY**ed. The other three were constructed because they're needed for dimensioning. (Plan ahead!)

In dimensioning the outside of the part, account for a possible large corner radius. You'll want to start your extension line at the start of the radius. To determine this point, **cradius** must be subtracted from either the **x** or **y** coordinate and formed into a list, as shown in lines **110** through **113**.

Line **114** tests to see if a center hole has been specified. If so, you'll need some dimension points. For a diametrical dimension, lines and arrows look best at 45 degrees. To do this, we've established **P9** point on the center hole circumference at 45 degrees (see line **115**, a continuation of the **if** statement).

Note: AutoLISP thinks in terms of radians, not degrees. When you see **(/ pi 4)** you're looking at 45 degrees.

Next, you must draw a leader at 45 degrees to one of the bolt holes, calling out its diameter or threads. Line **116** establishes that point **P10** determines this point for the bolt hole at **C4**, the upper left. From the arrow, you'll draw to **P11**, to the right at 45 degrees.

The length of this line is both a function of how far from the outside edge the bolt holes are inset and the scale at which the part is to be plotted (**ds**). Line **117** and its continuation on **118** establishes point **11**.

You'll also need a leader to call out the corner radius. Points **12** and **13** are required. The leader will be drawn from the lower left at 45 degrees to **P13**. (*** pi -0.75**) = -135 degrees.

Lines **123** through **127** calculate points for outside dimensioning. In linear dimensioning a third point is required to space the dimension away from the part. That is the purpose of **P18** in line **127**.

```
109 ;---------- DIMENSION POINTS -------------
110   (Setq P5 (List 0 (- SIDE2 CRADIUS)))
111 (Setq P6 (List SIDE1 (- SIDE2 CRADIUS)))
112 (Setq P7 (List (- SIDE1 CRADIUS) SIDE2))
113   (Setq P8 (List (- SIDE1 CRADIUS) 0))
114   (If ( CHOLE 0)
115 (Setq P9 (Polar MPT (/ Pi 4) (/ CHOLE 2))))
116   (Setq P10 (Polar C4 (/ Pi 4) (/ BOLTHOLE 2)))
117   (Setq P11 (List (+ (Car C4) INSET (/ DS 2))
118     (+ (Cadr C4) INSET (/ DS 2))))
119   (Setq P12 (Polar (List CRADIUS CRADIUS)
120     (* Pi -0.75) CRADIUS))
121   (Setq P13 (List (- 0.0 INSET (/ DS 2))
122     (- 0.0 INSET (/ DS 1.75))))
123 (Setq P14 (List 0 CRADIUS))
124   (Setq P15 (List Side1 CRADIUS))
125 (Setq P16 (List CRADIUS 0))
126   (Setq P17 (List CRADIUS SIDE2))
127 (Setq P18 (List (* DS -1.75) 0))
```

Dimensions

Dimensions usually are placed on a different layer. Line **129** places them on **LAYER 4** (a standard in our office).

Line **130** starts a horizontal dimension along the top from the upper left corner, **P5**, to the upper left bolt hole, **C4**. Next, you need a third point to place the dimension.

Oops, we forgot to construct the point in the previous section, but you can add it on the fly. Such flexibility is one of the nice features of AutoLISP! Remember the "" is a **(RETURN)**. You then **CONT**inue the dimension to the next bolt hole at **C3**, then to the right edge, **P6**.

Starting at line **134**, the same series of vertical dimensions are created.

Lines **138** and **139** dimension the center hole.

Line **140** annotates the upper left bolt hole with a leader if it has screw threads. If the hole is not tapped, the "callout" will be handled by line **142**.

Line **144** tests to see if a corner radius was specified. If so, it's first converted from the numerical value of **cradius** to text, then joined with **R** (**R**adius). A leader is drawn and the text entered.

```
128 ;---------- DIMENSIONS ------------
129    (Command "Layer" "M" 4 "")
130    (Command "Dim" "Hor" P5 C4
131 (List (Car P4) (+ (Cadr P4) (* 2 DS))) "")
132 (Command "Cont" C3 "")
133 (Command "Cont" P6 "")
134    (Command "Ver" P7 C3
135    (List (+ (Car P3) (* 2 DS)) (Cadr P3)) "")
136 (Command "Cont" C2 "")
137 (Command "Cont" P8 "")
138    (If ( CHOLE 0)
139    (Command "Dia" P9 ""))
140    (If (= TAP "Y")
141    (Command "Lea" P10 P11 "" TAPSTRING))
142    (If (/= TAP "Y")
143 (Command "Lea" P10 P11 "" HOLESTRING))
144 (If ( CRADIUS 0)
145 (Progn
146    (Setq CRADIUSTXT (Strcat +
          (Rtos CRADIUS 2 2) "R"))
147    (Command "Lea" P12 P13 "" CRADIUSTXT)))
148 (Command "Hor" P14 P15 P13 "")
149    (Command "Ver" P16 P17 P18 "")
150    (Command)
151    )
```

Now the overall dimensions of the plate are given in lines **148** and **149**.

Again, **(command)** at line **150** functions like **CTRL-C** to exit the dimensioning mode.

Finally the remaining parenthesis, **)**, on line **151** closes the **defun**, ending the routine.

The above is a simple example that would take an intermediate AutoLISP user six to eight hours to program. Aside from integration with engineering and manufacturing, it could conservatively save half an hour per drawing. Based on that time-savings, the payback for this program is 12 to 16 base plates.

The AutoCAD user for whom this program was developed makes 30 base plates a week. These drawings are accurate and mistake-free—another big payback. Never again will a dimension be omitted from a base plate drawing.

SUMMARY

Whether you automate part of a drawing, a design, or a series of drawings, or whether you program engineering into the drawings or integrate bill of materials and manufacturing, drawing automation is the pot of gold at the end of the rainbow, rewarding you with speed, accuracy and consistency.

AutoCAD was designed to be a "ready-to-use" program, but never meant to stagnate in that condition. The field of drafting and design is too diverse for any CAD program to completely fit your application.

One CAD user automated 80 hours of manual drafting. The same job is now done in two hours using a $100,000-per-terminal system. Now you can do exactly the same thing with AutoCAD. Think big!

With some creativity, AutoCAD can grow more useful every day. Who's going to work harder, you or your computer? AutoLISP allows you to do less with more. You can spend your time thinking of creative new ways to use your AutoCAD system while the computer cranks out drawings unattended.

Even more productivity can be gained when you link your CAD system with the rest of the company. Departmental barriers go down, communication goes up. CAD shouldn't be an island of productivity. Look for places where data are being recreated and establish a way for computers to share the data.

Have you seen a purchasing agent transposing information from your CAD drawing? Have you seen the technical illustrator redrawing an engineering drawing by hand because he wants it in a slightly different format? Have you seen the machinist taking the coordinates from your drawing and entering them into another computer? With customization, linkage and automation, you reap far more than you sow.

Productivity Tips and Tricks

IN THIS CHAPTER

Up to this point, we've discussed the following ways to increase CAD productivity:

1. Working with AutoCAD's latest version.

2. Updating hardware.

3. Learning your operating system.

4. Managing data in subdirectories.

5. Optimizing your hard disk.

6. Customizing your screen menus.

7. Writing macros with AutoLISP.

8. The "20/80" rule and RISC concepts.

9. Customizing AutoCAD's Advanced User Interface.

10. Customizing your tablet menu.

11. Programming a script file.

12. Using pull-down menus with AutoCAD's Advanced User Interface.

13. Automating your drawings.

14. Linking AutoCAD to other programs and departments.

15. Developing a critical mindset that helps you search for improvements.

That's a lot! But there's more, and it doesn't fit into a well-organized chapter. So Chapter Ten is a potpourri of tricks, tips and ideas for further improving CAD productivity. First, let's address some "people" issues, because you and your staff can be more productive when you're happy, challenged and cooperative.

PRODUCTIVITY IS A FRAME OF MIND

The point of reviewing the above list is to illustrate the many factors that influence CAD productivity — and there are more than 16 of them. You can't learn them all over-night.

But some of the most important influences on CAD productivity are the least tangible. We're talking about such "people" issues, such as attitude, work environment and frame of mind.

CAD productivity is more than just customization. It's a mindset for the CAD technician and management, a commitment to take hundreds of small steps on a never-ending learning path. The secret of CAD productivity lies not in a new tablet menu or a fancy AutoLISP routine, but in the hundreds of small steps that will improve your system over the years.

More Than Equipment

Often CAD systems are thrust upon employees with expectations for dramatic improvement in drawing speed, but without the commitment for training that this complex technology requires. Many systems are purchased when the companies are too busy to learn their proper use or customize them for most productive use. They're commonly thought of as a one-time expense, like fancy typewriters. These attitudes result in low productivity and unnecessary job stress.

CAD productivity is more than just equipment. It's the latest software upgrade, a faster CPU and time to develop a LISP routine. It's a trip to a trade show, a training class on advanced features, a users' group meeting, a yearly nationwide meeting of users in your multidivision company. It's using an applications program like CAM or CIM, reading a book or hiring a consultant to initiate a custom application.

CAD equipment has a useful life of two or three years, not because it becomes obsolete, but because something will always emerge that does the job better.

The CAD explosion has outpaced many managers' abilities. CAD management requires great care because CAD and related functions are at the very heart of what a company does. Users and managers alike must communicate their thoughts and needs to develop plans to keep CAD systems on the curve of ever-increasing productivity.

Today's desktop CAD systems are more capable and complex than yesterday's $150,000 systems. When you buy an expensive piece of equipment, you should gladly invest in the training and support required to protect that investment. A typical AutoCAD station costs $15,000 today. But be sure to include the necessary expenses of ongoing support and training in your planning.

More Than a CAD Operator

I dislike the term "CAD operator." A CAD technician, draftsman, designer, engineer — or whatever — is more than just an operator. You've been entrusted with an expensive, complex tool as a compliment to your intellect! Somebody believes in your ability. You've been given CAD so that your customers can benefit more from your work.

In the past, a draftsman was hired for his or her ability to produce good lettering and straight lines. With CAD, job advancement now depends more on your brain power. CAD is leverage for your mind, helping you communicate more ideas faster. You're no longer being used from the elbow out, but from the neck up!

You're no longer "spreading lead," but making mathematical computer models of ideas. This sounds like something professionals might do! And among professionals, mental work is prized over manual dexterity. For professionals, study and learning become a way of life. Would you go to a doctor who believes in on-the-job training?

All Work, No Play

...can make CAD a limited tool. Do you have a playful relationship with your CAD system? I do. Like Tom Sawyer tricking his friends into painting the fence, I try to dupe my friend the CAD system into working harder so that I can do other things.

It's on this level that you can make a mental link with the CAD system. Just as you take pleasure in learning a friend's idiosyncrasies and learning to anticipate a friend's needs and actions, you can learn to anticipate CAD. Once the mental link is established, CAD work can proceed much faster and be more fun. You know what the CAD system is going to do, you anticipate it and are three to five steps ahead of it.

Good CAD users go so fast they're always on the verge of making a mistake; in fact, they do, in about one of every 10 moves. If you let each CAD command become a big decision, you're not as productive as you should be — you haven't established the mental link. With UNDO, why worry about mistakes?

The best CAD users take the longest coffee breaks, because they've found a way to execute those three to five steps in advance. Of course, if instead of breaking for coffee they do some multitasking (other productive work or thinking of the next CAD commands), just imagine how much they can do in a day!

Protect Your Concentration

Unfortunately, there's a built-in barrier to this mental link — the AutoCAD menus!

First, they often interrupt the mental process. Let's say you want to **ERASE** the last item drawn. That's just one thought, one electrical impulse to your brain. To execute that thought using AutoCAD's screen menu, you must select the **EDIT** menu, the **ERASE** option and the **LAST** suboption. Then you'll probably need to return to the

DRAW menu and select another option. It takes five actions to execute one thought and return to the original drawing mode!

Second, if you use menus, you can execute only one command at a time because the menu "goes dead" until AutoCAD has finished. This forces you to watch the command execute before entering the next one. Many of us get so distracted by this boring wait that we don't even use the time to plan the next command, to mentally visualize it before executing.

What's the answer? It's the oldest input device: the keyboard. Thanks to the keyboard buffer, you can keep pecking while the computer works. Not only can you be thinking about the next command, but you also can enter it while the computer executes the previous command. The best CAD users love the keyboard.

The Right Environment

In the old days (a couple of years ago), CAD systems required raised computer floors, dedicated power lines, controlled humidity and precise air conditioning.

Desktop CAD appears to have far fewer demands. Plunk it on a desk and crank out drawings, right?

Not always. A recent study by an insurance company reports that 250,000 PCs were knocked out by electrical power problems last year. Obviously, when a CAD system is zapped electrically, it can't be productive. Line conditioners, surge protectors and standby power supplies are good investments. Not only can equipment be harmed, but data can be lost (by the way, tape backup is great).

Environment is more than just electrical power. More important to productivity are the human elements of environment. CAD requires concentration. Typical manual drafting rooms are "bull pens." With CAD everything can happen at "real-time" mental capacity — no time for fish stories. Noisy environments, phone calls and visual distractions can severely compromise CAD productivity.

In internal drafting operations, CAD productivity can be increased 15 percent by using a CAD system arranged in a "U" shape, with adequate drawers and table tops and with partial walls that absorb sound and block visual distractions. So the $2,000 spent to create a drafting station — including adequate furniture, accessories and indirect lighting — is a good investment.

The Morning Cup of Coffee — Good versus Great

A good AutoCAD user might arrive at the office, get a cup of coffee, then turn on the computer and load up a drawing only to watch a **REGEN** for the next few minutes.

The great AutoCAD user arrives at the office, turns on the computer. Then, using the "type ahead" feature, he types this (typical) sequence (first deleting the message file from the **ACAD** directory, **DEL *.MSG**):

From the DOS prompt,

```
ACAD        (RETURN)
2           (RETURN)
MYDWG       (RETURN)
ZOOM        (RETURN)
E           (RETURN) (RETURN)
.9X         (RETURN)
```

Then he goes for coffee. When he gets back, the drawing is up with a little free space around the edges. From then on, he uses **ZOOM DYNAMIC** to avoid any further **REGEN**s.

Both users get their coffee, but at the end of the day, who do you think has accomplished more? Differences like these separate a good AutoCAD user from a great one.

Another way to accomplish the same thing, but without the 16-character limitation of the keyboard buffer, is to use a startup script file (this allows you to avoid typos as well). Make the following ASCII text file called **START.SCR**:

```
ZOOM E
ZOOM .9X
LAYER N
1,2,3,4,5,6,7,8,9
```

Then to load up,

Type: ACAD (RETURN)

2   (RETURN)

MYDWG   (RETURN)

SCRIPT   (RETURN)

START   (RETURN)

Beep! No Mistake Here

While the computer executes a series of commands, you'd like to work on something else without looking back at the system. You can have AutoCAD beep when finished by simply configuring AutoCAD to beep on error. Then enter an erroneous keystroke at the end of your command sequence. AutoCAD will beep when the bad command is found!

If you don't like AutoCAD beeping every time you make a mistake, programs such as Norton Utilities have a beep function which can be installed in the **.PGP** file.

Mnemory Helpers

Mnemonics are abbreviations that help you remember. For example, if **ERASE LAST** were abbreviated "**EL**," you easily could remember it and type it in faster. Because it's only two letters, you'd make fewer typing mistakes and stack up more commands in the keyboard buffer.

You can use AutoLISP to abbreviate your commands. For a start, add these lines to an ASCII file called **ACAD.LSP** (it will automatically load):

```
(vmon);   (Turns on virtual memory.)
(defun C:L ()
(command "line"))
(Defun C:EL ()
(command "erase" "l" ""))
(defun C:ZV ()
```

```
(command "zoom" "w" (getvar "vsmin")
(getvar "vsmax")))
```

Start a new drawing, and **ACAD.LSP** will automatically load. Type **L** to draw some lines. Then type **EL** to **ERASE** the **LAST** line. In fact, once **EL** is entered, you can hit the space bar as fast as you like, causing items to be erased. Next, **ZOOM** in. Then type **ZV** to return to the full screen.

ZV is an interesting macro because it retrieves the corners of the virtual screen that AutoCAD uses for its fast zooms. When you **ZOOM** a **WINDOW** to these coordinates, you'll get the full picture without ever causing a **REGEN**.

Note: Since Release 9, you've been able to **UNDEFINE** and **REDEFINE** commands. So you can **UNDEFINE** the **LINE** command and **REDEFINE** it as **L**. Here's how. From the **Command:** prompt,

Type: UNDEFINE (RETURN)

Response: Command Name:

Type: LINE (RETURN)

Now you won't be able to use the **LINE** function unless you've defined **C:LINE** in AutoLISP or have a period precede the word "line," like this: **.LINE**. The period overrides the **UNDEFINE** for one usage of the command. To get the command back, use the **REDEFINE** command.

Another use of the above commands might be to restrict classroom students to certain AutoCAD commands.

The Built-in Calculator

By now you may realize that AutoLISP is on-line for your calculations at any time. Yet many users keep calculators at their CAD stations and never use this capability. Every time you place a right-facing parenthesis on the **Com-**

mand: line, you enter the AutoLISP interpreter. To add some numbers, try something like this:

```
Command: (+ 2 3 4)    (RETURN)
```

All math functions, including trig, work similarly. The LISP expressions can be used as an answer to a command. For example, when the **OFFSET** command asks for a distance, you could type **(/ 5 2)**, or **2.5**. Note the reverse notation.

You also can use AutoCAD as a graphics calculator by making the drawing first. Using **TRIM**, **EXTEND**, **FILLET**, **OFFSET** and **OBJECT SNAP**, AutoCAD can find the points for you. Then use ID and DIST to list any point and length you need.

Division by Two and Construction Lines

When you're drafting with CAD, you often must draw a part, such as a shaft, whose diameter you know. However, when you draw the plan view, you can draw lines **OFFSET** from a centerline. First, draw a circle centered on the centerline using the **DIA**meter option. Then use its quad points for construction purposes. **ERASE** the circle when finished.

For a shaft with several diameters, first draw circles spaced along the centerline at each shoulder. When done, create the end view of the shaft by moving the circles to a location off the end of the shaft, using "center" **OBJECT SNAP**. This is a great construction technique.

Throw Out Old Drafting Ideas: A New Way to Look at a Side View

To draw a side view of an object in manual drafting, you move to a clean spot on your paper and project lines from the existing view to the side view. You can do the same in CAD, and most people do. I did it this way for many years, and I kick myself for the lost productivity.

Throw out the old ideas and try this technique. Change **LAYER**s and **COLOR**s. Draw the side view directly on top of the existing view, using the existing view for **SNAP** points and reference. When you've obtained the required geometry, move it to where it should be. You may need to turn off some layers. Easy. With the new AutoLISP **FILTER** capability (Release 9 and later), you simply specify all lines on layer **X** and move them. For further uses of this capability, see **FILTER.LSP** in The AutoCAD Productivity Library.

What's a Construction Line?

In manual drafting, you draw faint lines called construction lines, then you "heavy them in." Many CAD systems even attempt to duplicate the process.

Now that you have AutoCAD, why not use real lines? You can create a lot of line work using **OFFSET**, **COPY** and **ARRAY.** Then, using **FILLET** with a **0** radius (we call it **JOIN**), **TRIM**, **EXTEND** and **BREAK**. Finally, quickly correct the line lengths. Voila! The construction lines become the permanent lines you want, in fewer steps than required by other CAD systems that use construction lines.

Alternatively, you could draw the construction lines on a unique **LAYER**. Then draw over them with appropriate **OBJECT SNAP** in another **LAYER**. Finally, delete the **LAYER** with construction lines.

AutoCAD is completely flexible; your thinking should be as flexible.

Help Yourself: Update HELP

As you customize AutoCAD, your system takes on a new personality. Remember to update the **ACAD.HLP** file, particularly if you're a developer who markets an AutoCAD enhancement. It's easy to add to **ACAD.HLP**, and taking a little time to do it as you go can save you a lot of time later. **HELP** and other information also can be added through AutoCAD's **.PGP** file. Just use the DOS **TYPE** command in **ACAD.PGP** and create an ASCII file.

Beyond Help ... Associated Databases?

When a change is made to the **HELP** file, an index is automatically created that searches through the lengthy file incredibly fast. What if ...? What if you created a brand-new **HELP** file from scratch that had unique part numbers with associated data instead of command names? You could point to a symbol using an AutoLISP routine and show a vast amount of associated data not stored with the drawing. In other words, the **HELP** file could evolve into more than just **HELP**; it could form the foundation of associated databases.

Here's an example from the oil patch. You could point to an oil well symbol on a map and see when it was drilled, the barrels per day, names of the partners, etc. This would be too much data to include as attributes. Yet an associated database for a drawing would make it practical.

Programming Hooks: Ins and Outs

Hook is a programmer's term for a "way to get information in and out of another program" and a "way to add new functionality." The graphic below shows all ways to get information in and out of AutoCAD. It's beyond the scope of this book to discuss all of these hooks in detail.

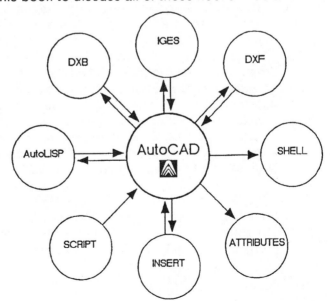

AutoLISP — You should know that AutoLISP can read, write and append to external ASCII text files. AutoLISP also can work on your drawing. That way, AutoLISP can read information from your drawing (perhaps using entity access) and store that information in a separate file on your hard drive.

The reverse also is true. You can use information stored in a file on the hard disk, commonly called a *parameter table*, to help create your drawing. For a comprehensive treatment of this capability, see *AutoLISP in Plain English*, by George O. Head.

Attributes — Attribute extraction is a one-way means of pulling information from your drawing. Attributes are textual information associated with graphic elements — **BLOCK**s. In building management, this information can be desks, their type and serial number.

Information can be copied to a file in a format easily used by other programs that can sort the data and more. For a comprehensive treatment of this subject, see *The AutoCAD Database Book*, by Frederic Jones and Lloyd Martin.

Here are some of the more commonly used hooks available with and for AutoCAD:

DXF — AutoCAD sets a de facto standard with its **DXF** format. When in a drawing, you use the **DXFOUT** command to translate your drawing from its binary files to an ASCII file that is well described and easily manipulated or created by other programs. **DXFIN** is the reverse process. At AutoCAD's **Command:** prompt, you can pull in a drawing created by another program (such as BASIC). One benefit of **DXF** over simpler script files is much greater speed. While other CAD programs kept users in the dark, AutoCAD gave this feature to the developers at the outset. **DXF** is one of the big reasons for AutoCAD's success.

IGES — IGES stands for the *Initial Graphics Exchange Specification*, a translator similar to **DXF** but not as rigid. Thus the translations may be a little unpredictable and more complicated for developers to use.

Scripts—Scripts are ASCII files in which you've recorded typical AutoCAD keystrokes. See previous discussions.

SHELL—**SHELL** is a hook because it allows the user to activate other programs. Those other programs could produce **DXF** files that could be input immediately into the current drawing.

INSERT—The AutoCAD command **INSERT** is mentioned because it's a primary method of bringing information into a drawing.

WBLOCK—**INSERT**'s companion command, **WBLOCK**, copies drawing information to a separate file in binary drawing format. Remember, if you create a **BLOCK** in a drawing, it's only accessible in that drawing, so it has to be **WBLOCKED** to its own spot on your hard disk.

DBX—**DBX** is a binary exchange file used for the now-defunct CAD camera product. Much of an AutoCAD drawing's intelligence (such as **LAYER** information) is lost through **DBX**.

A 3D Trick

If you configure your plotter as an ADI device, you'll be asked if you wish to plot in several formats, one being **DBX**. (Why doesn't AutoCAD offer a **DBXOUT** command?)

First, configure for a **DBX** plot. Now let's assume that you want a 3D drawing as a view on a drawing that has plan and elevation views. Make the 3D model, then rotate it to the proper viewing angle. Next, plot it to a file using hidden line removal. The **DBX** file created is the 3D model squashed flat in the proper view. Then **DBXIN** the model into any other drawing. It will be editable 2D line work. That's a lot faster than drawing in isometric.

Multiple Configurations Save Steps

Rather than reconfigure AutoCAD each time you **DBX**, or switch between a large digitizer and a small one, you can store a copy of the **ACAD.CFG** file in a separate directory. Here's how:

First, make a directory called **DBX**. Next copy your current **ACAD.CFG** file to **ACAD.SAV**. Now, run AutoCAD and configure for **ADI** and **DBX**. Quit AutoCAD. Then, at the DOS prompt, copy **ACAD.CFG** to the **DBX** directory and delete it from the current directory. Finally, rename **ACAD.SAV** to **ACAD.CFG**.

To run AutoCAD with the **DXB** configuration,

Type: `SET ACADCFG=C:\DBX`

To run with the standard configuration,

Type: `SET ACADCFG=C:\ACAD`

These statements could be executed in a **BATCH** file.

The Drawing Record

Think of an AutoCAD drawing as more than ink on paper. It's a database in your computer and can be used as the prime source from which all information flows. Thus, updating the drawing can update all departments where the information is used in different forms.

For example, electric utility maps could be the main record for

1. Location of each customer

2. Location of each piece of equipment (transformers, poles, etc.), tracked by a unique part number, an attribute

3. Conductor lengths, phase and sizes

4. Sections and nodes (engineering information)

5. Geography, subdivisions and highways

From this constantly updated drawing database, the engineering department can extract information to calculate loading and plan expansion. Maintenance can identify aging poles for replacement. During a storm, probable equipment failure can be shown on the CRT. Information can be extracted within tax boundaries. And so on.

For archiving, people who have relatively simple drawing tasks can insert all the piece part drawings into one drawing file. While the file gets larger, it keeps everything in one place.

Four Types of Symbols

There are four types of symbols. First, there are normal symbols that you want to scale and rotate arbitrarily. For example, a shrub drawn with a 1' radius can become any tree or shrub once it's scaled.

The second type of symbol is drawn at full size and should allow no scaling. A 36" shower stall should be drawn at 36," to help with design. When you place it, you'll know if it fits.

The third type is a schematic symbol. Its scale will vary with the final plot size. Electrical symbols on an architect's floor plan are drawn with the same plastic template regardless of drawing scale. Thus, there's a mathematical relationship between a schematic symbol and final plotted size.

Finally, there are parametric symbols, drawn with AutoLISP. Normally you are asked a series of questions, then the symbol is drawn. Parametrics are preferred in these circumstances:

1. When adjusting, the X and Y scale factors would not make an adequate symbol.

2. When storing, a symbol for each variation requires too much storage.

A door is a good example of a symbol that should be parametric. There are a lot of potential door widths. In *The*

AutoCAD Productivity Library, we've created an AutoLISP routine (Macro 65) that draws a door and cuts the opening without using a symbol. You can make the door any size imaginable.

A Time-saver: Attributes for the Title Block

Attributes usually are used for extraction to bill of materials programs; but there's another simple use. Draw the title block of your drawing sheet using attributes where variable text might appear — for instance, for the drawing number. Then, when you insert the title block on your drawing border, AutoCAD will ask you the drawing number, date, your initials, part name, etc.

The beauty of it is that you don't have to **ZOOM** in to see what you're doing. It also helps ensure consistency among all draftsmen and designers in your company.

The Prototype Drawing (or "Never Start at the Beginning")

You never have to start at the beginning if you understand AutoCAD's prototype drawing concept. Instead, you can start a drawing equal to any other drawing on your hard disk. That could be a blank drawing with certain layers and drawing layers, or starting a floor plan equal to one drawn for another customer. Even the geometry of every symbol can be immediately accessible. Let's explain:

In configuration — from the **MAIN** menu, **Option 8** — you can specify the prototype drawing, called **ACAD** by default. If you place the text **AIN'T AUTOCAD GREAT** in the **ACAD.DWG**, the message will appear every time you start a new drawing. **ERASE LAST** and go on with the new drawing.

The prototype drawing also remembers defaults such as **GRID, SNAP, LIMITS**, the menu and the **LAST VIEW**. So call up **ACAD.DWG**. Specify the **SNAP, GRID**s and **LIMITS**, then **ZOOM ALL** so the drawing **LIMITS** fill the screen. Call up the menu you wish to use and then **END** it.

You can have several prototypes, perhaps one for each discipline. For example, with **ELEPROTO.DWG** (for electrical), you could insert all your electrical symbols and erase them, leaving their descriptions in the prototype drawing.

When you use this drawing and insert a symbol, AutoCAD won't have to retrieve the symbol from the hard disk. In fact, you can archive all your symbols, then erase them from your hard disk—a nice way to manage lots of symbols. Be sure to **PURGE** your drawing or **WBLOCK** it to a file. This will compress the drawing size by eliminating unused blocks.

Here's how to use multiple prototype drawings without having to reconfigure AutoCAD each time. From AutoCAD's **MAIN** menu, **Option 1**, begin a new drawing and type in the drawing name as **NEWDWG = PROTO**, or **NEWBLDG = OLDBLDG**. You actually can start any new drawing equal to any existing drawing. Very handy!

If you choose not to use a prototype drawing, you can rely on AutoCAD's built-in defaults (no layers except 0, no blocks with drawing limits set to 12"x 9"). There are two ways to get this "clean sheet." First, you can use a period in place of the prototype drawing name during configuration, or you can start a new drawing and type the name like this: **NEWDWG =** . Note the "dangling" equal sign.

Play It Safe

Good users generally run with a safety or scratch floppy in their computers. They save their work on it several times per day, although not as often as to the hard disk. This is valuable insurance against accidental erasure of important data. The moment you complete a drawing, copy it to the project floppy. When you finish the project, make two floppy copies, then delete your drawings from the hard disk. Take one set of floppies off-site for storage. Through it all, you can reuse the scratch floppy.

AutoSave

Since Version 2.5, AutoCAD has allowed you to read the system clock. You can store the time in a variable with AutoLISP. Then you can come back later and check the variable against the current time to see how many minutes have elapsed. If the time is over 15 minutes, save the drawing. You can tie this function to an often-used command, such as **LINE** or **REDRAW**. Check out this macro in The AutoCAD Productivity Library.

New Hope for Read Error Recovery

Ah, the bane of all AutoCAD users, the **illegal read error**— your drawing is lost forever. Now there's some hope. A clever computer scientist has cracked the binary drawing file and can translate a drawing to **DXF** format without using AutoCAD. (He can plot, too.) The interesting point is that his program will generally read a drawing when AutoCAD won't! If you have a **read error**, you can use his program to **DXFIN** to a new drawing. He claims an 85 percent success rate. See Appendix D for more information.

Drawing Revisions

To keep a record of drawing revisions and avoid multiple drawing copies, place the parts of the drawing to be changed on a layer named **REV-A**, then draw in the revisions. Then, turn off **REV-A** (this could lead to a large drawing file).

Linetypes Unlimited

You can create all sorts of linetypes. You can even have multiple libraries of lines. You aren't restricted to **ACAD.LIN**. An easy way to get started is to copy **ACAD.LIN** to **MYLINES.LIN**, then edit it with a text editor. You could create line files for mapping, site planning, floor plans and schematics that would all use a linescale of **1**.

Here are two lines from the **ACAD.LIN** file:

```
*CENTER,____ _ ____ _ ____ _ ____ _ ____ _ ____ _ ____
A,1.25,-.25,.25,-.25
*SDOTS,........
A,0,-0.05
```

The first line, which begins with an asterisk, starts with the name of the line type followed by a description. The description is pure text. Underline dashes are used to give a visual sense of a center line. However, a worded description would be fine.

The second line starts with the type of alignment (the only available type is **A**). The next number is a dash. It must be positive or **0** (**0** produces a dot). These are the pen down movements. Negative numbers are pen up movements. You may have 12 dashes, provided they fit on an 80-character line.

To use **MYLINES.LIN** in a drawing, you first must use the **LINETYPE** command to load it (**ACAD.LIN** loads automatically).

A Concrete Problem

Why doesn't AutoCAD include a concrete hatching pattern? Or for that matter, a freehand font? Hatching patterns are like broken lines, only they're not stored in the database efficiently as broken lines; they're stored as individual line segments. That's why it's so easy to get **disk full** errors while crosshatching. So be careful about "tight" hatching patterns. A very pretty concrete pattern can be a big memory hog.

Like having multiple **.LIN** files, you can have multiple **.PAT** files. A concrete pattern is a random pattern of rocks and stipple. The rocks are triangles produced by the first three lines following the pattern name and description, in the code below.

The first number of each line is an angle. Angles 60, 120 and 0 degrees form the bases of equilateral triangles. In the first two lines, the next two numbers are the starting coordinate, **0,0**.

```
*C3,Concrete - type 3
60, 0,0, .3,.5196, .1,-.5
120, 0,0, .3,.5196, .1,-.5
0, .55,.0866, .3,.5196, .1,-.5
27, 0,0, .1,.1, .005,-.08
47, 0,0, .1,.1, .02,-.25
120, .05,0, .12,.08, .02,-.2
```

Add the above to the **ACAD.PAT** file, under the name **C3**.

Thus, the first two lines form a **V**. The starting coordinate of the "cap," in the third line, is **.55, .0866**. The next two numbers on any line are the offset and parallel distances between lines. The last two numbers describe the pen down and up movements of a broken line.

The last three lines of the pattern are random dots and dashes to fill in the stippling.

Shapes and Text: A Challenge

In the good old days (circa 1985), it was faster to use shapes than blocks. But shapes couldn't be edited or scaled independently on **x** and **y**. Worst of all, they had to be programmed in!

I believe it's better to throw hardware at a speed problem than to learn shapes as a replacement for symbols. So, I've never had a use for them until now. I have a customer who is a steel detailer and must "scrunch" up his fractional dimensions. The standard font doesn't allow this.

Fonts are shapes. So I've learned just enough to extend the **TXT** font file (**TXT.SHP** on support disk 2 in the source directory). It took two hours. I honestly can't tell you much about them, I don't want to learn shapes. By fiddling around (one approach to programming), I got everything adjusted to come out all right.

If you add the following code to the bottom of the **TXT.SHP** file and then recompile it (**Option 7** from the **MAIN** menu), you'll have proper fractions for steel detailing. If this inspires you to dig deeper into shapes, you're a better person than I am!

```
*130,18,1/16
3,2,2,8,(0,8),7,49,8,(-6,-8),7,49,7,54,4,2,0
*131,16,1/8
3,2,2,8,(0,8),7,49,8,(-5,-8),7,56,4,2,0
*132,18,3/16
```

```
3,2,2,8,(0,8),7,51,8,(-7,-8),7,49,7,54,4,2,0
*133,16,1/4
3,2,2,8,(0,8),7,49,8,(-5,-8),7,52,4,2,0
*134,18,5/16
3,2,2,8,(0,8),7,53,8,(-7,-8),7,49,7,54,4,2,0
*135,16,3/8
3,2,2,8,(0,8),7,51,8,(-5,-8),7,56,4,2,0
*136,18,7/16
3,2,2,8,(0,8),7,55,8,(-7,-8),7,49,7,54,4,2,0
*137,16,1/2
3,2,2,8,(0,8),7,49,8,(-5,-8),7,50,4,2,0
*138,18,9/16
3,2,2,8,(0,8),7,57,8,(-7,-8),7,49,7,54,4,2,0
*139,16,5/8
3,2,2,8,(0,8),7,53,8,(-5,-8),7,56,4,2,0
*140,20,11/16
3,2,2,8,(0,8),7,49,7,49,8,(-8,-8),7,49,7,54,4,2,0
*141,16,3/4
3,2,2,8,(0,8),7,51,8,(-5,-8),7,52,4,2,0
*142,20,13/16
3,2,2,8,(0,8),7,49,7,51,8,(-10,-8),7,49,7,54,4,2,0
*143,16,7/8
3,2,2,8,(0,8),7,55,8,(-5,-8),7,56,4,2,0
*144,20,15/16
3,2,2,8,(0,8),7,49,7,53,8,(-10,-8),7,49,7,54,4,2,0
```

Here's what was done: Line 1 of each shape begins with an asterisk followed by the number of elements on the following line(s), followed by a description of the shape (in this case, the fraction).

Line 2 uses the geometric description of the numbers (as described in Lines *48 through *57 of the whole font file), scales them by half and places them in the right positions (the coordinates are surrounded by parentheses).

To use this extended font, you must use a double percent sign preceding the shape number, like this:

3-%%144 is the same as 3-11/16

Assign them to menu squares for easy operation.

Synthesis

Most AutoCAD users can accomplish a great deal with AutoLISP, AutoCAD's internal programming language. However, if you have extensive need for drawing automation, a third-party program called Synthesis can easily pay for itself.

Synthesis works with **DXF** files to redraw a drawing to any new set of dimensions. You use AutoCAD to create a master drawing, but you substitute variable names for the numerical dimension text. Next you prepare a spreadsheet that uses the variable names and prompts for user-supplied information. You then execute the spreadsheet in its "runtime" mode. It functions like a program, asking you questions, looking up tabular data and calculating. Finally, a new drawing is created—synthesized.

The advantage Synthesis has over AutoLISP is that because of the master drawing technique, you don't have to program every point in your drawing. Synthesis is powerful. Some applications can be 20 to 200 times faster than manual drafting. For more information, see Appendix D.

Variables: Revising Values

Behind your pretty drawings, AutoCAD keeps track of everything. What was the last point you entered? What was the last text size used? And so on. This information is stored with the prototype drawing, so any change you make can become the system default every time you start a drawing (when saved in a prototype drawing).

When customizing and using AutoLISP, you want to retrieve and revise the values of those variables. Some of them are "read only," such as the **CLAYER** (the **C**urrent **LAYER**).

A handy example is **'setvar;snapunit;1,1**. This changes the **SNAP** to **1** unit in both **x** and **y**. The apostrophe allows you to change the **SNAP** transparently during a drawing command (such as **LINE**). For example, if you're set to **1/8" SNAP** and need 1/16," just use the transparent **setvar** command to change it on the fly.

Sometimes when I sit down at someone else's CAD system and try to **ERASE** something, the "pickbox" is too small. No need to cancel the **ERASE** command when a transparent **setvar** will do the job.

Here's one for changing mirrored text in a drawing. From the **MIRROR** command you can actually watch the text flip-flop dynamically. Just assign it to a menu.

```
'setvar;mirrtext;(abs (- (getvar "mirrtext") 1));
```

Plotting, Batch and Script Files

Today's plot spoolers can plot a drawing while you continue to draw. (See Appendix D). Spoolers work with plot files; you plot it to a file on your hard disk, which is much faster than sending it directly to the plotter.

You can use an AutoCAD script file to create these plot files automatically and unattended—say, overnight! Here's a typical script file—call it **PLOT.SCR**:

```
3
Dwg1
E
N


3
Dwg2
E
N


0
```

The **3** on the first line is the option for plotting in AutoCAD's start-up menu. **E** is to plot Extents. **N** answers the question **Do you want to change anything?** Be sure AutoCAD is set to plot the drawing to a file. The next two blank lines answer the pause for checking the plotter and the call for a (**RETURN**) at the end of the plot. Finally, an **0** returns AutoCAD to DOS. Because the commands are repetitive, you can use your editor to quickly copy the lines, then change the drawing names.

To execute it, type: **ACAD X PLOT**, where **X** is a drawing name (here it isn't really used) and **PLOT** is the name of a script file.

Script Files to the Rescue!

Imagine you have 300 drawings ready for final plots and your boss decides to change the company logo. Of course, he wants you to update all the drawings! How boring to call up all the drawings, one by one. Script files to the rescue!

Here's a script that would replace all the logos—unattended, where "**junk1**" and "**junk2**" are drawing names.

```
2
junk1
insert logo= (getvar "viewctr") 1 1 1
erase l

save

quit
y
2
junk2
insert logo= (getvar "viewctr") 1 1 1
erase l
```

```
save

quit
y
0
```

(Be sure to include the blank lines.)

You must insert the logo and erase it, because if you cancel, the **INSERT** command interrupts the script. We use the **viewctr** variable rather than a point like **0,0**, because if **0,0** were off the screen, you'd erase the wrong item.

Try this out. It's amazing — probably 1,000 percent faster than calling each one and making an edit!

Other Autodesk Products

Autodesk has other fine products that can help your business. For example, AutoSHADE can help you, your associates and clients visualize your ideas. One purpose of CAD is to communicate faster. Products like AutoSHADE can help you win jobs.

AutoFLIX can animate the AutoSHADE images for even more realism and marketing pizzazz.

AutoSKETCH is a low-cost, effective drafting tool that can pass drawings up to AutoCAD. For the infrequent user, it might be just the answer.

AutoSOLID is a full-featured solids modeling system for mechanical design, with integrated ties to CAM, Finite Element Analysis and, of course, AutoCAD.

AutoCAD AEC and Mechanical (HVAC) gives AutoCAD a personality for architecture, making AutoCAD much more productive for anyone working in the AEC marketplace.

In addition to Autodesk's growing product line, many "third-party" products are available that can greatly enhance productivity for a relatively low price. Modules and software packages are available for landscape design, numeric control, stress analysis, complex area calculations and a host of other tasks. Quality varies, so you'll want a demonstration from your local dealer or a satisfactory guarantee of quality.

Keep on Learning

Continuing education can keep you current and pay for itself many times over. Here are some suggestions: join or form a users' group; read *CADalyst* and *Cadence* magazines; log on to the AutoCAD forum on CompuServe; invest in training; attend AutoCAD Expo.

Know Thy AutoCAD Dealer

Keeping the goodwill of a dealer who supplies training and support for your customization efforts is one of the best investments you can make.

No AutoCAD system should be sold without some initial customization before delivery. This could include a symbol library, AutoLISP programs and entry of title sheets and standard drawings, or a commercial application package such as AutoCAD AEC. It's better to hit the ground running.

Purchasing AutoCAD from the cheapest source rarely buys the additional service that makes and keeps your AutoCAD system productive year after year.

SUMMARY

This chapter could go on and on. However, my intention is not to overwhelm, but to expand your horizons.

While you've been given some handy productivity tips throughout the book, the greater aim of this book is to provide the intellectual framework and conceptual tools to make your company productive with the use of AutoCAD. Be creative!

The second half of this book features even more routines to enhance your productivity. Modify them to best suit your needs and integrate them into a system of drafting and design.

Release 10
Tips and Tricks

AutoCAD's Release 10 is a full-fledged attack on the capabilities of larger CAD systems; and it's productivity has advanced by giant leaps. But with this advancement comes a whole new set of challenges.

Release 10 is such a departure from previous updates that we've dedicated a chapter to each aspect of its features and the ways in which this new system can be made even more productive.

The best way to learn Release 10 is to first take an overview of its organization and features and how they work together to get the job done; and then learn some tips and techniques, feature by feature, that can be used to customize your system and do the job more productively. Finally, we present some general techniques that apply to Release 10 as well as earlier releases.

This chapter isn't a complete lesson in 3D and Release 10; for a thorough tutorial, read *The AutoCAD 3D Book* (Ventana Press). However, you do need to look at Release 10 as a whole, so that you can see how the commands work and how they can be improved upon for greater productivity.

3D OR 2D?

Release 10 is advertised as being AutoCAD's full 3D version, and it is. But the first reaction of many users is that they don't really need 3D. So, what does Release 10 have for them?

Although Release 10 is a full 3D version of AutoCAD, it has wider implications than drawing in 3D or 2D; with Release 10, they're one and the same. The drawing database has been changed dramatically, so that nearly every entity has an X, Y and Z coordinate. Therefore you *are* drawing in 3D, but in plan view. 3D is really only the angle at which you view the object!

This is important. In Release 9 and earlier versions, you had to use specific commands and perform abnormal gyrations to simulate 3D. Now you're in 3D the first time you draw a line across the screen. Also, a whole host of new features has been added to help you draw and view that line—and this is the important difference. All the features touted as 3D features are also productivity tools that will help you draw and design faster and smarter.

CHANGES AND ENHANCEMENTS

Because Release 10 was developed as a 3D communication package, most of the enhancements have supported 3D. They were designed to make your work easier, but when you first look at them, you may wonder.

One of the first problems you encounter when trying to design a 3D model is the limitation of the input and output device. Both are 2D instruments. The input device is the most critical. There are some 3D input devices, but most people use mice or digitizers. These instruments can supply only the **X** and **Y** coordinates when a point is picked. As a result, AutoCAD had to find a way to indicate the **X, Y** plane upon which you're drawing.

In order to do this, AutoCAD lets you redefine your **X, Y** plane through the **User Coordinate System (UCS)**—you can redefine your point of origin, the direction of positive **X** and the direction of positive **Y**. Thus, by definition, you've been able to rotate in any direction the **X, Y** and **Z** planes. Now that the **X** and **Y** planes have been redefined, your input device can now produce the proper point in terms of **X** and **Y** anywhere in the drawing.

In other words, by redefining a new **UCS**, you're always drawing on **X** and **Y** *somewhere* in your drawing.

VIEWING YOUR DRAWING

Visualization is the key to productivity for any CAD system. That is what made the earlier attempts at 3D so unsuccessful—it was hard to visualize where you were in 3D space. But all that has changed in Release 10.

Dynamic View (DVIEW) provides this important visualization, which helps you see not only the actual drawing on the screen, but also enables you to redefine your **UCS**. You must be able to dynamically rotate your angle of view in relation to the object in 3D space.

DVIEW gives you an impressive collection of tools to position the object and camera in relation to each other. Other commands let you **PAN** and **ZOOM** in real time. And to give realism to the visualization, you can add **PERSPECTIVE** at any distance.

SPLITTING THE SCREEN

Rotating the object using **DVIEW** isn't the only change in visualization. You can now split the screen into as many as four screens. Each screen is independent regarding **SNAP, GRID, ZOOM, VIEW**, etc. What's more, you can begin a command in one window **(VPORT)** and continue that command in another window. This opens up an enormous number of possibilities.

One of the most efficient uses of **VPORTS** is to double-check where you're drawing in 3D space. It's possible for the drawing to "look right" in one window but be way out in space when viewed from another angle.

ASSORTED CHANGES AND IMPLICATIONS

Many of the changes in Release 10 are brought about not as much by commands that have actually been added or changed, but by the implications of what you can do with the new commands.

The biggest ones are the changes brought on by the **UCS**. The ability to change your coordinate system, for example, changes the way distances and angles are measured, the direction of text, the **CHANGE** command and many editing commands, which simply won't work all the time unless you understand how the entity must be made parallel to the existing **X, Y** plane.

CHPROP is one of these new commands. It contains almost all the suboptions of the **CHANGE PROPERTIES** command, but will work regardless of the entity's relation to the current **UCS X, Y** plane.

LET'S BE SPECIFIC

TIP 1: YOUR POINT OF ORIGIN

As you can see, the **UCS** can provide a lot of productivity. In fact, some productivity tricks using the **UCS** have nothing to do with 3D.

One of the hardest things to do gracefully in AutoCAD is to start a line or a point at a distance up and to the right of another known point. One way to do this with Release 9 is to draw two construction lines, using the relative @ first at 0 degrees, then another at 90 degrees. The endpoint of the second line would be your starting point. Then you'd erase your construction lines.

There are other ways to do this, but none is as easy as the **UCS** in Release 10. You want to redefine the point of origin at the known point. You can use whatever **OBJECT SNAP** is appropriate. Now that this point is the new point of origin, you can easily locate any other point in relation to it by absolute coordinates. Therefore, if you wanted to begin a line 2 1/2 units to the right and 3 1/4 up from the point, then you'd respond to the **From point** prompt with:

```
2.5,3.25 (RETURN)
```

Return to **UCS PREVIOUS** when finished.

TIP 2: CHANGING YOUR UCS

You should make liberal use of **UCS PREVIOUS** and of naming the **UCS**; this will dramatically increase your productivity. We suggest that you create several macros that restore standard named **UCS**s. For example:

```
(defun c:ls ()
(command "ucs" "r" "leftside"))
```

This isn't to say that every object should have the same **UCS**s. Each point of origin and **X, Y, Z** plane will be different. But if you get into the habit of giving them standard names, you can set up macros that will let you quickly "pop" from one to another.

TIP 3: AN ENDPOINT/INTERSECTION MACRO

One thing you'll notice when you start using **UCS** is that you'll be using **3POINT** more than most of the other subcommands. Another interesting thing is that you're almost always pointing to either **ENDPOINT** or **INTERSECTION**. Then why not set up a **UCS 3POINT** macro that changes to **INTERSECTION** and/or **ENDPOINT** and returns you to **NONE** at the end? You might use the following macros as a model:

```
(defun c:3p ()
(setvar "osmode" 32)
(command "ucs" "3" pause pause pause)
(setvar "osmode" 0))
```

If you set "**osmode**" to **33** instead of **1**, or **32** for **ENDPOINT** or **INTERSECTION**, it will let you use either **ENDPOINT** or **INTERSECTION**.

TIP 4: HANDLING TEXT

If you don't want your text to go in the direction of your entities in 3D, but would prefer for it to be parallel to the **X, Y** of the screen, use **UCS VIEW**. However, be careful of two things: First, be sure you put your text on another layer so that it can be frozen or turned off. Second, be sure you save that view so that you can return to it. The **VIEW** subcommand doesn't tell you where the text really is in 3D space in relation to the object.

TIP 5: TRANSLATING COORDINATES

You can also use **UCS** as a translating device of coordinates. Let's say you're a civil engineer working on a plat and need to put in information by coordinates, based on a fixed point of origin in your drawing. You could use the **UCS ORIGIN** subcommand and establish that point in your drawing as the new point of origin. Now you can input the other points and their coordinates.

But you need to know what those coordinates are in relation to where the point of origin was before you changed it. Simply change back to **UCS PREVIOUS** or **UCS WORLD**. All the new points you input will now carry the coordinates of the previous coordinate system. In this way you can create as many coordinate systems as you want and be able to query points as they exist in relationship to each other, translated to each coordinate system.

TIP 6: PLOTTING IN UCS

Be sure that you're in **UCS WORLD** when plotting. If you're not careful, strange things can happen to your plots as you try to position them on the paper. If you have a current **UCS** other than **WORLD**, you'll have trouble positioning the plot on the paper using the plot origin option. If you take the precaution of plotting everything from **UCS WORLD**, then your plotting sequence will be just as before.

TIP 7: WHEN Z GETS IN THE WAY

One common procedure you'll use is drawing or moving something "on top" of another entity. With Release 10, this can get tricky if you're simply trying to visualize and point to where an object ought to go.

The best procedure is to create a **UCS 3POINT** for the base object to be copied or moved. Then, if necessary, rotate the **UCS** around the **X** axis until **Y** is pointing above the object. Now simply use the relative @ command to move the object 90 degrees. Because the direction you want to move is on the **Y** axis, this is 90 degrees to the current **UCS**!

TIP 8: RELEASE 9 REVISITED

You may find that macros you've already written or third-party software don't seem to work the way they used to. This is probably not your imagination. Most of the problems can be traced back to confusion over the **UCS** (where exactly **X** and **Y** are).

AutoCAD has provided a workable solution, at least temporarily, with a new variable called **FLATLAND**. If **FLATLAND** is set to **1**, then new features, such as **UCS**, are disabled — this should allow old programs or procedures to continue to work until they can be updated. If **FLATLAND** is set to **0**, then all the features of Release 10 are active.

Don't get too comfortable with **FLATLAND**, because it won't be around for long (i.e., Autodesk will probably do away with **FLATLAND** with its next release).

TIP 9: STREAMLINING DVIEW

The problem with **DVIEW** is that it has too many options and desperately needs to be streamlined. You should set up several stand-alone **DVIEW** options that are single-purpose programs. AutoCAD has pointed the way by placing an icon for **DVIEW CAMERA** on the pull-down menus.

You could go a step further. Create several viewing angles that you might want to use routinely for most of your drawings. Of course, you'll still need the general-purpose **DVIEW CAMERA** routine so that you can choose any angle.

If you go into **DVIEW** while in a **UCS**, the **CAMERA** or **TARGET** angles are based on the current **UCS**, which may be unpredictable. So it's best to set **UCS** to **WORLD** going into **DVIEW** and to return to **UCS PREVIOUS** coming out.

A system variable called **WORLDVIEW** does this for you. When set to **1**, **WORLDVIEW** will change the **UCS** to **WORLD** going into **DVIEW** and return you to **UCS**

PREVIOUS as you return. We recommend that this system variable be set to **1**.

If you don't use **WORLDVIEW**, then notice how in the macro below, the **UCS** is set to **WORLD** going into **DVIEW** and **UCS PREVIOUS** coming out. If you use **WORLDVIEW**, remove those two lines.

```
(defun c:ca45 ()
  (command "ucs" "world")
  (command "dview" "" "ca" 45 35 "")
  (command "ucs" "p"))
```

TIP 10: WHAT'S YOUR POINT OF VIEW?

Even in simple drawings, it's sometimes hard to tell whether you're above the object looking down or below looking up. One solution is to hide your lines, but this can take a lot of time.

AutoCAD can help you with this. Look at your **UCS** icon pair of **X**, **Y** arrows. If they crisscross and form a box at their intersection, you're looking from the top down. If there's no crisscross box where they meet, you're looking from the bottom up. The **UCS** icon provides another clue. If there's a crisscross inside the box, then the icon is located at the point of origin.

TIP 11: SAVING/RESTORING THE VIEW AND UCS

Unfortunately, there isn't a **DVIEW SAVE** that will save the **UCS** in effect at the time. Therefore, to save a specific **DVIEW**, you must use the ordinary **VIEW SAVE** command.

But to restore the view with the same **UCS** in effect as when it was saved, you'll need to write a pair of macros that saves and restores both the **VIEW** and the **UCS** of the same name at the same time.

```
(defun c:dvsav ()
  (setq nam (getstring "\nDview name to save  "))
  (command "view" "s" nam)
  (command "ucs" "s" nam))
```

```
(defun c:dvres ()
  (setq nam (getstring "\nDview name to restore  "))
(command "view" "r" nam)
(command "ucs" "r" nam))
```

TIP 12: BROKEN-PENCIL ICON

From time to time while working with **DVIEW**, you'll see an icon that's a picture of a broken pencil, appearing in the lower left-hand corner of your screen. The broken-pencil icon means that you're viewing the object from within one degree of parallel of the current **X, Y** plane. This would be like looking at a sheet of paper on its edge.

When this happens, AutoCAD's letting you know that choosing objects may be difficult and/or inaccurate. Don't choose objects when this icon appears. Instead, go back into **DVIEW** and rotate the inclination.

TIP 13: PERSPECTIVE ON AND OFF

One of the most bothersome aspects of **DVIEW** is when you're working with **PERSPECTIVE ON**. It seems that no matter what you want to do, you get that infuriating message about **REGEN** with **PERSPECTIVE OFF** and are asked whether you want to proceed. If you type **NO**, then you can't issue your command. If you type **YES**, you lose your **PERSPECTIVE** and the drawing actually changes size sometimes.

The key to working with this is to issue the macro you created in **TIP 11** to save your **DVIEW**. Then let it **REGEN** with **PERSPECTIVE OFF**. When finished, restore your **DVIEW** and your **PERSPECTIVE** will be restored along with it, without having to go back through the **DVIEW DIS-TANCE** command.

TIP 14: FINDING YOUR OBJECT

From time to time, you'll "lose" your object — it will seem to completely disappear while in **DVIEW**. Of course, there's no certainty where it went, but it's probably behind you! If that's the case, the best way to retrieve it is by using **PAN** and **ZOOM**, which are part of **DVIEW**.

First, use **ZOOM** to reduce the object's size. This will make it look like a little speck on the screen. By moving your cursor back and forth, you'll see where the object is disappearing. Make the object as large as possible before it goes off the screen. Then use the **PAN** command. Pick the object and pull it to the center of the screen. Again use **ZOOM** to make the object larger. Repeat this several times, if necessary, until the object is the right size and placed where you want it on the screen.

TIP 15: A SHORTCUT TO DVIEW

You can often save a lot of time when using **DVIEW** if you don't have to actually see the object that you're rotating, zooming, clipping or setting **PERSPECTIVE** for. To use this shortcut, don't select objects when asked. Simply <**RETURN**>, and a picture of a house built by AutoCAD will appear. Because this is a simple object, the reaction time will be almost instantaneous. When you finally confirm with <**RETURN**>, your entire object will be redrawn in accordance with the settings created in **DVIEW**.

TIP 16: YOUR OWN DVIEW DEFAULT

If you don't select objects, and you'd rather see a different default drawing for **DVIEW**, you can design your own.

This is easy to do. First, design the drawing you want to use with a 1 × 1 × 1 unit area. Place the point of origin in the lower left corner of the object. Block your drawing with the name **DVIEWBLOCK**, then **WBLOCK** the drawing. Then insert this block into your prototype drawings, such as **ACAD.DWG**.

Now AutoCAD will use **DVIEWBLOCK** if it exists. If not, it will use the house drawing.

TIP 17: CHECKING YOUR DRAWING

Many people think that multiple viewports are a good idea, but realize the implications. **VPORTS** capabilities are one of the most productive new features of Release 10.

At least two viewports *must* be active while you're drawing in 3D. One of the viewports should be at a different angle from the primary viewport—the most important reason for this is error checking.

Drawing in 3D can be very frustrating, especially when you're just learning. If you're not careful, you might be on the wrong **X**, **Y** plane and not realize it. Therefore, what might appear to be correct in one viewport might be totally off when viewed from another angle. A good rule is that if it looks right from two or more angles, then it's probably correct.

TIP 18: USING VIEWPORT CONFIGURATIONS

VPORTS is still a useful command, even when you're not drawing in 3D. The power of multiple viewports is that you can begin a command in one viewport and continue that command in another. Also, each viewport is independent—each can have its own **VIEWS**, **ZOOMS**, **SNAP**, etc.

Therefore, you must decide exactly what should go into each viewport. If you're developing a 3D model, you might consider each side of the object and a plan view. If you're drawing in 2D, then a **ZOOM EXTENTS** should be in one window. You might prefer tight **ZOOMS** for several viewing areas.

Remember that each viewport can be changed. You can also save an entire viewport configuration, complete with the views that were in each window at the time. So you can develop several viewport configurations and swap between them.

TIP 19: UPDATING THE UCS ICON

The **UCS** icon doesn't automatically update in all viewports. To make sure they're updated, choose the **ALL** option under **UCSICON**.

Note: This isn't a toggle. You must issue it each time you choose a new option for **UCSICON**.

Therefore, if you want the **ALL** option to be executed when you turn **UCSICON ON** or **OFF**, use a macro that chooses the **ALL** option first. That way, you won't have to choose so many steps for such a simple operation.

TIP 20: ERRORS AND THE UCS

From time to time, you'll get errors that indicate the entity chosen isn't parallel to the current **UCS**. Unless you correct this situation, you won't be able to execute the **EDIT** command you've chosen.

The solution is to change the **UCS** in order to make the entity parallel to the current **UCS**. The easiest way to do this is to choose **UCS ENTITY** and pick the entity in question. This will change the current **UCS** to the one that was in effect when the entity was created. When you've finished the command, return to **UCS PREVIOUS**.

TIP 21: BLOCKS IN 3D

Many users need to plot multiple objects, view drawings, etc., on the same sheet, and they've developed systems that do this effectively. These generally involve **BLOCKS** or **WBLOCKS** inserted at different scales or in different positions on the same neutral drawing—generally a new sheet just for this purpose.

When you're working with 3D drawings, it's not that straightforward. If you try to bring in a 3D block, it doesn't necessarily come in the same way it was created. Therefore, to bring in the block as it was created, set the drawing to **UCS VIEW**, and it will come in as the view in which it was created. You can now **SCALE**, **MOVE**, **ROTATE** or otherwise use the block.

TIP 22: FINDING YOUR MACROS

As you develop your macros and customize your menu structure, you'll need to have a directory where the AutoLISP routines reside. The problem with earlier versions is that AutoLISP routines will not path; they're viewed by DOS as files, not programs. So, you need to hard-code their paths into your menu structure.

Although this is still a valid option with Release 10, you now have another choice. Release 10 has an environment variable that lets you set up one directory to hold any file you want to bring up in AutoCAD, regardless of your current directory.

To use this feature, you need to issue a **SET** command. The environment variable is **ACAD**. Therefore, if your AutoLISP directory is called **\LISP**, you'd put this line in your **AUTOEXEC.BAT** file:

```
SET ACAD=\LISP
```

TIP 23: OBJECT SNAP

Changing **UCS** isn't the only way that you can pick points when modeling in 3D. If your **UCS** isn't set properly, and you pick a point at random, it probably won't be on the correct plane, because it has no idea where **Z** is.

A more efficient option is choosing a point using one of the **OBJECT SNAPS** — this will always pick the three coordinates of that point. Therefore, if you can pick the points using some form of **OBJECT SNAP**, do it instead of changing the **UCS**.

TIP 24: REDIRECTING THE KEYBOARD

AutoCAD uses function keys **F6** through **F10** in addition to **F1** if you use the flip screen. That leaves **F2**, **F3**, **F4** and **F5** available as quick macros.

Of course, with a keyboard redirector, you can assign any key on the keyboard to any macro you wish. But keyboard redirectors cost money or memory or both.

DOS provides a "poor man's" keyboard redirector. It's free and takes up virtually no memory. It does require the following statement in a file on your root directory, called **CONFIG.SYS**:

```
DEVICE=ANSI.SYS
```

The **CONFIG.SYS** file is simply the text file described in Chapter One where you put the **FILES** and **BUFFERS** statement. After the above line is added, be sure that the file **ANSI.SYS** is located in the DOS root directory. If it isn't there, it should be on your original DOS floppy disk.

Once you add the line to the **CONFIG.SYS** file, you'll need to reboot the computer to make it active. To redirect the keyboard, you must know the extended codes for the function keys:

Fl	59
F2	60
F3	61
F4	62
F5	63
F6	64
F7	65
F8	66
F9	67
Fl0	68

The following is an example of how **F2** can be redirected to **OBJECT SNAP INTERSECTION** — at the DOS level, not in AutoCAD. You can place this line in the **AUTOEXEC.BAT** file.

```
prompt $e[0;60;"int";13p
```

The code **$e[0** is an ANSI escape sequence that indicates that you want to redirect one of the keys. **60** is the code for the **F2** key. "int" is the string you want to place in the **F2** key. **13** is the code for a **<RETURN>**. The final **p** ends the sequence. So for each function key you want to redirect, change the code number and the string.

Finally, be sure that the last prompt sequence is:

```
prompt $p$g
```

so that you can retrieve your standard prompt. If you forget this last prompt, then you'll be left with no prompt on the screen.

You don't have to accept the predetermined function keys that AutoCAD has set up. If you want to use them for something else, go right ahead. You'll soon find that using function keys for **OBJECT SNAP** is extremely productive, particularly in 3D.

TIP 25: PROTOTYPE DRAWINGS

As you can see, there are now many more variables and procedures to be set up in prototype drawings. If you have to set each of these from scratch, you may never start your drawing!

Remember that there are two ways to set up a prototype drawing. Simply set up a drawing, sometimes called **ACAD.DWG**, with everything pre-set. Then you can name this file in the AutoCAD configuration. But you may need to have more than one prototype drawing. You can start a new drawing using any prototype drawing by giving it the file name **NEWDRAWING=PROTOTYPE**, where **NEWDRAWING** is the name of your new drawing and **PROTOTYPE** is the name of any prototype drawing you want to use.

Here are some of the new items you can include in the prototype drawing:

    Viewport Configurations
    New Dimension Variables
    New Special Areas for TEXT
    Set New System Variables
    DVIEWBLOCK drawing

Of course, you'll set up your normal settings for **SNAP**, **GRID**, etc.

As you can see, you can make Release 10 more productive in many ways; the suggestions presented here are only a sample. As you work, you'll develop your own tips and tricks that work specifically with the way you draw.

Section II

THE
AutoCAD
Productivity
Library

How to Use the Library

The AutoCAD Productivity Library contains 80 carefully selected, time-saving macros and AutoLISP routines. Accompanying commentary provides explanations of each macro and suggested modifications that will further enhance creativity.

We selected macros and AutoLISP routines that illustrate all the features and power of customization. While a macro may not relate to your business, it may illustrate a concept you can apply to your quest for productivity. So you may wish to review each macro after you've selected the ones with immediate benefit. Generally, the routines become more complex toward the end of the library.

The macros are written for AutoCAD Release 9 and 10, and will require some modification to be downward compatible with earlier versions. We want the readers of this book to be the most productive AutoCAD users in the world and that meant sticking to the most productive version of AutoCAD at the time of this edition—Release 10. (The authors and Ventana Press cannot provide support for modifications to macros or for earlier versions of AutoCAD.)

Unless you've purchased *The AutoCAD Productivity Diskette*, you'll need to enter in the macros and AutoLISP routines with a text editor in ASCII format with no printer codes. EDLIN, which comes with the DOS operating system, produces such codes. Some word processors have a no-format, or nondocument format, that produces a pure ASCII file. A discussion of EDLIN is included in Chapters One, Two and Three and Appendix D.

Entering a macro and using it is a simple, straight-forward process. However, ensuring that every space, parenthesis and character is correct can be tedious and time consuming. We have collected all of the menus, macros and routines from both the library and Chapters One through Eleven on a diskette, which can save both time and frustration and increase your productivity. (An order form is available at the end of the book.)

If you're ready to enter the productivity enhancements from this library, we assume you have some basic knowledge of a text editor and the debugging process. Chapters One through Eleven provide step-by-step instruction for those procedures and we give you a mental framework around which you can mold the pieces of customization into a drawing/design *system*.

While *The AutoCAD Productivity Book* is not a LISP programming guide, you can become familiar with AutoLISP through our examples and explanations. Chapter Nine, "Automating Your Drawings," explains one example in detail. Appendix C describes the basic AutoLISP functions. If you want more AutoLISP training, we suggest *AutoLISP in Plain English*, by George O. Head, published by Ventana Press as part of The AutoCAD Reference Library. For more advanced users, Autodesk's *AutoLISP Programmer's Reference* is a handy guide.

Many routines or macros are intended to be placed in a menu. On the diskette, they're noted by their **.MNU** file extension. For example, Macro 2 has the filename **MACRO2.MNU**. To test this macro immediately, you can just use the AutoCAD command **MENU** and respond with the macro name, without the extension. You can even give it a drive letter and path, such as **A:MACRO2** or **C:\ACAD9\MACRO2**. After a macro is working on a stand-alone basis, you can use the "text merge" feature of your word editor to insert it into a larger menu file.

AutoLISP routines (programs) must end with the **.lsp** extension and must be loaded to be used. For example, to load the wall routine, you would type: **(load "macro64")** or **(load "a:macro64")** or **(load "c:/acad9/macro64")**, depending on your system's configuration. Note the intentional use of a forward slash in the path name.

Just as you group macros together in a menu file, you may want to group your LISP files. For example, an architect might place all LISP routines in a text file called **ARCH.LSP**. Then he/she would need to type only **(load "arch")** to have functions like doors, walls and windows at his/her fingertips. Two methods can be used to accomplish this. You can use the text merge feature of your text editor, or the DOS **COPY** command, like this:

```
COPY macro65.lsp + macro64.lsp + macro66.lsp arch.lsp
```

The contents of the **ARCH.LSP** file might look something like this:

```
(defun c:wall ()
etc.
)
(defun c:door ()
etc.
)
(defun c:window ()
etc.
)
```

Once loaded during a drawing, each one of these functions will remain active. If this file were named **ACAD.LSP**, it would load automatically every time you entered the drawing editor.

Note: Avoid loading one large LISP file every time you enter a drawing. (You can use a ^ **C** to halt the loading of **ACAD.LSP**.) See Macro 7, Loading AutoLISP Files, for a better solution.

We hope you'll use our ideas and parts of our code to create your own unique menus, macros and AutoLISP routines for even greater productivity. You'll be able to edit and recombine parts of macros to create new macros. Once you grasp these "cut and paste" techniques, you'll find that creating new macros takes much less time.

Macros and routines generally are presented as follows:

MACRO No.: Number corresponds to macro listed in Table of Contents.

NAME: Name referred to throughout tutorial chapters, indexes and appendices. You may change macro names to suit your needs.

PURPOSE: Describes macro's unique functions and benefits.

TO CREATE: Outlines actual macro to be entered into your computer, line by line.

The name in brackets **[MACRNAME]** will be displayed on the screen menu. Macros used in creating a tablet format are the same as screen macros. You may omit the **[BRACKETED]** name when creating tablet macros.

TO INVOKE: Indicates whether to load LISP file (**.LSP**) or add macro to menu.

LET'S TRY IT: Walks you through sample macro application, using routine just created.

TO REVISE: Identifies and explains changes you can make to further customize program.

TIPS: Gives pointers on further customizing macro. Also highlights peculiarities noted in operation of a particular macro.

MACRO

0

TROUBLESHOOTING

If you have trouble creating, editing or using these macros, please refer to Chapter Four ("Creating and Editing Macros") for assistance. If you want to know more about the operation of EDLIN, refer to Appendix A.

If you don't have a general understanding of DOS, particularly as it relates to AutoCAD and EDLIN, read Chapters One through Three before using The AutoCAD Productivity Library.

Customizing menus and automating drawings are covered in Chapters Four through Eleven.

The most common mistake in AutoLISP programming is a missing parenthesis or quotation mark. Either one will leave this prompt on the screen:

2>

And your computer will seem to be hopelessly locked. The **2** tells you two parentheses or quotes are missing. First, try typing in **))** followed by a (**RETURN**). Then try two quotation marks. Eventually some arbitrary pattern of parentheses or quotes will return control to you.

RULES OF THE ROAD

Before you begin using the macros and routines, review these important guidelines:

Rule 1. If you want to change the name of a macro, the name you assign it cannot exceed eight characters.

Rule 2. The screen menu holds only 20 menu items at one time, including blank spaces.

Rule 3. All symbols and notations must be typed exactly as they appear. Sometimes we include a parenthetical note to further explain the macro. These notes—placed far enough away to distinguish them from the macro—are not to be entered as part of the macro.

Rule 4. Enter <**RETURN**> after typing each line of text, including the last line of the macro.

Rule 5. When instructed to "enter AutoCAD and make a drawing," you may enter just a few lines or circles. You may even want to save a couple of **TEST** drawings—some with lines, some with circles—to test other routines you edit or create.

Rule 6. A ^C^C should prefix most macros to cancel any other macro or command you may be in. For example, if you're in the **LINE** command and want to **FILLET** the corners of a rectangle, you don't have to hit <**RETURN**> to exit **LINE** and enter into the **FILLET**. When you use ^C^C, selecting **FILLET** automatically cancels **LINE**.

The ^C^C feature augments productivity in two ways: 1) you have one less keystroke to enter; and 2) you don't have to remember to hit the final <**RETURN**>, then wonder why the **FILLET** command you just typed gave you an error!

Rule 7. If you're creating a macro to work in conjunction with another macro or to be invisible to the current command (such as **SNAP TOGGLES**), remember not to use ^C^C. It will cancel the current command. This will become obvious as you begin to use The AutoCAD Productivity Library.

Rule 8. If you intend to run AutoLISP routines, before booting AutoCAD (from **C:\ACAD>**),

Type:
```
SET LISPHEAP=30000    (RETURN)
SET LISPSTACK=15000   (RETURN)
SET ACADFREERAM=19    (RETURN)
```

Or add the above lines to your **AUTOEXEC.BAT** files, as described in Chapter Two.

AutoLISP routines have been created with uppercase and lowercase letters. Although initially it's best to enter all routines as shown, you may wish to use all uppercase or all lowercase letters as a matter of personal preference.

To aid beginners, typical AutoLISP indention, called pretty printing, has not been used on the AutoLISP routines. Experienced users may want to indent these routines to show logical sections of the programs. Programs on the optional floppy diskette *are* indented to aid understanding.

LET'S GET STARTED!

Consider the simple macros first, because they can save you a great deal of time and effort quickly—giving you a sense of accomplishment.

As you're looking for that missing parenthesis, quotation mark or space, consider the time you will save in the long run. Also remember that it will get much easier with the next macro you enter and debug.

Your efforts will result in greatly increased productivity.

MACRO 1 Help

PURPOSE: Allows access to AutoCAD's built-in **HELP** functions through a menu.

TO CREATE:

`[GENERAL]^C^CHelp;`

TO INVOKE: Add this macro to a space in your menu file.

LET'S TRY IT: Get into a drawing and select the **HELP** macro. When prompted **Command:**, enter **LINE**. All **HELP** for the **LINE** command is now displayed.

TO REVISE: The above macro will put you into the **HELP** command. After you're in **HELP**, make a choice: do you want a list of all AutoCAD commands or **HELP** for a specific command?

   If you want the list of commands, hit **RETURN**. If you need **HELP** for a specific command, enter that command at the prompt.

   You can make the **GENERAL** macro access the list of commands directly by adding an extra **RETURN**.

Example:

`[GENERAL]^C^CHelp;;`

TIPS: You can also obtain help for the command you are presently using by replacing the double **CONTROL C** (^C^C) with a single quote (').

Example:

`'Help;`

   This will give help for your command and prompt you to press **RETURN** (to continue with your command).

MACRO 2 Simple Entry of a Single Command

MENU

DRAW

PURPOSE: These simple macros cancel your previous command and enter the new command. They're easier and quicker than typing the command, eliminate typing errors and help new users learn by keeping the most frequently used commands visible.

TO CREATE:

```
[  LINE  ]^C^CLine;
```

TO INVOKE: Add this macro to a space in your menu file. Pick this command and it will be entered just as if you'd typed it from the keyboard.

LET'S TRY IT: Get into AutoCAD and start a new drawing. Type the **CIRCLE** command. Now select the **LINE** macro, which should cancel the **CIRCLE** command and prompt you for a point to start your line.

TO REVISE: You can edit this macro to perform many other functions simply by changing the **LINE** command to another command.

Example:

```
[COPY   ]^C^CCopy;
[MOVE   ]^C^CMove;
[ARRAY  ]^C^CArray;
[MIRROR ]^C^CMirror;
[ERASE  ]^C^CErase;
[BREAK  ]^C^CBreak;
[CHANGE ]^C^CChange;
[FILLET ]^C^CFillet;
[CHAMFER]^C^CChamfer;
[TRACE  ]^C^CTrace;
```

TIPS: The **LINE** command, if in a screen menu, should automatically invoke an optional submenu for **OBJECT SNAP**, **ORTHO** and **SNAP** toggles. The following shows how this might be accomplished:

```
[LINE]^C^CLine;$S=SUBMENU
**SUBMENU
[MIDPOINT]Midpoint;
[ENDPOINT]Endpoint;
[INTERSEC]Intersection;
[PERPENDI]Perpendicular;
[CENTER  ]Center;
[QUADRANT]Quadpoint;
[TANGENT ]Tangent;
[NEAR    ]Near;
[NODE    ]Node;
[INSERT  ]Insert;
[TOGGLES ]^Z
[SNAP    ]^B
[ORTHO   ]^O
[COORDS  ]^D
[LASTMENU]$S=
```

The tablet menus also can be used to toggle the screen menus, but you may prefer to have **OSNAP** on your tablet menu.

To make a command repeat (and save a keystroke), add an asterisk in front of the command. You can also use AutoCAD's automated new **WINDOW/CROSSING WINDOW** option. Finally, you can have a command operate on the first object or group of objects found. This is handy in most situations but limits the interactive editing features.

Example:

```
^C^C*Erase;AU;SI;
```

MACRO 3 Circles

PURPOSE: Automates AutoCAD's **CIRCLE** commands.

TO CREATE:

```
[CIR C,R ]^C^CCircle;
```

TO INVOKE: Add this macro to a space in your menu file.

LET'S TRY IT: Get into AutoCAD and begin a drawing. After picking the **CIR C,R** macro, pick a **Center point:** and **Radius:** (or a point representing the radius).

TO REVISE: Change this macro to draw the other four types of circles.

Example:

```
^C^CCircle;\D;
^C^CCircle;2P;
^C^CCircle;3P;
^C^CCircle;TTR;
```

TIPS: To make the command repeat in Release 9, add an asterisk in front of the command.

Example:

```
^C^C*Circle;\D;
```

4 Arcs

PURPOSE: Automates AutoCAD's many **ARC** commands. By making the macro do the keyboard work for you, you'll increase your speed in drawing an arc. The routine helps eliminate typing errors and errors resulting from not knowing available **ARC** choices.

TO CREATE:

```
[  3 Pt. ]^C^CArc;
```

TO INVOKE: Add this macro to a space in your menu file.

LET'S TRY IT: Select the **3 Pt.** macro and pick three points. With one selection, you've drawn a three-point arc.

TO REVISE: By adding the combinations of letters that represent the different options available for the **ARC** command, you can produce many other **ARC** macros.

Example:

`^C^CArc;\C;`	(Start, Center, End)
`^C^CArc;\C;\A;`	(Start, Center, Incl. Angle)
`^C^CArc;\C;\L;`	(Start, Center, Chord Len.)
`^C^CArc;\E;\R;`	(Start, End, Radius)
`^C^CArc;\E;\A;`	(Start, End, Incl. Angle)
`^C^CArc;\E;\D;`	(Start, End, Direction)
`^C^CArc;;`	(Continuation)

MACRO 5 Text Commands

PURPOSE: Automates the selection of different **TEXT** options. You can select desired justification while the macro simultaneously enters the **TEXT** command and the option you chose.

TO CREATE:

```
[TEXT  L ]^C^CText;
```

This is the same as Macro 2 ("Simple Entry of a Single Command") and is the only way to left-justify text.

TO INVOKE: Add this macro to a space in your menu file.

LET'S TRY IT: Get into an AutoCAD drawing and select the **TEXT** macro. At the prompt, **Starting Point:**, pick a point for your text to begin. After you answer the remaining questions, your text will be placed.

TO REVISE: To create macros that give different **TEXT** options, add the desired option to the end of the above macro.

Example:

```
[TEXT  R ]^C^CText;R;
```
(Right Justified)
```
[TEXT  C ]^C^CText;C;
```
(Center Justified)
```
[TEXT  A ]^C^CText;A;
```
(Aligned)
```
[TEXT  F ]^C^CText;F;
```
(Fitted)
```
[TEXT  M ]^C^CText;M;
```
(Middle Justified)

You can also specify the text height directly in the macro. The example below shows left justified, 1/8 high text.

Example:

```
[TEXT.125]^C^CText;\0.125;
```

TIPS: If you would like your text to be multiplied by **DIMSCALE**, add that option to the above macro.

```
[TEXT.125]^C^CText;\(* 0.125 (Getvar "Dimscale"));
```

MACRO 6 Repetitive Commands

PURPOSE: To use certain commands and options repeatedly without having to select more than once.

TO CREATE: Because of the widespread utility of these options, we'll give several examples and explanations. There are two different ways to cause a menu item to repeat. The first is the **MULTIPLE** option, which will cause any command to repeat. This is true of menu items; but also can be typed in at the **Command:** prompt. It will repeat only the actual command. If a menu item has options, only the command will be repeated.

```
[LINE]^C^CMultiple Line;
```

This lets you draw as many lines as you wish. As soon as you hit **RETURN** to end a line, AutoCAD will automatically go into another **LINE** command. This will continue until a **CANCEL** is issued.

```
[CIRCLE]^C^CMultiple Circle;
```

This line lets you draw as many circles as you wish. You don't need to hit **RETURN** to continue drawing, as you do with the **LINE** command. The instant you complete one **CIRCLE**, AutoCAD will automatically start the next one. This will repeat until a **CANCEL** is issued.

The second way to repeat commands is the *****. This option works *only* with menu items and will cause any menu item, regardless of complexity, to repeat. This option repeats both the command and all its specified options.

```
[CIRCLE]*^C^CCircle;\D;
```

This causes the **CIRCLE** command with the **CENTER DIAMETER** option to repeat. If you'd used **MULTIPLE**, the first circle would have been drawn with **CENTER DIAMETER** and the remaining ones as normal circles.

TO INVOKE: Add these options to any menu item. Selected items will repeat until you **CANCEL** them. **CANCEL** can be accomplished with

CONTROL C (^C) or by picking another menu item if that item is preceded with **^C^C**.

LET'S TRY IT: Get into a drawing and pick some of the commands to which you've added these options. You'll see how these simple routines can be some of your biggest time-savers.

TIPS: When using either one of the above options, be cautious. If you add the * to **ERASE LAST**, ***^C^CErase;L;;**, it erases your entire drawing one entity at a time. Don't add a **MULTIPLE** or * to the **SAVE** command. Don't add these options to any of the **UNDO** commands. Added to certain **ZOOM** functions, * or **MULTIPLE** could tie up a considerable amount of time. It's up to you to determine when it's appropriate to use them.

MACRO
7   Loading AutoLISP Files   .LSP

PURPOSE: Loads a file written in AutoLISP by picking the command and entering the filename.

    When loading an AutoLISP file, you usually must type **(LOAD "FILENAME")**, which includes the opening parenthesis, **LOAD**, opening quote, **FILENAME**, closing quote, closing parenthesis and a final **RETURN**. Often users forget at least part of this sequence and must retype it. With this macro, all you enter is the filename.

TO CREATE:

```
[LOADLISP]^C^C(Setq A+
(Getstring "Enter name of LISP file to load... "));\+
(Load A);
```

TO INVOKE: Add this macro to a space in your menu file.

LET'S TRY IT: To use this macro you must have created at least one working AutoLISP file (such as Macro 11). After picking the **LOADLISP** macro, enter your desired **FILENAME** without the **.LSP** extension. When you hit **RETURN**, the system will show the name of the macro on the **Command:** line.

TO REVISE: The following is a general loading routine for AutoLISP files. After each of these files is loaded you must type in the command to activate the routine. If you wish to program a square in your menu file to load *and* activate certain commands, use the following routine in a menu square. It first checks to see if the routine has already been loaded. If not, it loads it. After checking and loading, it will activate the routine if necessary.

This sequence saves a lot of time loading AutoLISP. First, you don't have to put all your AutoLISP commands in the **ACAD.LSP** file that loads automatically every time. Second, you load the individual commands only once and only if needed.

```
^C^C(If (Not C:R) (Load "Macro58"));R;
```

Note that the **C:R** is the actual function name and the **Macro58** is the name of the file containing the function.

MACRO
8 Editing a Single Selection Point

PURPOSE: Quickens the selection process when you're editing a specific selection set of entities in the drawing.

This macro is another step up the ladder in macro development. Some menus have you select a command, but you still must select the appropriate option (such as **L** for **LAST** or **W** for **WINDOW**). This macro automatically selects whichever option you've set. By using the **L** option, you can edit the **LAST** entity. The **W** option allows you to select a **WINDOW** full of entities for editing. And the **C** option allows a **CROSSING WINDOW**.

Release 9 offers new options. **BOX** lets you select one corner of a box, then ask for the second. If you move to the **LEFT**, the box will be a **CROSSING WINDOW**. If you move to the **RIGHT**, it will be a **WINDOW**.

Unlike most of the other options, **BOX** must be spelled out completely. **AU** stands for **AU**tomatic. This option allows you to pick a point. If there is an entity at that point, AutoCAD will select that entity. If there is no entity, it will go into the **BOX** option **AU**tomatically.

TO CREATE:

```
[ERASE L ]^C^CErase;L;;
[ERASE W ]^C^CErase;W;\\;
[ERASE C ]^C^CErase;C;\\;
[ERASE B ]^C^CErase;BOX;\\;
[ERASE AUTO]^C^CErase; AU;
```

TO INVOKE: Add this macro to a space in your menu file. By touching **ERASE L**, you erase the last object added to the drawing. **ERASE W, ERASE C** and **ERASE BOX** each allow you to select two points (\\) that describe the corners of the area, then erase according to the option selected.

These simple macros combine three actions into one: 1) type and enter the **ERASE** command; 2) type and enter the **DESIGNATED** option; and 3) enter a final **RETURN**, which erases the object(s) and returns you to the **Command:** prompt (that's why two semicolons are placed at the end of the line).

LET'S TRY IT: Boot up AutoCAD, start a new drawing and add a few random lines. Pick the **ERASE L** macro, either from the screen or tablet, and see what happens. The last object you drew should have been erased. Try it again. You'll step backward through the lines you drew, erasing them as you go. Pick the **ERASE W** macro. You'll be prompted for the points that describe the **WINDOW**. After selecting the points, AutoCAD will erase all entities that were entirely in the window. Try the other options. Isn't this easier than typing in **ERASE**, then the option?

TO REVISE: If you change **ERASE** to another command, this macro can perform many other editing functions.

Example:
```
[COPY  L  ]^C^CCopy;L;;
[MOVE  W  ]^C^CMove;W;\\;
[MOVE  AU ]*^C^CMove;AU;SI;
[ARRAY C  ]^C^CArray;C;\\;
[MIRROR B]^C^CMirror;BOX;\\;
```

TIPS: This macro works on specified entities only, and doesn't allow you to use AutoCAD's interactive selection process. If you wish to allow interactive selection after the option has been chosen, remove the last semicolon. If you remove the semicolon, it will leave two \\. Note that any time you have a line that ends with a backslash, you can get rid of it. In this case, you can remove both backslashes with the semicolon. You must then hit **RETURN** to indicate you've completed the selection process.

Example:
```
[COPY  L  ]^C^CCopy;L;
[MOVE  W  ]^C^CMove;W;
[ARRAY C  ]^C^CArray;C;
[MIRROR B]^C^CMirror;BOX;
```

MACRO 9 Break, 1 Point

PURPOSE: Lets you specify a single point to break an entity. This is often needed to break an object at only one point, such as when you're breaking lines in half.

TO CREATE:

[BREAK 1]^C^CBreak;\F;\@;

TO INVOKE: Add this macro to a space in your menu file.

LET'S TRY IT: Draw a line across your screen. Now you'll break this line into two pieces at its midpoint, leaving two lines of equal length sharing a common endpoint. Pick the macro, which prompts **Select object:**. Pick the line you just drew. It now prompts **Select first point to break:**. Using **OBJECT SNAP**, specify **MIDPOINT** and touch the line at any point. The line is broken in half. To make sure, erase half the line.

TIPS: In a screen menu, this command should invoke the same optional submenu for **OBJECT SNAP**, **ORTHO** and **SNAP** toggles as the **LINE** command in Macro 2.

MACRO 10 Break, 3 Points

PURPOSE: Allows you to break an entity by specifying two break points after the object has been selected.

TO CREATE:

[BREAK 3]^C^CBreak;\F;

TO INVOKE: Add this macro to a space in your menu file.

LET'S TRY IT: Draw a circle on the screen with a line running through it. Pick the macro. You are prompted **Select object:**. Pick the line by touching it anywhere. (It's safest to pick the line outside of the circle so you don't accidentally break the circle.)

   After picking the line, you're prompted **Enter first point:**. Using **OBJECT SNAP, intersection**, pick one of the intersections of the line and circle. You're now prompted **Enter second point:**. Pick the other intersection of the line and circle. Now you've removed the section of the line inside the circle.

Although this macro does the job just fine, there's an easier way. The **TRIM** command will usually break your lines more quickly and efficiently then the **BREAK** command. However, the **BREAK** macro will come in handy in a number of situations.

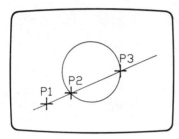 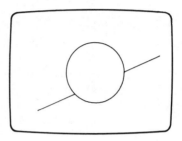

_{MACRO}
11 Erase All

ALL

PURPOSE: Erases the entire drawing without setting new criteria.

Sometimes you set up all your layers, linetypes, text styles, etc., in a new drawing, begin drawing, then decide you don't want the drawing but want to keep the criteria. This macro allows you to **ERASE ALL** and start over in the same drawing file.

TO CREATE:

```
(Defun C:Da () (Command "Erase" (Ssget "X") ""))
```

TO INVOKE: Create this macro as an AutoLISP file (**.lsp**).

LET'S TRY IT: Boot up AutoCAD, open a new drawing file and draw 20 to 30 random objects. Load **MACRO11 (Load "Macro11")**. Type **DA**. It will quickly erase everything you've drawn. If you change your mind, use the **OOPS** command to retrieve the drawing.

TO REVISE: By adding a question and an **if** statement to the beginning of the macro, you can change it to prompt whether you really want to **ERASE ALL**.

Example:

```
(Defun C:Da () (Initget 1 "Y N")
(Setq A (Getkword "Really want to delete all: "))
(If (= A "Y") (Command "Erase" (Ssget "X") "")))
```

TIPS: If you want to rename your new drawing, wait until you're finished and, using **File Utilities**, assign the new name. Or **SAVE** the drawing under a new name, then **Quit** to exit the drawing editor.

MACRO
12 Limits

PURPOSE: Allows you to set your **LIMITS** to either a specified preset size by making a single selection.

TO CREATE:

```
[36 X 24]^C^CLimits;0,0;36,24;
```

TO INVOKE: Add this macro to a space in your menu file.

LETS TRY IT: Get into a drawing and pick the **36 x 24** macro. Type **STATUS**, and you'll be switched to the **text** screen. A statement will read **Limits are: 0,0 36,24**.

TO REVISE: You can change this macro to include your most frequently used **LIMITS**.

Example:

```
^C^CLimits;0,0;1080,720;       (90' X 60')
```

Another helpful revision is to set the limits to a specified size according to the DIMSCALE.

If a drawing is to be plotted at a scale of 1/4" = 1'-0," then you normally would set your **DIMSCALE** to **48**. However, **LIMITS** of 36 x 24 would be too small. But you could set them at 36 x 24 x **DIMSCALE**. This would actually make the **LIMITS** 1728 x 1152. It would appear to be a 36" x 24" piece of paper at a scale of 1/4" = 1'-0".

Example:

```
^C^CLimits;0,0;+

(List (* 36 (Getvar "Dimscale")) (* 24 (Getvar "Dimscale")));
```

TIPS: Always give the coordinates of your **LIMITS** in the simplest form (such as inches), so they'll work regardless of the **UNITS** you're presently using.

MACRO 13 Snap and Grid

PURPOSE: Sets a desired **SNAP** or **GRID** value with a single pick.

Note: In the following examples, replace **SNAP** with **GRID** for changing the **GRID**.

TO CREATE:

```
[SNP .25]^C^CSnap;.25;
```

TO INVOKE: Add this macro to a space in your menu file.

LETS TRY IT: Get into a drawing and pick the **SNP .25** macro. Type **STATUS**, and you'll be switched to the **text** screen. A statement will read **Snap resolution: 0.25**.

TO REVISE: To allow this macro to set different values, choose a new number at the end of the macro.

Example:

```
^C^CSnap;.125;
```

```
^C^CSnap;.5;
```

```
^C^CSnap;12;
```

```
^C^CSnap;      (Allows you to specify the value.)
```

You can also revise this macro to make it transparent to the current command, which allows you to change **SNAP** value while in another command.

Example:

```
'Setvar;Snapunit;.25,.25;'Setvar;Snapmode;1;
```

```
'Setvar;Snapunit;.125,.125;'Setvar;Snapmode;1;
```

TIPS: You can switch parameters more quickly if you place at least five of your most commonly used **SNAP** values in your menu. Also, make sure all the values you specify are in simple **UNITS** (such as inches) so they can be used regardless of the type of **UNITS** you're using.

MACRO
14 Rotate Crosshairs

PURPOSE: Sets the **GRID** and **crosshair** rotation to a given angle.

This is useful when working with an extension a certain number of degrees from the main part. You can rotate the **GRID** and **crosshairs** the same angle as the extension.

When using this macro, please note that the point from which your **SNAP** and **GRID** is based is also the point from which your crosshatching begins. Normally your hatching is based through **0,0**. This will allow you to base crosshatching through any desired point.

The angle of your **crosshairs** and **GRID** is also the angle that your objects will copy when using **ARRAY**.

TO CREATE:

[XHR ROT]^C^CSnap;R;

TO INVOKE: Add this macro to a space in your menu file.

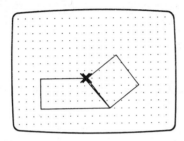 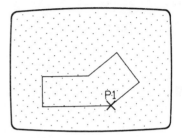

LET'S TRY IT: Get into AutoCAD, begin a new drawing and draw a series of lines. You'll draw a plate with a portion of that plate at an angle.

Type the following responses:

```
Command: Line
From point: 0,0
To point: 9.375,0
To point: @5<37.5
To point: @5<127.5
To point: @5<217.5
To point: 0,3.9667
To point: C
Command: Grid
Grid spacing (X) or ON/OFF/Snap/Aspect <.000>: 1
Command: Snap
Snap spacing or ON/OFF/Value/Aspect/Rotate/Style: .5
```

At this point, if you tried to draw a line with your cursor from the intersection at the bottom of the angle plate (where it breaks upward to its matching point on the top), you would have to turn **SNAP OFF**.

Now, you'll rotate your cursor so the **GRID BASE POINT** is at the lower intersection of the plate and the angle will match the angle of the plate.

Pick the **XHR ROT** macro. Type the following responses:

```
Command: SNAP
Snap spacing or ON/OFF/Value/Aspect/Rotate/Style<0.50>: R
Base point <0.0000,0.0000>: Intersection of 9.375,0
Rotation angle : 37.5
```

Your cursor is rotated and the **GRID** base has been moved from **0,0** to the intersection you chose. Now you can work on the angled part more easily.

TO REVISE: The above macro lets you pick the point to rotate the crosshair about, then specify the rotation angle either with keyboard input or using the crosshairs. However, you may want to specify several of the most commonly used angles so they can be accessed and set with a single pick. Several combinations exist; you decide which works best for you.

Example:

```
^C^CSnap;R;\0;
```

This allows you to pick the point to rotate about, then sets the rotation angle at zero.

Example:

```
^C^CSnap;R;\30;
```

Does the same as the previous macro, except it sets the rotation angle at 30 degrees.

Another revision would be to make this macro work transparently. First, set the desired base point (**Snapbase**). Next, set the angle by selecting a point (**Snapang**). The next line forces the **SNAP ON** (**Snapmode**). Finally, issue a **Redraw** (if the **REDRAW** isn't executed, the **SNAP** will be rotated but the **GRID** may not.)

Example:

```
'Setvar;Snapbase;\+
'Setvar;Snapang;(Getvar "Snapbase");\+
'Setvar;Snapmode;1;'Redraw
```

TIPS: If your current **SNAP** style is set to **ISOMETRIC**, change it back to standard before setting the **GRID BASE POINT** and **ROTATION**. This prevents an unexpected operation.

Example:

```
^C^CSnap;S;S;;;R;
```

This macro first enters the **SNAP** command, then chooses the **STYLE** option, changes the style to **standard**, reenters the **SNAP** command and finally enters the **ROTATION** option.

Here's a little known fact: setting the **GRID BASE POINT** to a point other than **0,0** will cause crosshatching to originate from another point. Great for staggering hatch patterns or making bricks line up!

MACRO
15 Osnap, Single Use

PURPOSE: Sets the **OBJECT SNAP** mode for picking one point.

You can use this on the screen menu we mention in Macro 2 ("Simple Entry of a Single Command").

TO CREATE:

```
[ENDPOINT]Endpoint;
```

TO INVOKE: Add this macro to a space in your menu file.

LET'S TRY IT: Draw a few random lines. While you're in the **LINE** command, pick the **ENDPOINT** macro and touch one of the lines. The last line you drew **SNAP**ped to the end of the line you touched.

TO REVISE: To use other types of **OSNAP**, simply place them in similar situations.

Example:

[MIDPOINT]Midpoint;

[INTERSEC]Intersection;

[QUAD]Quadrant;

[CENTER]Center;

Note: No ^C^C has been placed at the beginning of these macros, because it would cancel your current command. For example, if you drew a line, picked a starting point and wanted to go to the **ENDPOINT** of another line, it would cancel the **LINE** command and report the **ENDPOINT** as **invalid**.

TIPS: If you use a tablet menu and don't mind using a screen menu simultaneously, you can have the screen menu contain different **OBJECT SNAP** modes for easy access. But you can still place the **OBJECT SNAP** modes on a tablet (one of the more important tablet functions).

MACRO
16 Osnap, Multiple Use

PURPOSE: Sets the **OSNAP** to a desired option and allows you to activate one, or a combination of, **OSNAP** modes for use before entering a command. Picking **OSNAP** this way activates **OSNAP** each time AutoCAD requires a point as input. It remains activated until you turn it **OFF**.

TO CREATE:

[OSNAP]^C^COsnap;

TO INVOKE: Add this macro to a space in your menu file.

LET'S TRY IT: Get into a drawing, create a few random lines and pick the **OSNAP** macro. At the prompt, **Object Snap Modes:**, enter **endpoint**. When you return to your **LINE** command, each point picked will search for an **endpoint** to **SNAP**.

TO REVISE: If you're using a tablet menu, select this macro, then pick one of the macros created in Macro No. 15 ("Osnap, Single Use") to set your desired **SNAP**.

Note: The **RETURN** on the end of Macro 15 allows you to set only one type of **OSNAP**. If you want to select more than one **OSNAP** mode at a time, use a comma instead of a semicolon.

Example:
```
[MIDPOINT]Midpoint,\
[INTERSEC]Intersection,\
[  QUAD  ]Quadrant,\
[ CENTER ]Center,\
```

The comma allows you to string more than one mode together before the final **RETURN**. The **backslash** tells the computer to wait for your input.

TIPS: If you use some **OSNAP** modes more than others, you'll want to create macros that set **OSNAP** to those modes with a single pick.

Example:
```
^C^COsnap;Endpoint;          (OSNAP to Endpoints)
^C^COsnap;Midpoint;          (OSNAP to Midpoints)
^C^COsnap;Intersection;      (OSNAP to Intersections)
^C^COsnap;Off;               (OSNAP OFF)
```

When you use the multiple option **SNAP**s, remember the **none** option will turn it **OFF** for one freehand point.

The following example allows you to use **OBJECT SNAP** transparently.

Example:

```
'Setvar;Osmode;(insert sum of the following);
Object snap modes bit-code:
1=Endpoint      32=Intersection
2=Midpoint      64=Insert
4=Center        128=Perpendicular
8=Node          256=Nearest
16=Quadrant     512=Quick
```

If you want OSNAP set to **Endpoint** and **Midpoint**, enter the value **3**. If you want **Intersection** and **Quadrant,** enter the value **48**.

TIPS: If you set your mode while the system is waiting for point entry, the modes you choose won't be activated until you pick the point.

MACRO 17 Setting Relative Coordinate to a Specified Point

PURPOSE: Sets a reference point for use with relative and polar coordinates.

When a reference point is needed, many users draw a line or circle at that point, then erase it after establishing a new relative point. That will work but requires the user to erase a line.

This macro simply uses the **setvar** function to set the system variable **lastpoint** to a newly specified point.

TO CREATE:

```
(Defun C:Rel ()
```

```
(Setvar "Lastpoint" (Getpoint "\nNew relative point: "))
(Princ))
```

TO INVOKE: Create this macro as an AutoLISP file (.**lsp**).

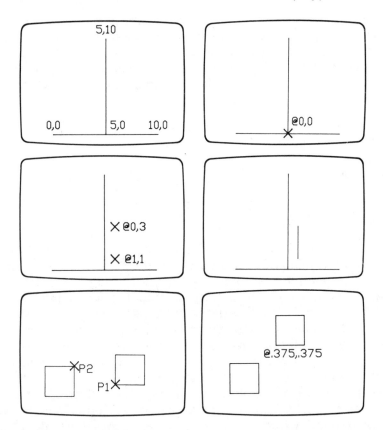

LET'S TRY IT: Enter AutoCAD and draw a line **From point: 0,0 To point: 10,0**. Then draw another line **From point: 5,0 To point: 0,10**. Now **ZOOM EXTENTS** so your drawing fills the screen.

Let's say you need a vertical line three units long, which starts one unit up and to the right of the intersection of your two lines.

Load **MACRO17 (Load "Macro17")**. Type **REL**. It will prompt **New relative point:**, at which time you enter the intersection of the two existing lines, using **OBJECT SNAP** to properly locate it. Enter the **LINE** command and you'll be prompted **From point**. Enter **@1,1**.

This tells the system you want to start your line one unit up and over from the last referenced point, which in this case is the intersection you set by using the macro. At **To point:** enter **@0,3** to move the line up the three required units.

TO REVISE: This macro is useful for setting the relative coordinate before entering a command you'd like to reference to a known point in your drawing. If you want to use it to reference a different point once you've entered into the command (or reference a point other than the current point), the macro must be created as an AutoLISP function instead of a command.

Example:

```
(Defun Rel ()
(Setq P1 (Getpoint "\nRelative from: "))
(Setq P2 (Getpoint P1 "\nTo point: "))
(Command P2) (Princ))
```

Once you load this function, you can use it anytime AutoCAD asks for a point by typing **REL**. This suspends the command while you pick a reference point. For example, get into a drawing and create two 1" squares. Now move one square so that the lower left corner is **.375,.375** above and to the right of the upper right corner of the other square. To do this you normally must know where the points are located. However, the above macro makes it easy. Type **MOVE** and select the objects you wish to move. When prompted **Base point:**, select the lower left corner of the square with **INTERSECTION**. When it prompts for **Second point:**, type (REL). Instead of specifying the point, reference the upper right corner of the other square. When prompted **Relative from:**, pick the upper right corner with **INTERSECTION**. It will now prompt **To point:**. Enter **@.375,.375**, which will move the first square to a point **.375,.375**. This will move the first square to a point **.375,.375** away from the second.

MACRO
18 Setting Relative Coordinate to a Midpoint

PURPOSE: Sets a reference point for use with relative and polar coordinates.

Like Macro 17, this macro allows you to set a relative, or "working," point between two specified points. Traditionally, such points have been determined by drawing a line from one point to another and using the midpoint. This macro lets you pick the two points, then sets the **Lastpoint** variable exactly in the middle of the two points you picked.

TO CREATE:

```
(Defun C:AH ()
(Setq P1 (Getpoint "Enter first point: "))
(Setq P2 (Getpoint P1 "Enter second point: "))
(Setvar "Lastpoint"
   (Polar P1 (Angle P1 P2) (/ (Distance P1 P2) 2)))
(Command "Line" (Getvar "Lastpoint") "") (Princ))
```

Note: The line command at the end of the macro forces the system to place a tick mark, or **BLIP** at the new point.

TO INVOKE: Create this macro as an AutoLISP file (**.lsp**).

LET'S TRY IT: Enter AutoCAD and create a 1" x 6" rectangle. Load **MACRO18 (Load "Macro18")**. Type **AH**. It will prompt "**Enter first point:** " at which time you select the lower left corner of the rectangle. Next, it will prompt "**Enter second point:** ". Select the upper right corner. A **blip** will appear in the middle of the rectangle. This point is now the point from which AutoCAD will base its next relative (or polar) coordinate if you don't change it.

Now that you've set the point, use **TEXT** with the **M** option (to middle justify). When asked for the middle point, type **@**. This tells the system to reference the **Lastpoint** variable which you just set. Finish the **TEXT** command in the normal fashion.

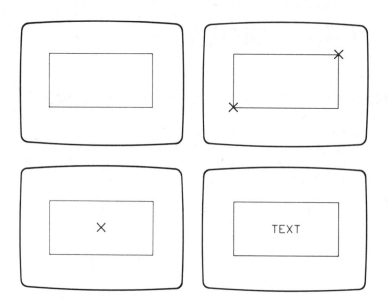

TO REVISE: Like Macro 17, this is useful for setting the relative coordinate before entering a command. If you want to use it to find a midpoint once you've entered into a command, you must create an AutoLISP function instead of a command.

```
(Defun AH ()
 (Setvar "Cmdecho" 0)
 (Setq P1 (Getpoint "\nEnter first point: "))
 (Setq P2 (Getpoint "\nEnter second point: "))
 (Setq P3 (Polar P1 (Angle P1 P2) (/ (Distance P1 P2) 2)))
 (Command P3) (Princ))
```

Once you load this function, you can use it anytime AutoCAD asks for a point by typing **(AH)**. This suspends the command while you pick the two points, then AutoLISP figures the midpoint. For example, get into a drawing and create a 1" x 6" rectangle. Place a string of text in the center of the box. To do this you normally would have to draw a line from one corner of the rectangle to the next, or use the above macro *before* entering the **TEXT** command. Type **TEXT**, then **M** (for middle justified). When asked for insertion point, type (AH). When prompted **Enter first point:**, touch the corner of the rectangle. At the **Enter second point:** prompt, touch the opposite corner of the rectangle. This will pick a point midway between the points selected for text placement.

MACRO
19 Units

PURPOSE: Saves you keystrokes by entering the **UNITS** command and setting the units to a commonly used type with a single menu pick.

TO CREATE: For the purpose of this macro, suppose you want to use architectural units (to the nearest 1/16th inch), angles measured as degrees, minutes and seconds to the nearest second, angles based from 0 degrees, and rotated counterclockwise.

```
[ARCHUNIT]^C^CUnits;4;16;2;4;0;N;Graphscr;
```

Each time you select the square for this macro it will set units exactly as you need them.

TO INVOKE: Add this macro to a space in your menu file.

LET'S TRY IT: Get into a new AutoCAD drawing, type **UNITS 2 4 1 2 0 N** then return to your drawing screen. Your coordinates dial will read in decimals. Pick the **ARCHUNIT** macro. Your coordinate dial now will read in feet and inches.

TO REVISE: This macro can set your **UNITS** to any type you use. Two types—architectural and decimal—are often used several times a day (and sometimes several times during one drawing).

We've made one for architectural; now let's make one for decimal. Set the decimal to the nearest 10,000th inch with angles measured in decimal to two decimal places.

Example:

```
^C^CUnits;2;4;1;2;0;N;Graphscr;
```

Using these two macros, you now can switch easily from one type of unit to another.

You may want to make this macro transparent to the current command.

```
'Setvar;Lunits;4;'Setvar;Luprec;4;+
'Setvar;Aunits;2;'Setvar;Aprec;4;+
'Setvar;Angbase;0;'Setvar;Angdir;0;+
'Graphscr;
```

MACRO 20 Blipmode

PURPOSE: With a single pick, you can quickly activate and deactivate the **BLIP** created at each point you pick with your cursor.

It doesn't affect any **BLIP** mark already on the drawing; only each point you pick after you've set the **BLIPMODE**. Some users don't like **BLIP**s because they make the drawing look cluttered and force them to **REDRAW** more often than necessary. However, **BLIP**s are often useful in allowing you to see where your **LAST** and **PREVIOUS** picks have been. This macro lets you turn the **BLIP ON** when you need it and **OFF** when you don't.

TO CREATE:

```
[BLIPMODE]^C^CSetvar;Blipmode;(Abs (- (Getvar "Blipmode") 1));
```

TO INVOKE: Add this macro to a space in your menu file.

LET'S TRY IT: Get into an AutoCAD drawing and draw a few lines. This will create the familiar blip marks at each point picked. Pick the **BLIP-MODE** macro and draw a few more lines. You'll notice the blips no longer appear. To continue "blipping," pick the **BLIPMODE** macro again.

TO REVISE: You can make this macro transparent to the current command by changing the ^C^C to '.

Example:

```
'Setvar;Blipmode;(Abs (- (Getvar "Blipmode") 1))
```

TIPS: Try this using **MIRROR**ed text, and you can see the text flip-flop between right-reading and mirrored.

Example:

```
'Setvar;Mirrtext;(Abs (- (Getvar "Mirrtext") 1))
```

MACRO
21 Toggles

PURPOSE: Enters most AutoCAD keyboard toggles as special characters, function keys and control characters from a menu.

TO CREATE:

[COORDS]^D	(Toggles the coordinate readout)
[GRID]^G	(Toggles the **GRID**)
[ORTHO]^O	(Toggles the **ORTHO** mode)
[SNAP]^B	(Toggles the **SNAP**)
[TABLET]^T	(Toggles the **TABLET** mode)
[ISOPLANE]^E	(Toggles **ISOPLANE**)

TO INVOKE: Add these macros to spaces in your menu file.

LET'S TRY IT: From a drawing, select any of these macros, and you'll see the appropriate response on your **Command:** line.

MACRO
22 Zoom Commands

PURPOSE: Performs specific zooms.

Some of AutoCAD's most often-used commands are the **ZOOM** functions. If you create them in a menu as macros, you can simply select the desired **ZOOM** (such as **ZOOM WINDOW, ZOOM PREVIOUS**), saving you steps and mental fatigue.

TO CREATE:

```
[Zoom W]'Zoom;W;
```

TO INVOKE: Add this macro to a space in your menu file. Pick this command; it will simultaneously enter the **ZOOM** and the **WINDOW W** option. This function is transparent to the currently active command.

LET'S TRY IT: After entering AutoCAD, add some lines and, before leaving the **LINE** command, pick the macro. You are prompted **First point:** then **Second point:**. Pick the two corners that describe the area you wish to **ZOOM.** Because the macro is transparent to the current command you can continue in the same **LINE** command without having to **exit, ZOOM** and reenter the command.

TO REVISE: You can change this macro to accomplish any other AutoCAD **ZOOM** function.

Example:

`'Zoom;`	(Allows you to specify **ZOOM** Factor)
`'Zoom;P;`	**(ZOOM PREVIOUS)**
`'Zoom;D;`	**(ZOOM DYNAMIC)**

```
'Zoom;E;
```
(ZOOM DRAWING EXTENTS)

```
'Zoom;A;
```
(ZOOM ALL)

TIPS: You may enter these commands from inside another command or at the **Command:** prompt. If you're in another command and select one of these, AutoCAD sometimes responds **** Requires a regen, cannot be transparent**. This means **ZOOM E** and **ZOOM A** won't work transparently (because they always cause a **REGEN**). Using them as if they're transparent will keep you from regenerating your drawing so often. Remember, the commands will work at the **Command:** prompt. If you're sure of yourself, you may want to put the ^C^C in front of **ZOOM ALL** and **ZOOM EXTENTS**.

Another tip is to add a space in your menu file to **ZOOM** the current view to **.75**, as shown below. This leaves extra working room around the edges of your drawing after selecting **ZOOM E** or **ZOOM A**.

Example:

```
Zoom;.75X;
```

Note: AutoCAD's **ZOOM EXTENTS** command sometimes prints the message: ****Second regeneration required by change in drawing extents.**

On a large drawing, your **ZOOM EXTENTS** regeneration could take an annoyingly long time. The following macro will **ZOOM** your drawing to its extents, eliminating this problem most of the time. It will also work transparently, allowing you to **ZOOM EXTENTS** while in another command. You'll save some time.

Example:

```
'Zoom;W;(Getvar "Extmin");(Getvar "Extmax");
```

MACRO
23 View

PURPOSE: Automates options of the **VIEW** command.

TO CREATE:

`[VIEW  R ]^C^CView;R;`

TO INVOKE: Add this macro to a space in your menu file. When you select this command, enter a **VIEW** name to be restored.

LET'S TRY IT: Get into an existing AutoCAD drawing, **ZOOM** in on an area of interest. Type **View S 1**. Now **ZOOM PREVIOUS**, to return to where you were and **ZOOM WINDOW** on another area of interest. Pick the **VIEW** macro and type **1**, which will return you to your first viewing area.

TO REVISE: The **VIEW** command has five options. **RESTORE** is used in the above macro. You can modify the macro to incorporate the other four options.

Example:

`^C^CView;S;`	(Stores **VIEWS**)
`^C^CView;D;`	(Deletes **VIEWS**)
`^C^CView;W;`	(Stores **VIEWS** by defined **WINDOW**s)
`^C^CView;?;`	(Lists all saved **VIEWS**)

You can also make these functions transparent to the current command. These transparent commands will work as long as AutoCAD doesn't need to regenerate the drawing in order to display the specified **VIEW**.

Example:

`'View;R;1;`

`'View;S;1;`

`'View;W;1;`

TIPS: If you want to save standard **VIEW**s with your drawing, you may want to include examples such as these in your prototype drawings:

```
^C^CView;R;Full
^C^CView;R;Kitchen
^C^CView;R;Riteside
```

MACRO
24 Slide

PURPOSE: Enters the two **SLIDE** commands from a menu.

TO CREATE:
```
[ VSLIDE ]^C^CVslide;    (View SLIDE)
[ MSLIDE ]^C^CMslide;    (Make SLIDE)
```

TO INVOKE: Add these macros to a space in your menu file. When you select either macro, be sure to supply the name of a **SLIDE**.

LET'S TRY IT: Get into a drawing and pick the **MSLIDE** macro. Enter 1 (for the name) and **ZOOM** in on an area of interest. Pick the **MSLIDE** macro again. Enter 2 (for the name). Now, pick the **VSLIDE** macro and enter 1. Pick it again and enter 2.

TO REVISE: No changes really benefit these macros.

TIPS: Assign your **SLIDES** numbers instead of full-length names— they're easier to type. While you work on one drawing, you can use a **SLIDE** to view another.

MACRO
25 Hatching

PURPOSE: Immediately accesses and implements the most commonly used crosshatching patterns.

TO CREATE:

```
[ BRICK  ]^C^CHatch;Brick;
```

TO INVOKE: Add this macro to a space in your menu file.

LET'S TRY IT: Get into AutoCAD and draw a square. Now pick your **BRICK** macro.

TO REVISE: Replace the **BRICK** pattern with any changes to any other **HATCH** pattern.

Example:

```
^C^CHatch;Escher;
```

The **HATCH** command has many options you may want to implement as macros. The following examples are macros you can customize in whole or in part.

Example:

```
^C^CHatch;Net,O;
```

Enters the HATCH pattern as **NET** and sets it to **HATCH** your outermost area.

Example:

```
^C^CHatch;Steel,I;
```

Enters the HATCH pattern as **STEEL** and sets it to ignore any internal structures in the area you define.

Example:

```
^C^CHatch;Mud;1;0;
```

Enters the HATCH pattern as **MUD**, sets the pattern scale at **1** and the pattern angle at **0**.

Example:

```
^C^CHatch;\1;0;
```

Allows you to specify the pattern name, then sets the pattern scale at 1 and the pattern angle at **0**.

The next example uses one macro to set an overall **SCALE** factor to be used for all other hatching.

Example:

```
^C^C(Setq HS+
(Getreal "Enter the scale for your Crosshatching patterns: "));
```

Pick this macro and set a SCALE to be used when hatching.

Example:

```
^C^CHatch;Grass;!HS;
```

This enters GRASS as the pattern and sets the scale as specified in the macro. It still allows you to input the hatching angle. You may want to create a macro that sets the overall hatching angle.

Note: If you don't set the scale factor at least once during each edit session, any macro containing that variable will dump and report an error.

TIPS: If you constantly use different **HATCH** patterns, you might want to invoke an **ICON** menu that contains several desired patterns. (With higher-resolution monitors you can put up to 16 patterns in the **ICON**.) This method is discussed in detail in Chapter 7.

Example:

```
[SHOW PAT]^C^C$i=HATCH $i=*
```

MACRO 26 Inserting Symbols

PURPOSE: Automates insertion of commonly used symbols.

There are three types of symbols: 1) annotative, 2) those that are always used at full scale, and 3) those scaled to a specified size.

Symbols are annotative when they're inserted at a scale determined by the final plotting scale (much like dimensions). Annotative symbols can be bubble callouts, title blocks, borders or electrical symbols on architectural drawings. These symbols are created at the scale you'd normally use and inserted at a scale equal to the **DIMSCALE**.

Symbols always at full scale may consist of furniture, pipe fittings, plumbing fixtures and cars. These are created at full scale and inserted at a scale of 1.

A few symbols scaled to a specific size are bolt heads, shrubs and plants, and ceiling fans. You should create this type of symbol so that it measures 1". This lets you easily adapt it to any drawing. Say you create a fan symbol 1" in diameter. Then, when you need a fan 52 inches in diameter, you simply insert it with of scale of 52.

TO CREATE:

```
[SYMBOL  ]^C^CInsert;Symbol;
```

TO INVOKE: Add this macro to a space in your menu file.

LET'S TRY IT: First, create a symbol and call it **SYMBOL**. (You can substitute **SYMBOL** with any name you like, but it must match the name you put into the macro.) Now pick the macro and insert the symbol as you normally would.

TO REVISE: This macro is versatile—you can make it automatically enter the **NAME, SCALE ROTATION** or any combination of these.

Example:

```
^C^CInsert;Symbol;Scale;(Getvar "Dimscale");
```

This scales the symbol according to the current DIMSCALE. Then, you can place and rotate it. This is used on annotative symbols.

Example:

`^C^CInsert;Symbol;\(Getvar "Dimscale");;`

This example scales the symbol after you've placed it, then lets you enter the rotation.

Example:

`^C^CInsert;\Scale;\0;`

This example lets you specify the name and scale the symbol before inserting it. Then it sets the rotation at 0.

TIPS: When you want the object you created to be inserted at full scale and **0** rotation every time, you can have the macro enter the (**RETURN**)s needed in the **INERT** command.

Example:

`^C^CInsert;Symbol;\;;;`

Or, if you wish it to insert any symbol, you can input the name and let the macro enter the rest of the (**RETURN**)s for you.

Example:

`^C^CInsert;\\;;;`

MACRO 27 Inserting With Breakout

PURPOSE: Lets you insert certain symbols into a **LINE** or **POLYLINE**. This macro will insert the symbol and break out a section of **LINE** in which to place it. Because there is no way to know what size the symbol is, it only works for the symbol specified in the macro.

TO CREATE:

```
(Defun C:IWB () (Setvar "Cmdecho" 0)
(Setq D (Getvar "Blipmode")) (Setq E (Getvar "Osmode"))
(Setvar "Blipmode" 0) (Setvar "Osmode" 512)
(Princ "\nPick insertion point and angle: ")
(Command "Insert" "Break" Pause "1" "1" Pause)
(Setq Pl (Getvar "lastpoint"))
(Setq A (Cdr (Assoc 50 (Entget (Entlast)))))
(Entdel (Setq B (Entlast))) (Setq F (SSget Pl))
(If (Boundp 'F) (Progn
(Setq C (Cdr (Assoc 0 (Entget (Ssname (Ssget Pl) 0)))))
(If (Or (= C "LINE") (= C "POLYLINE"))
(Command "Break" (Polar Pl (+ A Pi) 0.25)
(Polar Pl A 0.25))))) (Entdel B)
(Setvar "Osmode" E) (Setvar "Blipmode" D) (Princ))
```

TO INVOKE: Create this macro as an AutoLISP file (**.lsp**).

LET'S TRY IT: The above macro is written to insert a symbol named **BREAK** into a line. Start a new drawing called **BREAK**. Use the following command sequence:

```
Command:        Line
From point:     -.25,0
To point:       -.125,.25
To point:       .125,-.25
To point:       .25,0
```

```
To point:        <RETURN>
Command:         END
```

Now start another new drawing of any name and draw a line. Load **MACRO27 (Load "Macro27")**. Type **IWB**. You'll be prompted **Pick insertion point and angle:**. The **OBJECT SNAP** mode **NEAR** will be invoked for the points. (You can override it, if you wish, by typing another mode.) Pick a point on the line for the insertion point, and one that describes the angle of the line. It will break the desired section out of the line and put the symbol in its place.

TO REVISE: This can be made into a macro for a number of different symbols or used for any type of schematic drawing, piping applications and even architectural drawings. Because of its flexibility, you must modify it on your own.

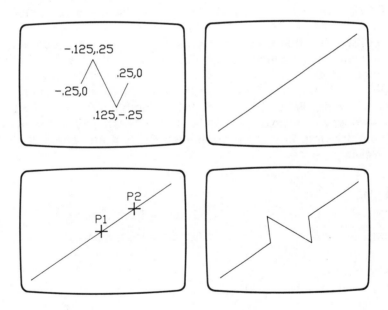

MACRO
28 Blocks

PURPOSE: Helps you understand and implement the **BLOCK** and **WBLOCK** commands.

TO CREATE:

```
[BLKNDRWG]^C^CBlock;
```

TO INVOKE: Add this macro to a space in your menu file.

LET'S TRY IT: Get into an existing drawing and pick the **BLKNDRWG** macro. Follow AutoCAD's prompts to create a **BLOCK** that can be inserted into the drawing.

To make certain you created a **BLOCK**, type **INSERT**. Answer AutoCAD's prompts and the **BLOCK** will appear where you placed it.

TO REVISE: The above macro lets you create a **BLOCK** of user-defined entities with a user-defined name. This block resides only within the drawing created.

Let's modify this to create a block on the disk from entities in the current drawing. **WBLOCK**, the AutoCAD command that allows this, works two ways: 1) picks the entities to **WBLOCK** and sends them to disk as a drawing; 2) takes a predefined **BLOCK** and sends it to disk as a drawing.

Example:

```
^C^CWblock;\;        (Option 1 from above)

^C^CWblock;          (Option 2 from above)
```

MACRO 29 Dimensions

PURPOSE: Automates the **DIM**ension commands so you don't have to type **DIM** and **EXIT** to get in and out of the **dimension mode**.

TO CREATE:

```
[  HORZ  ]^C^CDim;Hor;
```

TO INVOKE: Add this macro to a space in your menu file.

LET'S TRY IT: Get into an AutoCAD drawing and create some random lines. While still in the **LINE** command, pick the **HORZ** macro. This will cancel the **LINE** command and prompt you for the information needed to make a dimension. When the dimension is drawn, type **EXIT** to return to the **Command:** prompt.

If you use this with other items that begin with the sequence ^ **C** ^ **C**, then (at the **DIM:** prompt) pick one of those items to get you out of the **dimension** mode.

TO REVISE: Many companies create a set of standards for AutoCAD. One of these standards usually concerns the layer on which annotation and dimensions are placed. The following macro allows you to place dimensions without worrying whether they're on the correct layer.

In this example, all dimensions are placed on **Layer 4**. You can have the macro automatically set the current **Layer** to **4** before it actually enters the desired dimension command. In the example, you'll use the **Make** option. This option both creates the new layer (if it doesn't already exist) and sets it to the current layer. If the layer did not exist and the **Make** option created it, it would have the default color and linetype.

Example:

```
^C^CLayer;M;4;;Dim;Hor;
```

You also can create a macro that sets the layer for all dimensions each time you enter a drawing. This is particularly important if you're not going to place them on the same layer with each drawing.

Example:

```
^C^C(Setq DL+
(Getstring "Enter layer to place dimensions on: "));
```

Pick this macro and set the current layer for your dimensions. Now, incorporate this variable into one of your dimensioning macros.

Example:

```
^C^CLayer;M;!DL;;Dim;Hor;
```

Note: If you use the above example, set the layer at least once during each edit session. Otherwise, any macro containing that variable will dump and report an error.

TIPS: Dimensions can be associative or not depending on the **DIMASO** variable accessed from the **DIM:** prompt. Or, you can call up the prototype drawing and set **DIMASO ON**, which will become the default for all drawings. Datum line or baseline dimensions, isometric dimensions and dimensions that always put the text "between the uprights" (with arrows pointing inward) can be created with AutoLISP, although they won't be associative. (See the next three macros.)

MACRO 30 Baseline Dimensions

PURPOSE: Allows the user to place ordinate or **X Y** dimensions. This type of dimension is used to call out either the **X** or **Y** location from a given base point.

TO CREATE:

```
(Defun C:Baseline () (Setvar "Cmdecho" 0)
 (Setq DS (Getvar "Dimscale")) (Setq DL (Getvar "Dimlfac"))
 (Setq EX (Getvar "Dimexo")) (Setq TI (Getvar "Dimtih"))
 (Setq C '(= 0 (Cdr (Assoc 40
```

```
     (Tblsearch "Style" (Getvar "Textstyle"))))))
    (If (= nil BASE)
     (Setq BASE (Getpoint
      "\nPick point to base dimensions from: ")))
   (If (= 0 (Setq TX (Cdr (Assoc 40
     (Tblsearch "Style" (Getvar "Textstyle"))))))
    (Progn
     (Setq TX (Getvar "Dimtxt")) (Setq B (* (/ TX 2.0) DS)))
    (Setq B (/ TX 2.0)))
   (Command "Osnap" "End,Int,Cen")
   (Setq P1 (Getpoint "\nEnter first point: "))
   (Command "Osnap" "Off")
   (Setq P2 (Getpoint P1"\nEnter second point: "))
   (If
    (>(Abs (- (Car P1) (Car P2))) (Abs (- (Cadr P1) (Cadr P2))))
     (Progn (Setq P2 (List (Car P2) (Cadr P1))) (Basehorz))
     (Progn (Setq P2 (List (Car P1) (Cadr P2))) (Basevert)))
   (Command "Line" P1 P2 "") (Princ))

(Defun Basehorz () (Princ "\nDimension text < ")
 (Princ (Setq D (Rtos (* DL (Abs (- (Cadr P1) (Cadr BASE))))
   (Getvar "Lunits") (Getvar "Luprec"))))
 (Setq A (Getstring t ">: "))
 (If (= "" A) (Setq A D))
 (If (<(Car P2) (Car P1)) (Progn
   (Setq P1 (List (- (Car P1) (* EX DS)) (Cadr P1)))
   (Setq P3 (List (- (Car P2) B) (- (Cadr P2) B)))
   (If (Eval C) (Command "Text" "R" P3 (* TX DS) "0" A)
    (Command "Text" "R" P3 "0" A)))
     (Progn (Setq P1 (List (+ (Car P1) (* EX DS)) (Cadr P1)))
      (Setq P3 (List (+ (Car P2) B) (- (Cadr P2) B)))
    (If (Eval C) (Command "Text" P3 (* TX DS) "0" A)
     (Command "Text" P3 "0" A)))))

(Defun Basevert () (Princ "\nDimension text <")
```

```
(Princ (Setq D (Rtos (* DL (Abs (- (Cadr P1) (Cadr BASE))))
 (Getvar "Lunits") (Getvar "Luprec")))))
(Setq A (Getstring t ">: ")) (If (= "" A) (Setq A D))
(If (<= (Cadr P2) (Cadr P1))
 (Progn (Setq P1 (List (Car P1) (- (Cadr P1) (* EX DS))))
  (If <= (= TI 1)
   (Progn (Setq P3 (List (Car P2) (- (Cadr P2) (* 3 B))))
    (If (Eval C) (Command "Text" "C" P3 (* TX DS) "0" A)
     (Command "Text" "C" P3 "0" A)))
   (Progn (Setq P3 (List (+ (Car P2) B) (- (Cadr P2) B)))
    (If (Eval C) (Command "Text" "R" P3 (* TX DS) "90" A)
     (Command "Text" "R" P3 "90" A)))))
  (Progn (Setq P1 (List (Car P1) (+ (Cadr P1) (* EX DS))))
   (If (= TI 1) (Progn (Setq P3 (List (Car P2) (+ (Cadr P2) B)))
    (If (Eval C) (Command "Text" "C" P3 (* TX DS) "0" A)
                 (Command "Text" "C" P3 "0" A)))
   (Progn (Setq P3 (List (+ (Car P2) B) (+ (Cadr P2) B)))
    (If (Eval C) (Command "Text" P3 (* TX DS) "90" A)
     (Command "Text" P3 "90" A)))))))))
(Defun C:Baseorg ()
 (Setq BASE (Getpoint
 "\nPick point to base dimensions from: ")))
```

TO INVOKE: Create this macro as an AutoLISP file **(.lsp)**.

LET'S TRY IT: To try this, get into a drawing and create a part to dimension. Start a new drawing with any name. Follow the commands below:

```
Command:                  Line
From point:               0,0
To point:                 8,0
To point:                 8,4
To point:                 5,4
To point:                 5,3
To point:                 3,3
To point:                 3,4
```

To point:	0,4
To point:	C
Command:	Circle
3P/2P/TTR/<Center point>:	2,2
Diameter/<Radius>:	1
Command:	Circle
3P/2P/TTR/<Center point>:	6,1
Diameter/<Radius>:	.5
Command:	Zoom
All/Center/Dy.....	E
Command:	Zoom
All/Center/Dy.....	.5X
Command:	(Load "Macro30")

This macro uses some of the more important dimension variables, so you have control over the way it works. The following is a list of variables used. See the AutoCAD *User Reference* manual for a description of each. At this point you may need to change some of the following variables to suit your needs:

DIMSCALE

DIMEXO

DIMTIH

DIMTXT

DIMLFAC

Now, follow the prompts below:

Command:	Baseline
Pick point to base dim...	0,0
First point:	Touch one of the circles
Second point:	Go to the side you want the dimension placed
Dimension text <Default>:	Type in text or return

If you wish to respecify the point from which the dimensions are based, type **BASEORG**.

TIPS: If, when prompted for the **Dimension text < Default >:**, you enter something that begins with a parenthesis, it will report an error, **Can't reenter AutoLISP.** This is because AutoLISP is trying to evaluate what's contained in the parentheses. Because AutoLISP is busy, it can't evaluate it and will cause no harm.

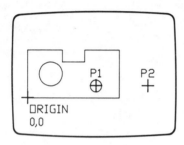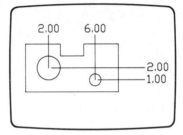

MACRO 31 Isometric Dimensions

PURPOSE: Adds dimensions to isometric drawings more efficiently.

For each of the three planes used in **ISO TOP**, **RIGHT** and **LEFT**, you're offered two ways to dimension: parallel and perpendicular to the plane. This creates a total of six ways to dimension the drawing. Because of this macro's complexity, it works only parallel to the top plane on the right or left.

TO CREATE:

```
(Defun C:Dimiso () (Setvar "Cmdecho" 0)
(Setq DS (Getvar "Dimscale"))
(Setq DA (Getvar "Dimasz")) (Setq DT (Getvar "Dimtxt"))
(Setq DE (Getvar "Dimexe")) (Setq DO (Getvar "Dimexo"))
(Setq A1 (/ Pi 180.0)) (Setq A2 (/ 180 Pi)) (Initget 1 "L R")
(Setq A (Getkword "\nLeft/Right: ")) (Setq P1 (Getpoint
"\nFirst extension line origin or RETURN to select: "))
(Cond ((= nil P1) (Setq P2 (Entsel)) (While (= nil P2)
```

```
(Princ "\nNo object found!") (Setq P2 (Entsel)))
(Setq P2 (Osnap (Cadr P2) "MID")) (Setq Pl (Osnap P2 "END"))
(Setq P2 (Polar Pl (Angle Pl P2) (* 2.0 (Distance Pl P2)))))))
((Boundp 'Pl) (Initget 1)
(Setq P2 (Getpoint "\nSecond extension line origin: "))))
(Initget 1) (Setq P3 (Getpoint "\nDimension line location: "))
(Cond ((= A "L")
(Setq B 150 C 30 G "ISOAROW2" H "ISOTEXT2" I 30) (Setpt)
(If (< (Cadr P6) (Cadr P7)) (Setq F -1) (Setq F 1)) (Dimit))
((= A "R")
(Setq B 30 C 150 G "ISOAROW1" H "ISOTEXT1" I 330) (Setpt)
(If (< (Cadr P6) (Cadr P7)) (Setq F -1) (Setq F 1)) (Dimit))))

(Defun Setpt ()
(Setq P4 (Inters Pl (Polar Pl (* Al B) 1) P3 (Polar P3
(* Al C) 1) Onseg))
(Setq P5 (Inters P2 (Polar P2 (* Al B) 1) P3 (Polar P3
(* Al C) 1) Onseg))
(Setq P6 (Polar P4 (Angle P4 P5) (/ (Distance P4 P5) 2)))
(Setq P7 (Polar Pl (Angle Pl P2) (/ (Distance Pl P2) 2))))

(Defun Dimit ()
(Command "Line" (Polar Pl (Angle Pl P4) (* DO DS))
(Polar P4 (Angle Pl P4) (* DE DS)) "" "Line" (Polar P2
(Angle P2 P5) (* DO DS)) (Polar P5 (Angle P2 P5) (* DE DS))
"" "Line" P4 P5 "")
(Setq P6 (Polar P6 (Angle Pl P4) (* F (* DT DS))))
(Setq Dl (Rtos (Distance P4 P5) (Getvar "Lunits")
(Getvar "Luprec")))
(Command "Insert" G P4 (* DS DA) "" (* A2 (Angle P4 P5)))
(Command "Insert" G P5 (* DS DA) "" (* A2 (Angle P5 P4)))
(Prompt "\nDimension text <") (Prompt Dl)
(Setq D2 (Getstring ">: "))
(If (= D2 "") (Setq D Dl) (Setq D D2))
(Command "Text" "S" H "C" P6 (* DS DT) I D))
```

TO INVOKE: Create this macro as an AutoLISP file (**.lsp**).

LET'S TRY IT: This macro requires you to create two text **STYLES** and two **ARROWHEAD**s. You also must set **SNAP** to the **ISOMETRIC** style. Let's do this with a prototype drawing. Start a new drawing called **ISOPROTO=**. Then follow the prompts.

```
Command:                              Solid
First point:                          0,0
Second point:                         1.0833,0.1443
Third point:                          0.9167,-0.1443
Fourth point:                         <RETURN>
Command:                              Block
Block name (or ?):                    ISOAROW1
Insertion base point:                 0,0
Select objects:                       L
Select objects:                       <RETURN>
Command:                              Oops
Command:                              Mirror
Select objects:                       L
Select objects:                       <RETURN>
First point of mirror line:           0,0
Second point:                         1,0
Delete old objects? <N>               Y
Command:                              Block
Block name (or ?):                    ISOAROW2
Insertion base point:                 0,0
Select objects:                       L
Select objects:                       <RETURN>
Command:                              Style
Text style name(or ?)<Def>:           Isotext1
Font file <Def>                       Take default or type in name.
Height <Def>:                         0
Width factor <Def>:                   1
Obliquing angle <Def>:                30
Backwards? <N>                        <RETURN>
Upside-down? <N>                      <RETURN>
Vertical? <N>                         <RETURN>
Command:                              Style
Text style name(or ?)<Def>:           Isotext2
Font file <Def>:                      Take default or type in name.
```

```
Height <Def>:                         0
Width factor <Def>:                   1
Obliquing angle <Def>:                -30
Backwards? <N>                        <RETURN>
Upside-down? <N>                      <RETURN>
Vertical? <N>                         <RETURN>
Command:                              Snap
Snap spacing or.../Style:             S
Standard/Isometric <Def>:             I
Vertical Spacing <Def>:               1
Command:                              End
```

Now you're ready to start a new drawing. Pick **Option 1** and enter the name you wish to use, followed by =ISOPROTO, ("FILENAME=ISOPROTO"). Load **MACRO31** (**Load "Macro31"**). Now create some isometric lines to be dimensioned. This macro uses several of the normal dimension variables; so change the variables to suit your needs. Type **DIMISO**.

The first prompt (**Left/Right**) determines whether you want to go to the left or right of the line. **Left** means the dimension extension lines will be placed at an angle from the bottom right to the upper left of the screen. **Right** goes from bottom left to upper right. From here the macro works like AutoCAD's **DIM** commands.

TO REVISE: Because we gave you only the code for the **TOP ISOPLANE**, it's up to you to create the rest of the code. The only real secret is determining which **ISOPLANE** you're on when you invoke the macro. You can easily find this out using the **getvar** function (**getvar "ISOPLANE"**). Then you can use conditional statements to branch into parts of the program written for each plane.

TIPS: If you have a layer on which you place dimensions, add it into the function.

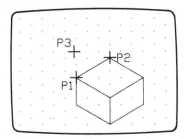
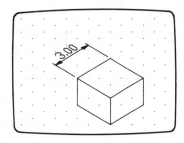

MACRO 32 Forced Fitting Dimensions

PURPOSE: Replaces AutoCAD's dimensioning function for certain uses. For example, have you ever dimensioned an item, only to watch AutoCAD throw the dimension **TEXT** and **ARROWHEAD**s outside the extension lines? You knew there was plenty of room inside the extension lines so you repositioned the **ARROWHEAD**s and **TEXT** yourself. This macro forces **ARROWHEAD**s and **TEXT** inside the extension lines, even if they won't fit!

(This macro places horizontal dimensions only and doesn't work on circles. In the **TO REVISE:** section, you'll learn how to make it work vertically.)

TO CREATE:

```
(Defun C:Fhdim () (Setvar "Cmdecho" 0)
(Setq AN1 0) (Setq AN2 (* Pi 0.5)) (Setq AN3 (* Pi 1.5))
(Setq BM (Getvar "Blipmode")) (Setq DS (Getvar "Dimscale"))
(Setq DA (* DS (Getvar "Dimasz")))
(Setq DT (* DS (Getvar "Dimtxt")))
(Setq DE (* DS (Getvar "Dimexe")))
(Setq DO (* DS (Getvar "Dimexo"))) (Setq P1 (Getpoint
"\nFirst extension line origin or RETURN to select: "))
(Cond ((= nil P1) (Setq P2 (Entsel)) (While (= nil P2)
(Princ "\nNo object found!") (Setq P2 (Entsel)))
(Setq P2 (Osnap (Cadr P2) "MID")) (Setq P1 (Osnap P2 "END"))
(Setq P2 (Polar P1 (Angle P1 P2) (* 2.0 (Distance P1 P2)))))
((Boundp 'P1) (Initget 1)
(Setq P2 (Getpoint "\nSecond extension line origin: "))))
(Initget 1) (Setq P3 (Getpoint "\nDimension line location: "))
(Setvar "Blipmode" 0)
(Setq P4 (Inters P1 (Polar P1 AN2 1) P3 (Polar P3 AN1 1)
Onseg))
(Setq P5 (Inters P2 (Polar P2 AN2 1) P3 (Polar P3 AN1 1)
Onseg))
```

```
(Setq P3 (Polar P4 (Angle P4 P5) (/ (Distance P4 P5) 2)))
(If (< (Cadr P4) (Cadr Pl)) (Setq F -0.5) (Setq F 0.5))
(Command "Line" (Polar Pl (Angle Pl P4) DO) (Polar P4
(Angle Pl P4) DE) "" "Line" (Polar P2 (Angle P2 P5) DO)
(Polar P5 (Angle P2 P5) DE) "" "Line" P4 P5 "")
(Setq P3 (Polar P3 (Angle Pl P4) (* F DT)))
(Setq Dl (Rtos (Distance P4 P5) (Getvar "Lunits")
(Getvar "Luprec")))
(Command "Solid" P4 (Polar (Polar P4 (Angle P4 P5) DA) AN3
(* DA (/ 1.0 6.0))) (Polar (Polar P4 (Angle P4 P5) DA) AN2
(* DA (/ 1.0 6.0))) "" "")
(Command "Solid" P5 (Polar (Polar P5 (Angle P5 P4) DA) AN3
(* DA (/ 1.0 6.0))) (Polar (Polar P5 (Angle P5 P4) DA) AN2
(* DA (/ 1.0 6.0))) "" "")
(Prompt "\nDimension text <") (Prompt Dl)
(Setq D2 (Getstring ">: "))
(If (= D2 "") (Setq D Dl) (Setq D D2))
(Command "Text" "C" P3 DT 0 D) (Setvar "Blipmode" ·BM) (Princ))
```

TO INVOKE: Create this macro as an AutoLISP file (**.lsp**).

LET'S TRY IT: Use this the same way you'd use any of AutoCAD's dimension commands.

TO REVISE: By changing a few angles, you can create a function that does vertical dimensions. Below, we show the existing line followed by the changed line.

```
EX:(Setq ANl 0) (Setq AN2 (* Pi 0.5)) (Setq AN3 (* Pi 1.5))
CH:(Setq ANl (* Pi 0.5)) (Setq AN2 0)) (Setq AN3 Pi)

EX:(If (< (Cadr P4) (Cadr Pl)) (Setq F -0.5) (Setq F 0.5))
CH:(If (< (Car P4) (Car Pl)) (Setq F -0.5) (Setq F 0.5))

EX:(Command "Text" "C" P3 DT 0 D) (Setvar "Blipmode" BM)(Princ))
CH:(Command "Text" "C" P3 DT 90 D) (Setvar "Blipmode" BM)(Princ))
```

TIPS: If you have placed dimensions on a specific layer, you can add that layer into the macro.

33 Balloons

PURPOSE: Places balloons with leaders at user-specified points (particularly useful when calling out parts in an assembly drawing).

TO CREATE:

```
(Defun C:Balloon () (Setvar "Cmdecho" 0)
(Setq DS (Getvar "Dimscale"))
(Initget 1) (Setq P1 (Getpoint "\nFrom point: "))
(Initget 1) (Setq P2 (Getpoint P1 "\nTo point: "))
(If (<= (Car P2) (Car P1)) (Setq B (* -0.25 DS))
(Setq B (* 0.25 DS)))
(Setq P3 (List (+ (Car P2) B) (Cadr P2)))
(Setq P4 (List (+ (Car P3) (/ B 2)) (Cadr P3)))
(Command "Dim1" "Leader" P1 P2 P3 ^C ^C)
(Command "Circle" P4 (/ (Abs B) 2))
(Initget 1) (Setq C (Getstring t "\nText for bubble: "))
(Command "Text" "M" P4 (* 0.125 DS) 0 C) (Princ))
```

TO INVOKE: Create this macro as an AutoLISP file (**.lsp**).
   The size of the arrowhead placed at the other end of the line is determined by a combination of the **DIMSCALE** and **DIMASZ**.

LET'S TRY IT: Get into a new AutoCAD drawing. Load **MACRO33** (**Load "Macro33"**). Type **Balloon**.

```
From point:    (Pick a point)
To point:      (Pick a point)
```

   Next you'll be prompted **Text for bubble:**. Enter desired text.

TO REVISE: A good revision to this macro forces it to place your balloon on a given layer automatically (**LAYER 4** in this example). First you must determine the current layer and store that value, so you can reset that layer when the macro is finished. The following contains the added lines in boldface with a few other lines as reference.

```
(Setq DS (Getvar "Dimscale"))
(Setq CL (Getvar "Clayer"))
(Command "Layer" "M" "4" "")
     .
     .
     .
(Command "Layer" "S" CL "")
(Princ)
```

MACRO 34   Parts List

PURPOSE: Automates the drawing and completion of a parts list. This macro doesn't create data that go into the parts list, but asks you for information, then completes it.

TO CREATE:

```
(Defun C:Plist () (Setvar "Cmdecho" 0)
(Setq F (Getvar "Blipmode")) (Setvar "Blipmode" 0)
(Setq A (Getvar "Dimscale")) (Initget 7) (Setq B (Getint
"\nEnter number of items in list: ")) (Initget 1) (Setq Pl
(Getpoint "\nPick a point for lower right corner: "))
(Command "Line" (Polar Pl (* Pi 0.5) (* A 0.3125))
(Polar (Getvar "Lastpoint") Pi (* A 7.62)) "" "Copy" "L" "" "0,0"
(Polar (List 0 0) (* Pi 0.5) (* A 0.3125)))
(Command "Text" "M" (List (+ (Car Pl) (* A -7.3075)) (+ (Cadr Pl)
(* A 0.4687))) (* A 0.125) 0 "ITEM")
```

```
(Command "Text" "M" (List (+ (Car P1) (* A -6.7762)) (+ (Cadr P1)
(* A 0.4687))) (* A 0.125) 0 "QTY")
(Command "Text" "M" (List (+ (Car P1) (* A -6.0575)) (+ (Cadr P1)
(* A 0.4687))) (* A 0.125) 0 "NUMBER")
(Command "Text" "M" (List (+ (Car P1) (* A -2.9506)) (+ (Cadr P1)
(* A 0.4687))) (* A 0.125) 0 "DESCRIPTION")
(Command "Text" "M" (List (+ (Car P1) (* A -3.81)) (+ (Cadr P1)
(* A 0.1563))) (* A 0.156) 0 "PARTS LIST")
(Command "Text" "M" (List (+ (Car P1) (* A -0.1719)) (+ (Cadr P1)
(* A 0.5388))) (* A 0.08) 0 "SIZE")
(Command "Text" "M" (List (+ (Car P1) (* A -0.1719)) (+ (Cadr P1)
(* A 0.3987))) (* A 0.08) 0 "DWG")
(Setq P1 (List (- (Car P1) (* 0.34375 A)) (+ (Cadr P1)
(* 0.3125 A))))
(Setq P2 (List (- (Car P1) (* 5.21375 A)) (Cadr P1)))
(Setq P3 (List (- (Car P2) (* 1.00 A)) (Cadr P2)))
(Setq P4 (List (- (Car P3) (* 0.4375 A)) (Cadr P3)))
(Setq P5 (List (- (Car P4) (* 0.625 A)) (- (Cadr P4)
(* 0.3125 A)))) (Setq A1 (* 0.5 Pi)) (Setq D (* 0.25 A))
(Setq E (+ (* 0.3125 A) (* D B))) (Command "Line" P1
(Polar P1 A1 E) "" "Line" P2 (Polar P2 A1 E) "" "Line" P3
(Polar P3 A1 E) "" "Line" P4 (Polar P4 A1 E) "" "Line" P5
(Polar P5 A1 (+ (* 0.6250 A) (* D B))) "")
(Setq P1 (Polar P5 A1 (* 0.875 A)))
(Command "Line" P1 (Polar P1 0 (* 7.62 A)) "")
(Command "Array" "L" "" "R" B "" (* 1 D))
(Setq P1 (List (+ (Car P1) (* 0.3125 A)) (- (Cadr P1)
(* 0.1875 A)))) (Setq P2 (Polar P1 0 (* 0.53125 A)))
(Setq P3 (Polar P2 0 (* 0.71875 A)))
(Setq P4 (Polar P3 0 (* 0.5625 A)))
(Setq P5 (Polar P4 0 (* 5.203125 A))) (Setq C 1)
(Repeat B (Command "Text" "C" P1 (* 0.125 A) "0" (Itoa C))
(Prompt "\nQuantity for item ") (Princ C) (Prompt ": ")
(Setq G (Read-line)) (Command "Text" "C" P2 (* 0.125 A) "0" G)
(Prompt "\nPart number for item ") (Princ C) (Prompt ": ")
```

```
(Setq G (Read-line)) (Command "Text" "C" P3 (* 0.125 A) "0" G)
(Prompt "\nDescription for item ") (Princ C) (Prompt ": ")
(Setq G (Read-line)) (Command "Text" P4 (* 0.125 A) "0" G)
(Prompt "\nDrawing size for item ") (Princ C) (Prompt ": ")
(Setq G (Read-line)) (Command "Text" P5 (* 0.125 A) "0" G)
(Setq P1 (List (Car P1) (+ (Cadr P1) D)))
(Setq P2 (List (Car P2) (+ (Cadr P2) D)))
(Setq P3 (List (Car P3) (+ (Cadr P3) D)))
(Setq P4 (List (Car P4) (+ (Cadr P4) D)))
(Setq P5 (List (Car P5) (+ (Cadr P5) D))) (Setq C (+ 1 C)))
(Setvar "Blipmode" F) (Princ))
```

TO INVOKE: Create this macro as an AutoLISP file (**.lsp**).

LET'S TRY IT: Get into a drawing and load **MACRO34** (**Load "Macro34"**). Type **PLIST**. Enter the number of items you want to place in the list. Pick a point for the **lower right corner**. Follow the prompts and the parts list will be completed.

TO REVISE: The only revision that might improve this macro would be to add layers, as in the previous macro.

MACRO
35 Autonumber

PURPOSE: Allows you to place numbers either randomly or patterned in a drawing.

TO CREATE:
```
(Defun C:Number () (Setvar "Cmdecho" 0)
(Setq G (Getvar "Blipmode")) (Setvar "Blipmode" 0)
(Setq A (Getint "\nStarting number: "))
(Setq B (Getint "\nEnding number: "))
```

```
(If (> A B) (Setq E -1) (Setq E 1))
(Setq D (Getdist "\nText height: "))
(Setq I (Getreal "\nRotation angle: "))
(Initget "R L") (Setq H (Getkword "\nRandom/<Linear>: "))
(Cond ((Or (= nil H) (= "L" H)) (GIP)
(Setq C (Getdist Pl "\nDistance between numbers: "))
(Setq Al (Getangle Pl "\nAngle to run numbers: "))
(Repeat (1+ (Abs (- A B))) (Setq F (Itoa A))
(If (/= (Type PlT) 'List) (Command "Text" PlT Pl D I F)
(Command "Text" Pl D I F)) (Setq A (+ A E))
(Setq Pl (Polar Pl Al C)))) ((= "R" H) (GIP) (Repeat
(1+ (Abs (- A B))) (Setq F (Itoa A)) (If (/= (Type PlT) 'List)
(Command "Text" PlT Pl D I F) (Command "Text" Pl D I F))
(Setq A (+ A E)) (If (/= F (Itoa B)) (Cond ((= PlT "C")
(Setq Pl (Getpoint "\nCenter point: "))) ((= PlT "M")
(Setq Pl (Getpoint "\nMiddle point: "))) ((= PlT "R")
(Setq Pl (Getpoint "\nEndpoint: "))) ((= (Type PlT) 'List)
(Setq Pl (Getpoint "\nStart point: ")))))))))
(Setvar "Blipmode" G) (Princ))

(Defun GIP () (Initget 1 "C M R") (Setq PlT (Setq Pl (Getpoint
"\nStart point or Center/Middle/Right: ")))
(Cond ((= PlT "C") (Setq Pl (Getpoint "\nCenter point: ")))
((= PlT "M") (Setq Pl (Getpoint "\nMiddle point: ")))
((= PlT "R") (Setq Pl (Getpoint "\nEndpoint: ")))))
```

TO INVOKE: Create this macro as an AutoLISP file (**.lsp**).

LET'S TRY IT: After getting into an AutoCAD drawing, load **MACRO35** (**Load** "Macro35"). Type **NUMBER**. You'll be prompted for **starting number** and **ending number**. These numbers can go from smaller to larger or vice versa, including negative numbers.

After specifying the numbers, answer the prompts for **TEXT HEIGHT** and **ROTATION**. Next you'll be prompted **Random/<Linear>:**   First type **R** for Random. You'll receive the normal AutoCAD prompt for text location. After selecting desired location, you'll be asked to select points for numbers to be placed.

Let's try the macro again. Hit **RETURN** to accept the default (or type **L**). With **LINEAR**, you'll need **Distance between numbers:** (enter the distance or pick a point on the screen) and **Angle to run numbers:** (type in an angle or pick a point on the screen at the desired angle). The last prompt is the same as the last prompt of the **RANDOM** section.

```
              5
              4
              3
              2
    5 4 3 2 1 2 3 4 5
              2
              3
              4
              5
```

```
    1      8
                    5

    9    2   6         7

    3      10    4
```

MACRO
36 Layers

PURPOSE: Sets a new **LAYER** with a single pick.

You'll use numbered **LAYER** names in this macro. To use named **LAYERS**, simply substitute names for the numbers. You also use the **Make** option for **LAYER** instead of **Set**. This option won't report an error if the layer doesn't exist. It will automatically create the layer, then set it as the current layer (if it doesn't exist). An existing layer will simply be set as **CURRENT**. If the macro creates the layer, it will use AutoCAD's default color (white) and linetype (continuous).

TO CREATE:

```
[LAYER 1 ]^C^CLayer;M;1;;
```

TO INVOKE: Add this macro to a space in your menu file.

LET'S TRY IT: Get into a new drawing and create **LAYER 1** (or use your existing **LAYER 1**), then switch to **LAYER 0**. Pick the **LAYER 1** macro. You're now on **LAYER 1**.

TO REVISE: To set a different **LAYER**, change the name of the **LAYER** used in the macro.

Example:

```
^C^CLayer;M;2;;    (Sets to LAYER 2)
^C^CLayer;M;3;;    (Sets to LAYER 3)
```

The above macro is a simple **MENU** function. The next example is an AutoLISP function that lets you set your **LAYER** by typing in the name or touching an entity on the layer you wish to set as current.

```
(Defun C:SCL () (Setvar "Cmdecho" 0)
(Setq A (Entsel "\nTouch entity on new layer: "))
(If A (Progn (Setq A (Cdr (Assoc 8 (Entget (Car A)))))
(Command "Layer" "S" A "") (Princ))
```

To use this macro, load **MACRO36** (**Load** "Macro36"). Type **SCL**. When prompted **Touch entity on new layer:**, pick any entity on the layer you wish to set as **CURRENT**.

TIPS: For Versions after 2.5, you can mix **COLORS** and **LINETYPES** on the same **LAYERS**, for which macros can be created.

```
^C^CColor;Blue
^C^CLinetype;S;Hidden
```

MACRO
37 Move Object to New Layer

PURPOSE: Selects object(s) to move to a specified layer.

During a drawing session you may end up with some entities on an undesired layer. Many users intentionally place entities on the wrong layer so they won't have to set to a certain layer, then reset to the previous layer. This macro helps avoid such gymnastics!

TO CREATE:

```
(Defun C:O2LA () (Setvar "Cmdecho" 0) (Setq A (SSget))
(If A (Progn (Setq B (Getstring "\nEnter name of new layer: "))
(If (= nil (Tblsearch "Layer" B))
(Progn (Princ (Strcat "\nLayer " B " does not exist!"))
(Initget 1 "Y N")
(Setq C (Getkword "\nWould you like to create it: "))
(If (= "Y" C) (Command "Layer" "N" B "" "Change" A "" "P" "LA"
B ""))) (Command "Change" A "" "P" "LA" B "")))) (Princ))
```

TO INVOKE: Create this macro as an AutoLISP file (**.lsp**).

LET'S TRY IT: Start a new drawing and create two **LAYERS, 1** and **2**. Give **LAYER 1** color **1 (RED)** and **LAYER 2** color **2 (YELLOW)**. Set **LAYER 1** as the **CURRENT** layer. Now draw a few random objects. Load **MACRO37 (Load "Macro37")**. Type **O2LA**. At **Select objects:**, select one or all objects. At the next prompt, **Enter name of new layer:**, enter **2**. The objects are now transferred to **LAYER 2**.

Let's try the same thing again, but this time specify a layer that doesn't exist. When prompted **Layer ? does not exist! Would you like to create it:**, answer **Y** to create the layer and change the selected objects to that layer, or **N** to do nothing.

TO REVISE: Replacing the question about what layer to put the items on is a useful change to this macro. Instead of specifying the layer name, you touch an entity that exists on the layer you want to move the objects to. This is a simple rendition of Macro 36.

```
(Defun C:O2LB () (Setvar "Cmdecho" 0) (Setq A (SSget))
(If A (Progn (Setq B (Entsel "\nTouch entity on new layer: "))
(If B (Progn (Setq B (Cdr (Assoc 8 (Entget (Car B)))))
(Command "Change" A "" "P" "LA" B ""))))) (Princ))
```

MACRO
38 Delete Layer

PURPOSE: Lets you delete all entities on a specified layer. Using AutoCAD, turn off all layers except the one you wish to delete, erase everything on the screen, then turn all the other layers back on.

TO CREATE:

```
(Defun C:DellayA () (Setvar "Cmdecho" 0)
(Setq A (Getstring "\nEnter name of layer to delete: "))
(Command "Erase" (Ssget "X" (Cons (Cons 8 (Eval A)) TEMPWORD))
"") (Princ))
```

TO INVOKE: Create this macro as an AutoLISP file (**.lsp**).

LET'S TRY IT: Create or get into a drawing that has several layers, with entities on each layer. Load **MACRO38 (Load "Macro38")**, and type **DELLAYA**. You will be asked to enter the name of a layer to delete (this will delete everything on the layer specified, even if the layer is **FROZEN** or **OFF**).

TO REVISE: Using the same format as the above macro, you can create one that lets you delete an entire layer just by picking an entity on that layer.

```
(Defun C:DellayB () (Setvar "Cmdecho" 0)
(Setq A (Entsel "\nTouch entity on layer to delete: "))
(If A (Progn (Setq A (Cdr (Assoc 8 (Entget (Car A)))))
```

```
(Command "Erase" (Ssget "X" (Cons (Cons 8 (Eval A)) TEMPWORD))
"")))  (Princ))
```

To use this, load **MACRO38** (**Load** "**Macro38**") and type **DELLAYB**.
When you pick an entity on the layer to be deleted, everything on that
layer will be deleted.

_{MACRO}
39 Edit Text

PURPOSE: Allows you to edit the spelling of an entire string of text or
a specific part.

TO CREATE:
```
(Defun C:Ct () (Setvar "Cmdecho" 0) (Setq B 0)
(Initget 1 "E S") (Setq F (Getkword "Entire line/String: "))
(Setq A (Ssget)) (If A (Cond ((= F "E") (Repeat (Sslength A)
(If (/= "TEXT" (Cdr (Assoc 0 (Setq E
(Entget (Setq C (Ssname A B)))))))) (Setq B (1+ B)) (Progn
(Command "Select" C) (Setq G (Strlen (Setq D (Getstring t
"\nEnter new text: ")))) (Setq H (Cdr (Assoc 1 E))) (Cond
((And (/= D "") (= "<>" (Substr D 1 2)))
(Setq D (Strcat H (Substr D 3 (- G 2)))))
((And (/= D "") (= "<>" (Substr D (- G 1) 2)))
(Setq D (Strcat (Substr D 1 (- G 2)) H)))) (If (/= D "")
(Progn (Setq E (Subst (Cons 1 D) (Assoc 1 E) E)) (Entmod E)))
(Setq B (1+ B)) (Command "")))))) ((= F "S") (Progn
(Setq D (Strlen (Setq C (Getstring t "\nOld string: "))))
(Setq G (Getstring t "\nNew string: ")) (Princ "\nWorking.")
(Repeat (Sslength A) (Princ ".") (If (= "TEXT"
(Cdr (Assoc 0 (Setq E (Entget (Ssname A B)))))) (Progn
(Setq K (Cdr (Assoc 1 E))) (Setq H 1) (If (= C (Substr G
```

```
(- (Strlen G) (- (Strlen C) 1)))) (Setq I D) (Setq I 0))
(While (= D (Strlen (Setq J (Substr K H D)))) (Princ ".")
(If (= J C) (Progn (Setq K (Strcat (Substr K 1 (1- H)) G
(Substr K (+ H D)))) (Setq H (+ (- (Strlen G) 1) H I))
(Setq H (1+ H)))) (If (/= K (Cdr (Assoc 1 E))) (Progn
(Setq E (Subst (Cons 1 K) (Assoc 1 E) E)) (Entmod E)))))
(Setq B (1+ B)))))))) (Princ))
```

TO INVOKE: Create this macro as an AutoLISP file (.lsp).

This macro offers three ways to edit text. You can revise the entire line; you can append a string to the beginning or end of the existing string; or you can change a portion of the text string. Each method is described below.

LET'S TRY IT: Place several strings of text in your drawing. Load **MACRO39 (Load "Macro39")**. Type **CT**. The first prompt you'll see is **Entire line/String:**. To change the entire line in this example, hit **E**. You're then asked to select text. Do this in any manner you wish. If you select the text in pieces, you'll revise them in the order of selection. If you select it with a **W**indow, **C**rossing or **B**ox, revisions will follow in the order of the original drawing.

Don't worry about other objects you might have selected inadvertently because the macro will ignore them. After selecting the objects, you'll be prompted **Enter new text:**. If you wish to leave the text as is, hit **RETURN** and you'll be walked through each of the objects you selected.

In this second example, you'll append text to the beginning and the end of an existing string. The routine works just like the one above, except that at the **Enter new text:** prompt, you type < > **new text** instead of typing a new string of text. The < > tells the command to add to the end of the current string. If you type **new text** < >, the command will add text that precedes the < > to the beginning of the string.

For this last example, place a string of text in your drawing that reads **I visited Ted at the office**. Type **CT**. At the **Entire line/String:** prompt, pick **S**. When you're asked to select the strings of text you wish to change, pick the string you just placed. Type **Ted** at the **Old string:** prompt and **Jim** at the **New string:** prompt. It will change the string to read **I visited Jim at the office**. This routine lets you select as many text segments as you wish.

TIPS: When you use the last option explained above, be careful if you plan to revise more than one string at a time. For example, if you change "is" to "as" in several strings, the change will be made in every line you selected.

MACRO 40 Text Fitting

PURPOSE: Allows you to fit a piece of text into a designated area by adjusting the width. This routine lets you move and fit a piece of existing text simultaneously.

TO CREATE:

```
(Defun C:Tfit ()
(Setq S (Entsel
"\nSelect insertion point of text to fit: "))
(Setq S (Car S)) (Setq E (Entget S))
(Setvar "Orthomode" 1)
(Setq P1 (Cdr (Assoc 10 E)))
(Setq P3 (Getdist P1 "\nTouch end of text: "))
(Setq P1 (Getpoint "\nEnter new 1st point: "))
(Setq P2 (Getpoint P1 "\nEnter 2nd point: "))
(Setq OLD (Assoc 41 E))
(Setq RATIO (* (/ (Distance P1 P2) P3) (Cdr OLD)))
(Setq RATIO (Cons 41 RATIO))
(Setq E (Subst Ratio OLD E))
(Setq P1 (Cons 10 P1))
(Setq P2 (Cons 11 P2))
(Setq OLD (Assoc 10 E))
(Setq E (Subst P1 OLD E))
(Setq OLD (Assoc 11 E))
(Entmod (Subst P2 OLD E)) (Print))
```

TO INVOKE: Save this macro as an AutoLISP file (**.lsp**).

LET'S TRY IT: Get into a new drawing and place several text items. Load **MACRO40 (Load "Macro40")**. Type **TFIT** and follow the prompts:

```
Select insertion point of text to fit:    (Touch one of the text
                                            items you entered.)
Touch end of text:      (Stretch the line to the end of your text.)
Enter new 1st point:    (Touch a new beginning point for the text.)
Enter new 2nd point:    (Touch a point to be the end of your text.)
```

Your text now will be moved to the new location and placed between the first and second points selected.

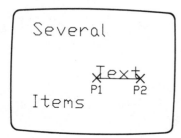 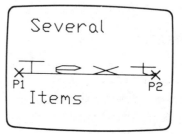

TIPS: This macro helps fit your dimensional text between leader lines after AutoCAD has thrown the text outside their limits.

MACRO 41 Change Text Style

PURPOSE: Allows you to change the text style by 1) changing all text of one style to another, and 2) changing all selected text, regardless of style. You can accomplish the same thing with AutoCAD's **CHANGE** command, but this is faster.

TO CREATE:

```
(Defun C:Ts () (Setvar "Cmdecho" 0) (Initget 1 "SE ST  ")
(Setq G (Strcase (Substr (Getkword "SElection/<STyle>: ")1 2)))
(Cond ((= G "SE") (Setq A (Ssget)) (Setq B (Sslength A))
(Initget 1) (Setq C (Getstring "\nEnter new text style: "))
(Extang C) (While (> B 0) (Setq B (1- B)) (Setq D (Ssname A B))
(Setq D (Entget D)) (Setq E (Assoc 7 D)) (Setq F (Cons 7 C))
(Setq D (Subst F E D)) (Setq H (Assoc 51 D)) (Setq I (Cons 51 J))
(Entmod (Subst I H D))) (Setq A nil)) ((Or (= G "ST") (= G ""))
(Initget 1) (Setq A (Strcase (Getstring
"\nEnter text style to change: "))) (Initget 1)
(Setq C (Getstring "\nEnter new text style: "))(Setq D (Entnext))
(Extang C) (While D (Princ ".") (Setq E (Entget D)) (If
(And (= "TEXT" (Cdr (Assoc 0 E))) (= A (Cdr (Assoc 7 E))))
(Progn (Setq F (Assoc 7 E)) (Setq G (Cons 7 C))
(Setq E (Subst G F E)) (Setq H (Assoc 51 E)) (Setq I (Cons 51 J))
(Entmod (Subst I H E)))) (Setq D (Entnext D))))) (Princ))


(Defun Extang (A) (Setq A (Tblsearch "STYLE" A))
(Setq J (Cdr (Assoc 50 A))))
```

TO INVOKE: Save this macro as an AutoLISP file (**.lsp**).

LET'S TRY IT: Get into a new drawing and create several text styles. Now create several lines of text in each style. Load **MACRO41** (**Load "Macro41"**). Type **TS**. First pick the way you wish to change text: **SElection/STyle:**.

   SE lets you select the text with AutoCAD's normal interactive selection process. You can select any text string. The strings that you select can be of the same or different styles. After you've selected each string you wish to change, you'll be prompted **Enter new text style:**. Enter the new style.

   The other option, **ST**, lets you enter a style, search the entire database for each string of that style and change those strings to the style you specify.

MACRO
42 Change Text Height

PURPOSE: Allows you to change the height of text. This function works exactly the same as the previous function (Macro41, Changing Text Styles) except that it changes heights instead of styles.

TO CREATE:

```
(Defun C:Tsz (/ G A B C D E F)
 (Setvar "Cmdecho" 0)
 (Initget 1 "S H ")
 (Setq G (Strcase (Substr (Getkword "Height/<Select>: ")1 1)))
 (Cond
  ((Or (= G "S") (= G ""))
   (Setq A (Ssget))
   (Setq B (Sslength A))
   (Initget 7) (Setq C (Getdist "\nEnter new text size: "))
   (While
    (> B 0)
     (Setq B (1- B))
     (Setq D (Ssname A B))
     (Setq D (Entget D))
     (If (= "TEXT" (Cdr (Assoc 0 D)))
      (progn
      (Setq E (Assoc 40 D))
      (Setq F (Cons 40 C))
      (Entmod (Setq D (Subst F E D)))))))
  )
  (Setq A nil)
 )
 ((= G "H")
  (Initget 7) (Setq A (Getdist "\nEnter text size to change: "))
  (Setq B (Fix (* 100 A)))
  (Initget 7) (Setq C (Getdist "\nEnter new text height: "))
```

```
(Setq D (Entnext))
(Setq E (Cons 40 C))
(While
 D
  (Princ ".")
  (Setq F (Assoc 0 (Entget D)))
  (If
   (= "TEXT" (Cdr F))
    (Progn
     (Setq F (Assoc 40 (Entget D)))
     (Setq G (Fix (* 100 (Cdr F))))
     (If
      (= B G)
      (Entmod (Subst E F (Entget D)))
     )
    )
   )
   (Setq D (Entnext D))
  )
 )
)
(Princ)
)
```

TO INVOKE: Save this macro as an AutoLISP file (**.lsp**).

LET'S TRY IT: Get into a new drawing and create several lines of text of varying heights. Load **MACRO42 (Load "Macro42")**. Type **TSZ**. First pick the way you wish to select the text to be changed, **Height/<Select>:** .

H lets you enter the height you wish to change, search the entire database for each string of that height, and change each of those strings to the height that you specify.

S will let you select the text with AutoCAD's normal interactive selection process. Any strings you select can contain characters of the same height or each of a different height. After you've selected each string you wish to change, you'll be prompted **Enter new text height:**. Enter the desired height.

TIPS: This macro will also change the height of text styles defined with a **FIXED** height. AutoCAD's **CHANGE** command can't do this. So if you use this macro to change **FIXED** height, you also must use it to change it back.

MACRO 43 Delete Leading Zero

PURPOSE: Allows you to remove the first character from a string of text. For those creating drawings to **MIL-SPEC**, this routine is useful for taking the leading zero from dimensions.

TO CREATE:
```
(Defun C:Rlc () (Setvar "Cmdecho" 0)
(Setq A (Entsel "Touch text: ")) (If A (Progn
(Setq A (Entget (Car A))) (If (= (Cdr (Assoc 0 A)) "TEXT")
(Progn (Setq B (Assoc 1 A)) (Setq C (Cons 1 (Substr (Cdr B) 2
(Strlen (Cdr B)))) (Entmod (Subst C B A))))) (Princ))
```

TO INVOKE: Save this macro as an AutoLISP file (**.lsp**).

LET'S TRY IT: Get into AutoCAD and create several strings of text. These can be created either with the **TEXT** command or with a dimension function. Load **MACRO43 (Load "Macro43")**. Type **RLC**. You'll be prompted to touch the text you wish to change. If you touch anything other than text, the macro will do nothing.

TIPS: One problem you may encounter while using this macro is that it won't work on **ASSOC**iative dimensions. Release 9 offers no easy way to modify a string of text in an **ASSOC**iative Dimension (and leave it **ASSOC**iative).

MACRO 44 Place Text Between Two Parallel Lines

PURPOSE: Lets the user place text between two parallel lines. It makes text parallel to the specified lines, with text height half the distance between the lines. This is handy for labeling roadways on street maps.

TO CREATE:
```
(Defun C:Tbpl () (Setvar "Cmdecho" 0) (Initget 1)
(Setq P1 (Osnap (Getpoint "\nTouch first line: ") "Nea"))
(Setvar "Lastpoint" P1) (Initget 1)
(Setq P2 (Osnap (Getpoint "\nTouch second line: ") "Per"))
(Initget 1) (Setq STR (Getstring t "Enter text: "))
(Setq H (/ (Distance P1 P2) 2.0))
(Setq P3 (Polar P1 (Setq A (Angle P1 P2)) H))
(Command "Text" "M" P3 H (- (/ (* A 180.0) Pi) 90) STR)
(Princ))
```

TO INVOKE: Save this macro as an AutoLISP file (**.lsp**).

LET'S TRY IT: Get into a drawing and create two parallel lines (using **OFFSET** or Macro 64, Parallel Lines. Load **MACRO44** (**Load "Macro44"**) and type **TBPL**. The bottom of the text will appear closest to the first line you touch. The second line determines the angle and distance of the two lines. Then enter your text, which will be placed midway between the lines, with **MIDDLE** justification.

TO REVISE: If you require a set text height, you can either hardcode the height into the macro or create a prompt that asks for it.

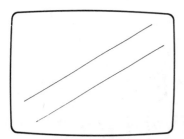 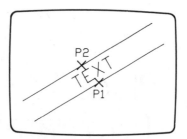

45 Import

PURPOSE: Allows you to input an ASCII text file into your drawing, controlling text height, line spacing and justification.

TO CREATE:

```
(Defun C:Import ()
 (Setvar "Cmdecho" 0)
 (If (= JUST nil) (Setq TSIZE 0.156 LSPACE 0.375 JUST "L"))
 (If (= EFNAM nil) (Setq EFNAM ""))
 (Setq X (Getstring (Strcat "\nEnter the ASCII text file name< "
  EFNAM ">: ")))
 (If (/= X "") (Setq EFNAM X))
 (Setq EFPNT (Open EFNAM "r"))
 (If
  (= EFPNT nil)
   (Princ (Strcat "\n"(Chr 34) EFNAM (Chr 34) ": Can't open file"))
   (Progn
    (Initget 6)
    (Setq X (Getdist (Strcat "\nEnter the text height< "
```

```
 (Rtos TSIZE 2 3) ">: ")))
(If (/= X nil) (Setq TSIZE X))
(Initget 2)
(Setq X (Getdist (Strcat "\nEnter the line spacing< "
 (Rtos LSPACE 2 3) ">: ")))
(If (/= X nil) (Setq LSPACE X))
(Initget 1 "C M R")
(Setq X (Getpoint "\nStart point or Center/Middle/Right: "))
(Cond
 ((= (Type X) 'List) (Setq P1 X) (Setq JUST "L"))
 ((= X "C") (Setq JUST X)
 (Initget 1)
 (Setq P1 (Getpoint "\nCenter point: "))
 )
 ((= X "M") (Setq JUST X)
 (Initget 1)
 (Setq P1 (Getpoint "\nMiddle point: "))
 )
 ((= X "R") (Setq JUST X)
 (Initget 1)
 (Setq P1 (Getpoint "\nEnd point: "))
 )
)
(Setq CRNTL (Read-line EFPNT))
(While
 CRNTL
  (If
   (= JUST "L")
     (Command "Text" P1 TSIZE 0 CRNTL)
     (Command "Text" JUST P1 TSIZE 0 CRNTL)
  )
  (Setq P1 (List (Car P1) (- (Cadr P1) LSPACE)))
  (Setq CRNTL (Read-line EFPNT))
 )
(Close EFPNT)
```

```
        )
    )
  (Princ)
)
```

TO INVOKE: Save this macro as an AutoLISP file **(.lsp)**.

LET'S TRY IT: Get into an AutoCAD drawing and load **MACRO45 (Load "Macro45")**. Because **MACRO45.LSP** is an ASCII text file, let's **IM-PORT** it into your drawing. Type **IMPORT** and follow the prompts:

```
Enter the ASCII text filename <DEF>: IMPORT.LSP
Enter the text height <DEF>: .125
Enter the line spacing <DEF>: .25
Start point or Center/Middle/Right: (Your choice)
```

The **MACRO45.LSP** file will be placed into your drawing line by line.

TIPS: When you enter a filename, enter the entire name, including any path and extension.

MACRO
46 Export

PURPOSE: Allows you to pick text from a drawing and **EXPORT** it to an ASCII file for further processing. You then can use Macro 45 (Import) to retrieve it.

TO CREATE:

```
(Defun C:Export () (Setvar "Cmdecho" 0)
(Setq A (Getstring "\nEnter the file name: "))
(Setq B (Open A "r")) (If B (Progn
(Princ "\nFile already exists.") (Close B) (Initget "Y N")
```

```
(Setq X (Getkword "\nWould you like to over-write? <N>
"))
(If (= X "Y") (Write-it))) (Write-it)) (Princ))
(Defun Write-it () (Setq C (Open A "w"))
(Prompt "\nFile now open")
(Prompt "\nPick items in order to write to file") (Setq D 0)
(Setq E (Ssget)) (Setq F (Sslength E)) (Repeat F
(Setq G (Ssname E D)) (Setq H (Entget G))
(Setq I (Cdr (Assoc 1 H))) (Write-line I C) (Setq D (+ 1 D)))
(Close C))
```

TO INVOKE: Save this macro as an AutoLISP file (**.lsp**).

LET'S TRY IT: Get into a drawing and load **MACRO46** (**Load "Macro46"**). Input text into the drawing, type **EXPORT** and follow the prompts:

```
Enter the filename: (Enter a filename to store the text in—any
                     DOS-supported name, with or without paths
                     and extensions.)
```

If the file already exists the system will prompt:

```
File already exists.
Would you like to over-write it? <N>: (Y or N or DEFAULT)
File now open
Pick items in order to write to file
```

```
Select objects:        (Pick the text you want to write to the file. You
                       should pick one item at a time, because pick-
                       ing items with a WINDOW might reverse the
                       text. When you've selected the objects, hit
                       RETURN and your selections will be written
                       to the file.)
```

TIPS: If you accidentally pick an entity that is not text, this routine won't work.

MACRO 47　List Length

PURPOSE: When you need to know a line length, you can use AutoCAD's **LIST** command, which gives you length, angle, start point, end point, delta X change, and so on — often more information than you want.

TO CREATE:

```
(Defun C:Llen () (Setvar "Cmdecho" 0)
(Setq A (Entsel "\nPick line: "))
(If A (Progn (Setq B (Entget (Car A))) (If
(= "LINE" (Cdr (Assoc 0 B))) (Progn (Setq Dl (Rtos
(Distance (Cdr (Assoc 10 B)) (Cdr (Assoc 11 B)))
(Getvar "Lunits") (Getvar "Luprec")))
(Princ (Strcat "\nLength of line is " Dl ".")))
(Princ "\nSelected entity is not a LINE")))
(Princ "\nNo entity found at that location")) (Princ))
```

TO INVOKE: Save this macro as an AutoLISP file (**.lsp**).

LET'S TRY IT: Get into AutoCAD and draw a few lines. Load **MACRO47** (**Load** "**Macro47**") and type **LLEN**. At the prompt, select a line. If you select an object that isn't a line, you'll be prompted **Selected entity is not a line**.

MACRO 48 Included Angle

PURPOSE: Places an angular dimension to give you the angle between two lines—a function AutoCAD forgot to give us. After reading it, you **ERASE** it. Cumbersome, no? This function quickly determines an included angle.

TO CREATE:

```
(Defun C:Iang () (Setvar "Cmdecho" 0)
(Setq A (Entsel "\nTouch first line: "))
(If A (Progn (Setq B (Entget (Car A))) (If
(= "LINE" (Cdr (Assoc 0 B))) (Progn
(Setq C (Entsel "\nTouch second line: "))
(If C (Progn (Setq D (Entget (Car C)))
(If (= "LINE" (Cdr (Assoc 0 D))) (Progn
(Setq P1 (Osnap (Cadr A) "MID")) (Setq P2 (Osnap (Cadr C) "MID"))
(Setq P3 (Inters (Cdr (Assoc 10 B)) (Cdr (Assoc 11 B))
(Cdr (Assoc 10 D)) (Cdr (Assoc 11 D)) ONSEG))
(Setq ANG (- (Angle P3 P2) (Angle P3 P1)))
(Setq ANG (Angtos ANG (Getvar "Aunits") (Getvar "Auprec")))
(Princ (Strcat "\nIncluded angle is " ANG ".")))
(Princ "\nObject selected is not a LINE")))
(Princ "\nNo object found at that location")))
(Princ "\nObject selected is not a LINE")))
(Princ "\nNo object found at that location")) (Princ))
```

TO INVOKE: Save this macro as an AutoLISP file (**.lsp**).

LET'S TRY IT: Get into AutoCAD and draw a few lines. Load **MACRO48** (**Load** "**Macro48**") and type **IANG**. You'll be asked to **Touch first line**, then **Touch second line**. The included angle will be reported.

TIPS: This macro works counterclockwise. The correct angle will be reported for lines picked in that direction; the complementary angle will be reported for lines chosen clockwise. Also, this routine won't measure or subtract parallel lines.

MACRO 49 Change Line Length

PURPOSE: Lets you quickly add to the length of a line.

TO CREATE:

```
(Defun C:Cll () (Setvar "Cmdecho" 0)
(Setq OM (Getvar "Orthomode")) (Setvar "Orthomode" 0)
(Setq A (Entsel "\nPick line to change: "))
(If A (Progn (Setq B (Entget (Car A)))
(If (= "LINE" (Cdr (Assoc 0 B))) (Progn
(Setq P1 (Osnap (Cadr A) "END")) (Setq P2 (Osnap (Cadr A) "MID"))
(Initget 1)
(Setq D1 (Distance (Cdr (Assoc 10 B)) (Cdr (Assoc 11 B))))
(Setq D1 (Rtos D1 (Getvar "Lunits") (Getvar "Luprec")))
(Princ (Strcat "\nLine is currently " D1))
(Setq D2 (Getdist P1 "\nAmount to add to line: "))
(Setq P3 (Polar P1 (Angle P2 P1) D2))
(Command "Change" (Car A) "" P3))
(Princ "\nObject selected is not a LINE")))
(Princ "\nNo object found at that location"))
(Setvar "Orthomode" OM) (Princ))
```

TO INVOKE: Save this macro as an AutoLISP file (**.lsp**).

LET'S TRY IT: Get into AutoCAD and add a few random lines. Load **MACRO49 (Load "Macro49")**. Type **CLL**. At the prompt, pick the line you wish to change near the end you wish to lengthen.

The line length will be reported, then you'll be asked how much you want to add. You can add that amount either by specifying a number or selecting a point.

TIPS: Turn **ORTHO OFF** before using this routine.

MACRO
50 AutoSave

PURPOSE: Automatically saves a drawing file for a specified length of time.

TO CREATE: To create this, we will use the LISP code and either modify a menu or create a new one. First the LISP.

```
(Defun C:AUSV () (Setvar "Cmdecho" 0) (If (= SAVETIME nil)
(Progn (Initget "Y N")
(Setq A (Getkword "\nDo you wish to invoke AutoSAVE <Y>: "))
(If (Or (= A nil) (= A "Y")) (Progn (Initget 1)
(Setq SAVETIME (Getreal "\nEnter minutes between saves: "))
(Setq SAVETIME (/ SAVETIME 1440.0))
(Defun C:Ausv () (If
(> (- (Getvar "Date") (Getvar "Tdupdate")) SAVETIME)
(Progn (Princ "\nSaving drawing file.....") (Command "Save" "")
)) (Princ))) (Defun C:Ausv () (Princ))))) (Princ))
```

Now for the menu item (if you have an existing menu, you can modify it as described below). For example, you might have a square for **LINE** that currently reads: ^C^CLine;. You should change this to include the AutoSAVE feature like this: ^C^CAusv;Line;. Now each time you pick **LINE**, your drawing will be saved if needed. Add this to several of the more commonly used commands on your menu. **ERASE**, **ZOOM**, **CIRCLE** and **CHANGE** are a few good candidates.

IMPORTANT NOTE: Once you've loaded AutoSAVE (either via **ACAD.LSP** or manually), you must invoke it. If you don't, AutoCAD will report an error, which will have no effect on the operation or the drawing file, but can be annoying.

TO INVOKE: Save this macro as an AutoLISP file (**.lsp**).

LET'S TRY IT: Get into a drawing and make sure that **MACRO50** is loaded. If not, load it (**Load "Macro50"**). Now pick the **LINE** command. You'll be asked if you wish to invoke AutoSAVE. If **Yes**, you'll be asked for the number of minutes between each save.

TIPS: This macro must be loaded into the drawing file each time you enter the drawing editor (for easier loading, you can place it into the **ACAD.LSP** file). Next it must be activated. The best way to do this is to add it to certain items in a menu file. If you add it to a tablet menu square that invokes the **LINE** command, each time you pick the **LINE** command it will check the amount of time since you last saved and **SAVE** if needed. This causes no noticeable time degradation if saving isn't required.

MACRO
51 Filter

PURPOSE: Lets you select objects in the drawing database by **FILTER**ing. You can select by entity type, **LAYER**, **COLOR** or any combination. For example, you can easily select all **LINE**s on **LAYER 1**, or all **CIRCLE**s on **LAYER 2** with the color **3** (Green). You may wish to select *all* lines in a drawing. This macro allows this and more.

TO CREATE:
```
(Defun C:FILTER () (Setvar "Cmdecho" 0)
(Setq ENTITY nil LAYER nil COLOR nil FLTRLIST nil)

(Menu) (Princ))
```

```
(Defun Menu () (Textscr) (Repeat 6 (Terpri))
(Princ "                    FILTER  MENU\n") (Terpri)
(Princ "               A = Enter an Entity type\n")
(Princ "               B = Enter a Layer name\n")
(Princ "               C = Enter a Color number\n")
(Princ "               X = Build filter list\n")
(Princ "              XX = Exit filter program\n")
(Repeat 7 (Terpri)) (Initget "A B C X XX")
(Setq LETR (Getkword "\n=======>>Select and Enter Letter: "))
(Cond ((= LETR "A")
(Setq ENTITY (Strcase (Getstring "\nEnter the Entity type: ")))
(Setq ENTITY (Cons 0 (Eval ENTITY))) (Menu)) ((= LETR "B")
(Setq LAYER (Strcase (Getstring "\nEnter the Layer name: ")))
(Setq LAYER (Cons 8 (Eval LAYER))) (Menu)) ((= LETR "C")
(Setq COLOR (Getreal "\nEnter the color number: "))
(Setq COLOR (Cons 62 (Eval COLOR))) (Menu))
((= LETR "XX") (Ender)) ((= LETR "X") (Build))
((/= LETR nil) (Menu))))


(Defun Ender () (Graphscr) (Command))


(Defun Build ()
(If (/= ENTITY nil) (Setq FLTRLIST (List (Eval 'ENTITY))))
(If (And LAYER FLTRLIST) (Setq FLTRLIST (Cons LAYER FLTRLIST)))
(If (And (= FLTRLIST nil) LAYER)
(Setq FLTRLIST (List (Eval 'LAYER))))
(If (And COLOR FLTRLIST) (Setq FLTRLIST (Cons COLOR FLTRLIST)))
(If (And COLOR (= FLTRLIST nil))
(Setq FLTRLIST (List (Eval 'COLOR)))) (Action))


(Defun Action () (Textscr) (Repeat 6 (Terpri))
(Princ "  What do you want to do with this selection set??\n")
(Terpri)
(Princ "            A = Erase\n")
(Princ "            B = Move\n")
```

```
(Princ "              C = Copy\n")
(Princ "              D = Change layer\n")
(Princ "              E = Change color\n")
(Princ "              F = Count\n")
(Princ "              XX = Exit and build selection set\n")
(Repeat 6 (Terpri)) (Initget "A B C D E F XX")
(Setq LETR (Getkword "\n=======>>Select and Enter Letter: "))
(If (= LETR "A") (Command "Erase" (Ssget "X" FLTRLIST)))
(If (= LETR "B") (Command "Move" (Ssget "X" FLTRLIST)))
(If (= LETR "C") (Command "Copy" (Ssget "X" FLTRLIST)))
(If (= LETR "D") (Command "Change" (Ssget "X" FLTRLIST)
"" "P" "LA")) (If (= LETR "E") (Command "Change"
(Ssget "X" FLTRLIST) "" "P" "C")) (If (= LETR "F")
(Progn
(Princ "\nYou have selected ")
(Princ (Sslength (Ssget "X" FLTRLIST))) (Princ " items.")
(Princ)))
(If (= LETR "XX") (Ssget "X" FLTRLIST)))
```

TO INVOKE: Save this macro as an AutoLISP file (**.lsp**).

LET'S TRY IT: Get into a drawing of some complexity (if you don't have one, call up one of AutoCAD's DEMO drawings). Create several entities of differing colors on different layers. Then, load **MACRO51** (**Load "Macro51"**). Type **FILTER.** You will be asked to choose one of many menu options. If you want to **ERASE** all lines on a given layer, pick **A,** enter **LINE,** then pick **B** and enter the layer name.

When finished, pick **X** to build the selection set. You'll be asked to make a choice from a menu. To **ERASE** entities, pick **A.** Each item filtered out will be chosen and highlighted. Now you'll be able to use AutoCAD's interactive selection process to remove or add to the selection set. When finished, hit (**RETURN**). This macro is complex, so you may need to work with it a bit.

TO REVISE: This is just a short version of what could really be done with the **ssget** function. For more ideas, see the *AutoLISP Programmer's Reference.*

TIPS: This routine works only on one layer and one entity type at a time.

MACRO
52 Clean !

PURPOSE: Cleans the AutoLISP **Atomlist** to provide more room for functions and variables. This macro should be used only if you aren't using (**vmon**) in your **ACAD.LSP** file. If you're not using (**vmon**) in the **ACAD.LSP** file (which you should), this macro shouldn't be used under any circumstances, as it will destroy the existing **Atomlist**.

TO CREATE:

```
(Defun C:Clean () (Setq Atomlist (Member 'Inters Atomlist)) (Gc))
```

TO INVOKE: Save this macro as an AutoLISP file (**.lsp**).

LET'S TRY IT: First, get into a drawing and create some variables. At the **Command:** prompt, type:

```
(Setq A 1 B 2 C 3)
```

Now type **!ATOMLIST** to view the three variables you've just set. You should see a list of all functions and assigned variables, with your three listed first. (Actually they're the last ones added because AutoLISP puts them in reverse order.)

To clean the **Atomlist**, load **MACRO52** (**Load "Macro52"**), and type **CLEAN**. Type **!ATOMLIST** again, and your variables will be gone.

TO REVISE: This macro works well when loaded before the **Atomlist** is cleaned. However, if you wait until you get an error from AutoLISP concerning space limitations, you may not have enough room left to load the function. If you can't load it, you can't use it. One way around this problem is to make a menu item instead of an AutoLISP item. This means that it's never loaded into the drawing, but can be used at any time from a tablet. The tablet item would read:

```
^C^C(Setq Atomlist (Member 'Inters Atomlist));(Gc);
```

TIPS: Be forewarned that **CLEAN**ing **Atomlist** with this function will remove any other functions you've loaded, including **Atomlist**.

MACRO
53 Play

PURPOSE: Demonstrates the use of **grread** and **grdraw** functions. The line work it creates doesn't really exist. If the macro appears to ruin a drawing, **REDRAW** will return you to the original drawing.

TO CREATE:
```
(Defun C:Play ()
(Initget 7) (Setq CLR (Getint
"\nEnter color number that you wish to play with: "))
(Initget 1) (Setq PNT (Getpoint "\nEnter point to play at: "))
(While t (Grdraw PNT (Cadr (Grread 5)) CLR) (Princ)))
```

TO INVOKE: Save this macro as an AutoLISP file (**.lsp**).

LET'S TRY IT: Get into any AutoCAD drawing and load **MACRO53** (**Load** "**MACRO53**"). Type **PLAY**. Choose a color and type a number that represents it. Pick a working point. Vectors will be generated from the point you selected to the current position of your cursor in the specified color. Vectors will continue to be generated until you hit any key, which will cause an error and stop the macro.

MACRO
54 Timer

PURPOSE: Tells you how fast your machine **REGEN**s or **REDRAW**s. This can be useful when testing different variables or equipment.

TO CREATE:

```
(Defun C:Timer () (Setvar "Cmdecho" 0) (Setvar "Gridmode" 0)
(Initget 1 "RED REG") (Setq X (Getkword "REDraw/REGeg: "))
(If (= X "RED") (Setq X "REDRAW") (Setq X "REGEN")) (Initget 7)
(Setq A (Getint "\nEnter number of times for average: "))
(Setq B (Getvar "Tdusrtimer")) (Repeat A (Command X))
(Setq C (* 86400.0 (- (Getvar "Tdusrtimer") B))) (Setq D (/ C A))
(Setq C (Rtos C 2 3)) (Setq D (Rtos D 2 3)) (Textscr)
(Princ (Strcat "\nTotal time for " X "(s) was " C " seconds."))
(Princ (Strcat "\nAverage time for " X " was " D " seconds."))
(Princ))
```

TO INVOKE: Save this macro as an AutoLISP file (**.lsp**).

LET'S TRY IT: Get into an AutoCAD drawing and load **MACRO54** (**Load "Macro54"**). Type **TIMER**, then indicate whether you want to time **REGEN** or **REDRAW**. You'll be asked how many times you want to time them so the macro can figure an average. Finally, the macro will report the total elapsed time and the average for each.

TO REVISE: It's best to run this test on the same drawing each time. You might even add a second function to the macro that creates the drawing you'll time. Let's add a function that generates a 33 by 33 matrix of circles to be timed. Simply add this function to the file that contains **TIMER**.

```
(Defun C:Circ ()
  (Setvar "Cmdecho" 0)
  (Command "Circle" "0,0" "0.5")
  (Command "Array" "L" "" "R" "33" "33" "1.25" "1.25")
  (Command "Zoom" "E")
 (Princ)
)
```

MACRO 55 Chamfer with Angle

PURPOSE: AutoCAD lets you create chamfered corners on objects by specifying the distance along each line from the corner. Most chamfers are specified a certain distance from the corner along one line and a specified angle from the same line. This macro lets you specify in this manner.

TO CREATE:

```
(Defun C:Cmfang () (Setvar "Cmdecho" 0)
(Setq A (Getdist "\nDistance along first line: "))
(Setq B (Getangle "\nAngle from first line: "))
(Setq B (* A (/ (Sin B) (Cos B))))
(Setq C (Entsel "\nFirst line: "))
(If C (Progn (Setq D (Entget (Car C))) (If
(= "LINE" (Cdr (Assoc 0 D))) (Progn
(Setq E (Entsel "\nSecond line: ")) (If E (Progn
(Setq F (Entget (Car E))) (If (= "LINE" (Cdr (Assoc 0 F)))
(Progn (Command "Chamfer" "D" A B)
(Command "Chamfer" (Cadr C) (Cadr E)))
(Princ "\nObject selected is not a LINE")))
(Princ "\nNo object found at that location")))
(Princ "\nObject selected is not a LINE")))
(Princ "\nNo object found at that location")) (Princ))
```

TO INVOKE: Save this macro as an AutoLISP file (**.lsp**).

LET'S TRY IT: Get into AutoCAD and create a 5 X 3 rectangle. Load **MACRO55 (Load "Macro55")**. Type **CMFANG**. You will be prompted:

```
Distance along first line:  1
Angle from first line:     30
```

First line:	(Pick left vertical line.)
Second line:	(Pick top horizontal line.)

The macro now calculates the distance needed for the second line using the first distance and the angle you specified.

TIPS: This macro works properly only on 90 degree angles.

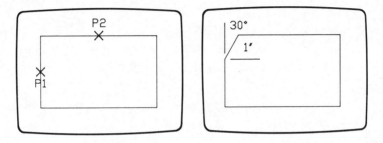

MACRO 56 3DBox

PURPOSE: Lets you create a three-dimensional box anywhere in space. This box can be created with **3DLINE**s or **3DFACE**s.

TO CREATE:

```
(Defun C:3dbox () (Setvar "Cmdecho" 0)
(Initget 7) (Setq W (Getreal "\nEnter width (X) of box: "))
(Initget 7) (Setq H (Getreal "\nEnter height (Y) of box: "))
(Initget 7) (Setq D (Getreal "\nEnter depth (Z) of box: "))
(Setq B (* W H D)) (Initget "L F")
(Setq A (Getkword "\nCreate box with 3dLine/3dFace>: "))
(Initget 17) (Setq Pl (Getpoint "Corner of box: "))
```

```
(Setq P2 (List (+ W (Car Pl)) (Cadr Pl) (Caddr Pl)))
(Setq P3 (List (Car P2) (+ H (Cadr P2)) (Caddr Pl)))
(Setq P4 (List (Car Pl) (Cadr P3) (Caddr Pl)))
(Setq P5 (List (Car Pl) (Cadr Pl) (+ D (Caddr Pl))))
(Setq P6 (List (Car P2) (Cadr P2) (Caddr P5)))
(Setq P7 (List (Car P6) (Cadr P3) (Caddr P5)))
(Setq P8 (List (Car P4) (Cadr P4) (Caddr P5)))
(Cond ((Or (= A nil) (= A "F"))
(Command "3dface" Pl P2 P3 P4 P8 P7 P6 P5 Pl P2 "")
(Command "3dface" Pl P5 P8 P4 "" "3dface" P2 P6 P7 P3 ""))
((= A "L") (Command "3dline" Pl P2 P3 P4 Pl P5 P8 P7 P6 P5 "")
(Command "3dline" P2 P6 "" "3dline" P7 P3 "" "3dline" P8 P4 "")))
(Princ "\nThe volume of this box is ") (Princ (Rtos B 2 4))
(Princ " square units.") (Princ))
```

TO INVOKE: Save this macro as an AutoLISP file (**.lsp**).

LET'S TRY IT: Get into an AutoCAD drawing and load **MACRO56** (**Load "Macro56"**). Type **3DBOX**. You'll be prompted:

```
Enter width (X) of box:          (Enter width.)
Enter height (Y) of box:         (Enter height.)
Enter depth (Z) of box:          (Enter depth.)
Create box with 3dLine/<3dFace>: (L or F.)
Corner of box:                   (Pick a point.)
```

A box will then be constructed (if constructed from **3DLINES** you'll get a wire frame model; if from **3DFACES**, it will appear as a solid box if you use the **HIDE** command).

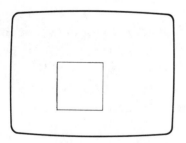
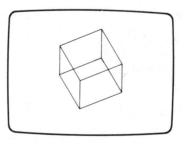

57 3DCircle

PURPOSE: Release 10 can now draw any entity anywhere in 3D space. This macro is for those who don't have Release 10 but would like to draw a circle on any plane. This macro creates a three-dimensional circle on any of the three planes.

TO CREATE:

```
(Defun C:3dC () (Setvar "Cmdecho" 0) (Setq A (/ Pi 18))
(Initget 1 "XY XZ YZ")
(Setq B (Getkword "Which plane, XY/XZ/YZ: "))
(Initget 17) (Setq P1 (Getpoint "Center point: "))
(Initget 7) (Setq R (Getdist P1 "Radius: ")) (Cond
((= B "XY") (Setq P2 (List (+ (Car P1) R) (Cadr P1) (Caddr P1)))
(Setq P3 (List (+ (Car P1) (* (Cos A) R)) (+ (Cadr P1)
(* (Sin A) R)) (Caddr P1))) (Repeat 36
(Command "3dline" P2 P3 "") (Setq P2 P3) (Setq A (+ A (/ Pi 18)))
(Setq P3 (List (+ (Car P1) (* (Cos A) R)) (+ (Cadr P1)
(* (Sin A) R)) (Caddr P1))))) ((= B "XZ")
(Setq P2 (List (+ (Car P1) R) (Cadr P1) (Caddr P1)))
(Setq P3 (List (+ (Car P1) (* (Cos A) R)) (Cadr P1)
(+ (Caddr P1) (* (Sin A) R)))) (Repeat 36
(Command "3dline" P2 P3 "") (Setq P2 P3) (Setq A (+ A (/ Pi 18)))
(Setq P3 (List (+ (Car P1) (* (Cos A) R)) (Cadr P1)
(+ (Caddr P1) (* (Sin A) R)))))) ((= B "YZ")
(Setq P2 (List (Car P1) (Cadr P1) (+ (Caddr P1) R)))
(Setq P3 (List (Car P1) (+ (Cadr P1) (* (Sin A) R))
(+ (Caddr P1) (* (Cos A) R)))) (Repeat 36
(Command "3dline" P2 P3 "") (Setq P2 P3) (Setq A (+ A
(/ Pi 18)))
(Setq P3 (List (Car P1) (+ (Cadr P1) (* (Sin A) R))
(+ (Caddr P1) (* (Cos A) R))))))) (Princ))
```

TO INVOKE: Save this macro as an AutoLISP file (**.lsp**).

LET'S TRY IT: Get into an AutoCAD drawing and load **MACRO57 (Load "Macro57")**. Type **3DC**. You can put your **CIRCLE** on any of three planes, **xy**, **xz**, and **yz**. (Imagine you are standing inside a box. If you look at the box top and bottom, you see the **xy** plane. Looking forward or backward, you see the **xz** plane. You face the **yz** plane when you look to the left and right.) Now enter the center point and radius, and a circle will be generated, composed of small **3DLINE** segments.

TO REVISE: This macro currently draws each circle as **3D** segments. If you wish it to draw more or fewer segments, replace the number **36** everywhere it occurs with the number of sides you want. Replace each occurrence of the number **18** with a number equal to one half the number of sides.

TIPS: For a more elaborate routine, see AutoCAD's bonus disk (Release 9).

MACRO
58 Rectangles and Squares

PURPOSE: Creates squares and rectangles by specifying two corners or lengths of the sides. This macro saves time by doing all the line work you usually must do manually. Unlike AutoCAD's screen **RECTANGLE** command, these macros draw rectangles and squares as **POLYLINE**s instead of **BLOCK**s.

TO CREATE:

```
(Defun C:R () (Setvar "Cmdecho" 0)
(Setq Pl (Getpoint "\nFirst corner: ")) (Initget 1 "E")
(Setq P3 (Getcorner Pl "\nEdge/ <Other corner>: "))
(If (/= "E" P3) (Progn
(Command "Pline" Pl (List (Car P3) (Cadr Pl)) P3
(List (Car Pl) (Cadr P3)) "C")) (Progn
(Setq A (Getdist "\nLength of first side: "))
(Initget "F") (Setq B (Getdist
"\nLength of second side/<Default=First side>: "))
(If (Or (= B nil) (= B "F")) (Setq B A))
(Command "Pline" Pl (Polar Pl 0 A)
(Polar (Getvar "Lastpoint") (/ Pi 2) B)
(Polar (Getvar "Lastpoint") Pi A) "C")))
(Princ "nRotation angle: ")
(Command "Rotate" "L" "" Pl Pause) (Initget "Y N")
(Setq C (Getkword "\nDo you wish to EXPLODE Pline <Y>: "))
(If (Or (= C nil) (= C Y)) (Command "Explode" "L")) (Princ))
```

TO INVOKE: Create this macro as an AutoLISP file (**.lsp**).

LET'S TRY IT: Get into an AutoCAD drawing and load **MACRO58** (**Load "Macro58"**). Type **R**. When prompted **First corner:**, pick a point for one corner of the rectangle. At the next prompt, **Edge/<Other corner>:**, you have a couple of choices. First, pick a point representing the diagonal corner point of the rectangle. If you would rather define the rectangle by specifying the lengths of the two sides than by picking the **Other corner:**, enter **E** for edge. Now you'll be asked for **Length of the first side:**, then prompted **Length of second side/<Default=First side>:**. Either specify a length or hit (**RETURN**) to leave it the same as the first. A rectangle will then be drawn as a **PLINE**. Next, specify a rotation angle for the rectangle. You can do this either with the cursor or by entering an angle from the keyboard. Finally, at **Do you wish to EXPLODE Pline <Y>:**, answer **Y** or **N** to the prompt.

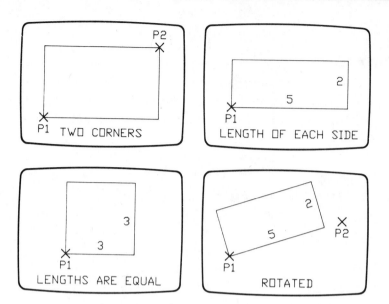

MACRO
59 Circle Tangent to Circle at Any Angle

PURPOSE: Allows you to draw a circle tangent to a circle (inside or outside an existing circle) at a specified radius and angle.

TO CREATE:

```
(Defun C:Ctc () (Setvar "Cmdecho" 0)
(Initget 1) (Setq A (Entsel "\nTouch circle: "))
(If A (Progn (Setq B (Entget (Car A))) (If
(= "CIRCLE" (Cdr (Assoc 0 B))) (Progn
(Setq P2 (Cdr (Assoc 10 B)))
(Setq P1 (Polar P2 0 (Cdr (Assoc 40 B)))) (Initget 1 "I O")
(Setq P3 (Getpoint "\nInside or Outside: ")) (Cond ((= P3 "I")
(Setq P3 (Polar P2 0 (/ (Cdr (Assoc 40 B)) 2.0)))) ((= P3 "O")
(Setq P3 (Polar P2 0 (* (Cdr (Assoc 40 B)) 2.0)))))
(Initget 7) (Setq CR (Getdist "\nCircle radius: "))
```

```
(Initget 1) (Setq AG (Getangle "\nCenter to center angle: "))
(Setq D1 (Distance P2 P1)) (Setq D2 (Distance P2 P3)) (If
(< D1 D2) (Setq D3 (+ D1 CR)) (Setq D3 (- D1 CR)))
(Command "Circle" (Polar P2 AG D3) CR))
(Princ "\nItem selected is not a CIRCLE")))
(Princ "\nNo item found at that location")) (Princ))
```

TO INVOKE: Add this macro to a space in your menu file.

LET'S TRY IT: Get into an AutoCAD drawing. Draw a **CIRCLE** with the center point anywhere you wish and a radius of **5**. **ZOOM EXTENTS** and load **MACRO59 (Load "Macro59")**. Type **CTC**. At the prompt, **Touch circle:**, touch the circle anywhere.

At the prompt, **Inside or Outside**, enter **I** or **O** or pick a point indicating whether your new circle will be inside or outside the old circle. Continue to follow the prompts:

```
Circle radius:          2
Center to center angle: 45
```

Now you've created a 2-inch radius circle tangent to the other circle on either the inside or outside (whichever you picked), with a 45 degree angle center-to-center.

TIPS: If you're drawing a circle inside an existing circle with a radius larger than the original circle's radius, the macro will draw a circle tangent to the original around its outside edge.

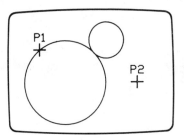
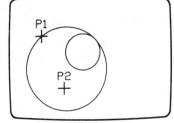

MACRO 60 Slots

PURPOSE: Creates a slot, including placement point, radius, length and angle.

TO CREATE:

```
(Defun C:Slot () (Setvar "Cmdecho" 0)
(Initget 1) (Setq Pl (Getpoint "\nInsertion point of slot: "))
(Initget 7) (Setq A (Getdist Pl "\nRadius: "))
(Initget 7) (Setq B (Getdist Pl "\nLength: "))
(Setq C (Getangle Pl "\nAngle: "))
(Command "Arc" "C" Pl (Polar Pl (+ (/ Pi 2) C) A) "A" "180")
(Command "Line" "" (Polar (Getvar "Lastpoint") A B) "")
(Command "Arc" "" (Polar (Getvar "Lastpoint") (+ (/ Pi 2) C)
(* 2 A)))
(Command "Line" "" (Polar (Getvar "Lastpoint") (+ Pi C) B) "")
(Princ))
```

TO INVOKE: Create this as an AutoLISP file (**.lsp**).

LET'S TRY IT: Get into an AutoCAD drawing and load **MACRO60 (Load "Macro60")**. Type **SLOT**. You'll be prompted:

```
Insertion point of slot: (Pick a point.)
Radius:        (Pick a point or enter a radius.)
Length:        (Pick a point or enter a length.)
Angle:         (Pick a point or enter an angle.)
```

Now, a slot will be drawn according to your specification.

MACRO 61 Beams

PURPOSE: Automates the drawing and coping of standard beams.

TO CREATE:

```
(Defun C:Beam () (Setvar "Cmdecho" 0)
(Initget 7) (Setq H (Getdist "\nEnter overall height of beam: "))
(Initget 7) (Setq FT (Getdist "\nEnter flange thickness: "))
(Initget 1) (Setq P1 (Getpoint "\nFrom point: "))
(Initget 1) (Setq P2 (Getpoint P1 "\nTo point: "))
(Setq P1 (Polar P1 (Setq A1 (+ (Angle P1 P2) (* 0.5 Pi)))
(* H 0.5))) (Setq P2 (Polar P2 A1 (* H 0.5)))
(Setq P3 (Polar P1 (Setq A2 (- (Angle P1 P2) (* 0.5 Pi))) H))
(Setq P4 (Polar P2 A2 H)) (Command "Line" P1 P2 "")
(Setq A (Entlast)) (Command "Copy" A "" P1 (Polar P1 A2 FT))
(Command "Line" P3 P4 "") (Setq A (Entlast))
(Command "Copy" A "" P3 (Polar P3 A1 FT))
(Command "Line" P1 P3 "" "Line" P2 P4 "") (Princ))
(Defun C:Cope () (Setvar "Cmdecho" 0)
(Initget 7) (Setq DC (Getdist "\nDepth of cut: "))
(Initget 7) (Setq LC (Getdist "\nLength of cut: "))
(Initget 1) (Setq P1 (Osnap (Getpoint "\nTouch Corner: ") "Int"))
(Initget 1) (Setq P2 (Osnap (Getpoint P1
"\nTouch point on flange surface: ") "Nea"))
(Initget 1) (Setq P3 (Osnap (Getpoint P1
"\nTouch end of beam: ") "Nea"))
(Setq P2 (Polar P1 (Angle P1 P2) LC))
(Setq P3 (Polar P1 (angle P1 P3) DC))
(Setq P4 (Polar P3 (Angle P1 P2) LC))
(Command "Line" P2 P4 "") (Setq A (SSadd (Entlast)))
(Command "Line" P4 P3 "") (Setq A (Ssadd (entlast) A))
(Command "Trim" A "" (Osnap P1 "END") (Osnap P1 "END")
(Osnap P1 "END") "") (Princ))
```

TO INVOKE: Create this macro as an AutoLISP file (**.lsp**).

LET'S TRY IT: Get into an AutoCAD drawing and load **MACRO61** (**Load "Macro61"**). This macro is actually two separate macros. The first creates the beam according to the sizes that the user inputs. The second copes the ends that the user picks. Let's start by drawing a beam. Type **BEAM**.

```
Enter overall height of beam:     (Enter a distance in inches.)
Enter flange thickness:           (Enter a distance in inches.)
From point:                       (Pick a point.)
To point:                         (Pick a point.)
Command: Zoom Extents
```

Now that the beam is created, let's cope one of the corners. Type **COPE**.

```
Depth of cut:                     (Enter a distance)
Length of cut:                    (Enter a distance)
```

These next three points are very important.

```
Touch corner:           (At this point you need to make sure you touch
                          the very corner of the end you are coping.)
Touch point on flange surface:    (You must touch the outside
                                   edge of the flange that you
                                   are coping.)
Touch end of beam:      (Touch the line that represents the end
                         of the beam that you are coping.)
```

At this point, AutoCAD will draw in the lines that represent the edges of the coped end and trim any lines that need to be trimmed.

TIPS: We have found there are times when the coping portion of this macro doesn't work. That has to do with the size of the object on the screen. If the lines that represent the flange thickness appear as one, it may not function properly. If so, you may need to **ZOOM** in a little bit to make them separate. If the lines are too far apart, it will tend to leave one line untrimmed. It is very easy to use the **TRIM** function to clean up this line. Remember, these macros are for general use and you should build upon them to create exactly what you want.

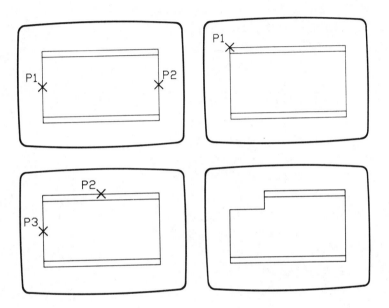

<h1>MACRO
62 Round to Round
Transitions</h1>

PURPOSE: Calculates and draws the flat pattern layout of a round-to-round transition. It will also draw the side view. This is a good example of a program that will perform the engineering calculations normally done manually.

TO CREATE:

```
(Defun C:RTR () (Setvar "Cmdecho" 0)
(Setq DS (Getvar "Dimscale"))
(Setq LOD (Getreal "\nLarge O.D.: "))
(Setq SOD (Getreal "\nSmall O.D.: "))
(Setq H (Getreal "\nHeight of transition: "))
(Setq PL (Getreal "\nPlate thickness: "))
(Setq P5 (Getpoint "\nStarting point: ")) (Setq D (- LOD PL))
(Setq D1 (- SOD PL)) (Setq B (/ (- D D1) 2.0))
(Setq C (Sqrt (+ (* H H) (* B B)))) (Setq R1 (/ D1 2.0))
(Setq ALPHA (Atan (/ B H))) (Setq E (/ R1 (Sin ALPHA)))
(Setq R (+ C E)) (Setq BETA (* 360.0 (/ (/ D 2.0) R)))
(Setq P1(Polar P5(- (* Pi 0.5) (* Pi (/ (/ BETA 2.0) 180.0))) R))
(Setq P2(Polar P5(+ (* Pi 0.5) (* Pi (/ (/ BETA 2.0) 180.0))) R))
(Setq P3(Polar P5(- (* Pi 0.5) (* Pi (/ (/ BETA 2.0) 180.0))) E))
(Setq P4(Polar P5(+ (* Pi 0.5) (* Pi (/ (/ BETA 2.0) 180.0))) E))
(Command "Line" P1 P3 "" "Line" P2 P4 "" "Arc" P1 "E" P2 "A"
BETA "Arc" P3 "E" P4 "A" BETA)
(Setq P1 (List (- (Car P2) (* 4.0 DS)) (Cadr P4)))
(Setq P2 (Polar P1 Pi LOD))
(Setq P3 (List (+ (Car P2) (/ (- LOD SOD) 2.0)) (+ (Cadr P2) H)))
(Setq P4 (Polar P3 0 SOD)) (Command "Line" P1 P2 P3 P4 "C")
(Princ))
```

TO INVOKE: Create this macro as an AutoLISP file (**.lsp**).

LET'S TRY IT: Get into a new AutoCAD drawing and load **MACRO62** (**Load "Macro62"**). Type **RTR**. You'll be prompted:

```
Large O.D.: 24
Small O.D.: 12
Height of transition: 12
Plate thickness: .25
Starting point: 0,0
```

TO REVISE: You could add dimensions to the macro (as in Macro 68, "Baseplates").

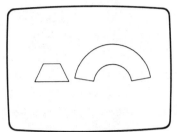

```
Large O.D.=24
Small O.D.=12
Height=12
Plate=.25
```

MACRO
63 Flanges

PURPOSE: Automates the process of drawing common types of flanges with user-specified data. This macro creates an all-purpose flange that you can customize to your own needs. The example below shows how to set up the geometric construction and information prompts.

TO CREATE:

Note: This macro has several "human factors" functions built in.

1) It won't let you enter an inside diameter larger than the outside diameter.

2) It won't let you create a bolt circle larger than the outside diameter or smaller than the inside diameter.

3) It won't let you create a bolt hole size that would cut through the inside or outside edge of the flange.

4) It won't allow more bolt holes of the specified size than would fit on the flange.

```
(Defun C:Flange () (Setvar "Cmdecho" 0) (Setq OR 0) (Setq IR 0)
(Setq BC 0) (Initget 1)
(Setq P1 (Getpoint "\nEnter center of flange: ")) (Initget 7)
(Setq OR (Getdist P1 "\nOutside radius: "))
(Command "Circle" P1 OR) (Initget 7)
(Setq IR (Getdist P1 "\nInside radius: ")) (While (> IR OR)
(Prompt "\nInside radius larger than outside: ") (Initget 7)
(Setq IR (Getdist P1 "\nInside radius: ")))
(Command "Circle" P1 IR) (Setq BAD t) (While BAD (Setq A nil)
(Setq B nil) (Initget 7) (Setq BC (Getdist P1
"\nBolt circle radius: ")) (If (> BC OR) (Prompt
"\nBolt circle larger than O.D.: ") (Setq A t)) (If (< BC IR)
(Prompt "\nBolt circle smaller than I.D.: ") (Setq B t)) (If
(And A B) (Setq BAD nil))) (Command "Circle" P1 BC) (Setq BAD t)
(While BAD (Setq A nil) (Setq B nil) (Initget 7) (Setq SH
(Getreal "\nBolt hole diameter: ")) (If (>= (* 0.5 SH) (- BC IR))
(Prompt "\nBolt hole cuts through inside edge: ") (Setq A t)) (If
(>= (* 0.5 SH) (- OR BC)) (Prompt
"\nBolt hole cuts through outside edge: ") (Setq B t)) (If
(And A B) (Setq BAD nil))) (Initget 7) (Setq NHI (Getint
"\nNumber of bolt holes: ")) (Setq NH (Float NHI)) (Setq NUM
(Fix (/ (* Pi (* BC 2.0)) (+ 0.5 SH)))) (While (> NHI NUM) (Princ
(Strcat "\nToo many holes, maximum allowed is " (Itoa NUM)))
(Initget 7) (Setq NHI (Getint "\nNumber of bolt holes: "))
(Setq NH (Float NHI))) (Initget 5) (Setq SA (Getangle
P1 "\nStarting angle of first hole: ")) (Command "Circle"
(Polar P1 SA BC) "D" SH) (Command "Array" "L" "" "C" P1
(/ 360.0 NH) NHI "") (Princ))
```

TO INVOKE: Create this macro as an AutoLISP file (**.lsp**).

LET'S TRY IT: Get into a new AutoCAD drawing and load **MACRO63**
(**Load** "**Macro63**"). Type **FLANGE**.

Enter center of flange:	(Pick a point.)
Outside radius:	(Pick a point or enter a number.)
Inside radius:	(Pick a point or enter a number.)
Bolt circle radius:	(Pick a point or enter a number.)
Bolt hole diameter:	(Enter the diameter.)
Number of bolt holes:	(Enter an integer value.)
Starting angle of first hole:	(Pick a point or enter a number.)

TO REVISE: This macro draws everything on the current layer, in one color and one linetype. You can use this format, then change the properties of the entities to suit your needs.

MACRO 64 Parallel Lines, Double off One Side

PURPOSE: Allows you to draw a pair of lines that represents a wall or pipeline in the same manner as you would draw a single line. This macro draws a **PLINE** along specified points, then **OFFSET**s the **PLINE** according to your previous specifications. It prompts for the distance between lines, then acts in the same manner as the **LINE** command. Points can be entered in any direction you wish.

TO CREATE:

```
(Defun C:Wall () (Set
var "Cmdecho" 0) (Initget "S C E")
(Setq B (Getkword "\nJustification-Specify 2/Center/<Edge>: "))
(If (= nil B) (Setq B "E")) (If (Or (= B "E") (= B "C")) (Progn
(Prompt "\nEnter width of wall <")
(Princ (Rtos (Getvar "Userr1") 2 3))
(Initget 6) (Setq A (Getdist ">: "))
(If (= nil A) (Setq A (Getvar "Userr1")) (Setvar "Userr1" A)))
(Progn (Initget 7)
(Setq A1 (Getdist "\nEnter first thickness: "))
```

```
(Initget 7) (Setq A2 (Getdist "\nEnter second thickness: "))))
(Initget 1) (Setq P1 (Getpoint "\nFrom point: ")) (Initget 1)
(Setq P2 (Getpoint P1 "\nTo point: ")) (Command "Pline" P1 P2)
(Setq P4 t) (While (Boundp 'P4) (Initget "U C")
(Setq P4 (Getpoint (Getvar "Lastpoint") "\nTo point: ")) (Cond
((= nil P4) (Command "")) ((= "C" P4) (Command "CL")
(Setq P4 nil)) ((= "U" P4) (Command "U")) ((= 'LIST (Type P4))
(Command P4)))) (Cond ((= B "E") (Setq E2 (Entlast))
(Setq P2 (Getpoint "\nSide to offset wall: "))
(Command "Offset" A P1 P2 "") (Setq E3 (Entlast))) ((= B "C")
(Setq E1 (Entlast)) (Command "Select" "L" "")
(Command "Offset" (/ A 2) (Polar P1 (Angle P1 P2)
(/ (Distance P1 P2) 2)) (Polar (Getvar "Lastpoint")
(+ (/ Pi 2) (Angle P1 P2)) (/ A 2)) "") (Setq E2 (Entlast))
(Command "Offset" A (Getvar "Lastpoint")
(Polar (Getvar "Lastpoint") (+ (/ Pi 2) (Angle P2 P1)) A) "")
(Setq E3 (Entlast))) ((= B "S") (Setq E1 (Entlast))
(Command "Select" "L" "") (Prompt "\nSide for ")
(Princ (Rtos A1 2 4)) (Setq P2 (Getpoint " offset: "))
(Command "Offset" A1 P1 P2 "") (Setq E2 (Entlast))
(Prompt "\nSide for ") (Princ (Rtos A2 2 4))
(Setq P2 (Getpoint " offset: ")) (Command "Offset" A2 P1 P2 "")
(Setq E3 (Entlast)))) (If (Or (= B "S") (= B "C")) (Progn
(Prompt "\nWhat would you like to do with the center line?")
(Initget "E L M") (Setq A (Getkword
"\nErase it/Leave as is/<Make centerline>: ")) (Cond ((= A "E")
(Command "Erase" "P" "")) ((Or (= A "M") (= A nil))
(Command "Change" "P" "" "P" "LA" "CENTER" "")))))
(Initget "Y N") (Setq A (Getkword
"\nWalls are PLINES, Do you wish to EXPLODE them, N/<Y>: "))
(If (Or (= A "Y") (= A nil))
(Command "Explode" E2 "Explode" E3 "Explode" E1 ^C)) (Princ))
```

TO INVOKE: Create this as an AutoLISP file (**.lsp**).

LET'S TRY IT: Get into a new AutoCAD drawing and load **MACRO64** (**Load "Macro64"**). Create a new layer, **CENTER**. Type **WALL**. You'll be prompted **Justification-Specify 2/Center/<Edge>:**. Options are described below, beginning with the default **Edge**.

Type **E** or hit **RETURN**. You'll be prompted **Enter width of wall <Default>:**. Specify the width or hit **RETURN** for default. Now pick your points as you would with the **LINE** command (you're allowed to use Undo and Close options). When you've drawn your wall, hit **RETURN** to stop or **C** to Close.

When asked **Side to offset wall:**, pick the side of the line on which you'll place the other side of the wall.

The next example describes the **CENTER** option. Type **C** for **CENTER**. This option works the same as **EDGE** up to the point after you **Close** or **RETURN** to terminate. You're not asked for **Side to offset wall**. Instead, the routine **OFFSET**s a thickness half the distance from each side of the line. Next, you're asked **What would you like to do with the center line? Erase it/Leave as is/<Make centerline>:**. **E** erases the centerline, **L** will leave it as you drew it, and **M** or a **RETURN** changes it to layer **CENTER**. (Layer **CENTER** must already exist in your drawing). The final example shows the Specify option in action. Type **S** for **SPECIFY**. Enter a number at the **Enter first thickness:** and another at **Enter second thickness:**. The rest of the macro works the same as Center except when it **OFFSET**s the lines. Instead of automatically **OFFSET**ting, it prompts **Side for <dist1> offset:**. Here you pick a point describing which side to offset (the same is true for **Side for <dist2> offset:**).

The last prompt in each of these examples is **Walls are PLINES, Do you wish to explode them N/<Y>:** If you answer the default Yes, lines created in the macro will be **EXPLODE**d into each of its individual parts. If you answer **No**, they'll be left as **POLYLINE**s.

TO REVISE: If you don't want the line to go to layer **CENTER**, change the word **CENTER** to another name in the macro.

TIPS: If you use other macros to clean up corners or intersecting walls, you will need to **EXPLODE** the walls.

MACRO 65 Doors, Windows and Openings

PURPOSE: Inserts a door, window or opening into a pair of parallel lines that represents a wall (a door construction is used as our example). Manual creation of doors, windows and similar construction consumes a lot of time. Many users insert doors as symbols, then go back and break out wall sections, which saves some time, but can be cumbersome if many different symbol sizes and styles are used.

This macro calculates every point necessary to draw the door, then automatically breaks out the wall section where the door is to be placed. It works for doors of any width, placed in any wall thickness at any angle.

TO CREATE:

```
(Defun C:Sssa () (Setvar "Cmdecho" 0) (Initget 7)
(Setq A (Getdist "\nEnter width of door: "))
(Initget 1) (Setq P1 (Osnap (Getpoint
"\nEnter hinge point of door: ") "Nea"))
(Setvar "Lastpoint" P1) (Initget 1) (Setq P2 (Osnap (Getpoint
"\nTouch point on opposite side of wall: ") "Per"))
(Initget 1) (Setq P3 (Osnap (Getpoint
"\nShow side of hinge you wish to place door: ") "Nea"))
(Setq A1 (Angle P1 P3)) (Setq P3 (Polar P1 A1 A))
(Setq A2 (Angle P1 P2)) (Setq P4 (Polar P3 A2 (Distance P1 P2)))
(Setq P5 (Polar P1 (+ Pi A2) A))
(Command "Break" P1 P3 "Break" P2 P4)
(Command "Line" P1 P2 "" "Line" P3 P4 "" "Line" P1 P5 "")
(Command "Arc" P3 "E" P5 "D" (Polar P3 (+ Pi A2) A)) (Princ))
```

TO INVOKE: Create this macro as an AutoLISP file (**.lsp**).

LET'S TRY IT: Get into a new AutoCAD drawing and create a pair of parallel lines representing a typical wall. Load **MACRO65** (**Load "Macro65"**). Set **UNITS** to Architectural.

```
Command: Line
From point: 0,0
To point: 60,0
To point: RETURN
Command: Copy
Select Object Window or Last: L
Select Object Window or Last: RETURN
Base point or displacement: 0,6
Second point of displacement: RETURN
Command: Zoom
Magnification or type (ACELPW): E
Command: RETURN
Magnification or type (ACELPW): .75X
Command: Door
Enter width of door: 2'
```

Enter hinge point: 6,6   (This can be any point on which you want to locate your door hinge.)

Touch opposite wall: (Touch the opposite line at any point.)

Side of hinge for door: (On the top line, touch a point that shows the side of the first point on which the door should be placed. This should be on the same line as the first point every time you use this macro.)

TO REVISE: Add commonly used symbols and notations to the end of this macro. The example below inserts a symbol called **DINFO** (**door information**) into your drawing. It scales the symbol according to the current **DIMSCALE**, then lets you place it. The example shows the last few lines of code with the new code added in boldface type.

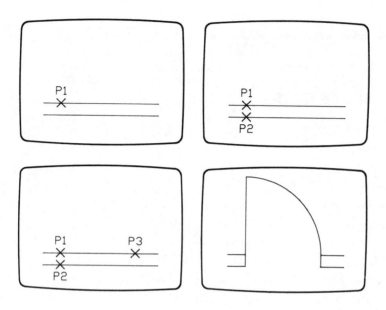

```
(Command "Insert" "Dinfo" "Scale" (Getvar "Dimscale") Pause 0)
(Princ)
)
```

Note: Before you run this revised version, you must create a symbol called **DINFO**. You can also put attributes in your symbol for bill of materials extraction. **DINFO** can even be invisible, yet contain all necessary information.

TIPS: The **DOOR** macro can be modified to break out openings only or to insert a window.

```
(Defun C:Open () (Setvar "Cmdecho" 0)
(Initget 7) (Setq A (Getdist "\nEnter width of opening: "))
(Initget 1) (Setq P1 (Osnap (Getpoint
"\nEnter insertion point of opening: ") "Nea"))
(Setvar "Lastpoint" P1) (Initget 1) (Setq P2 (Osnap (Getpoint
"\nTouch point on opposite side of wall: ") "Per")) (Initget 1)
(Setq P3 (Osnap (Getpoint
```

```
"\nShow side of point you wish to place opening: ") "Nea"))
(Setq Al (Angle Pl P3)) (Setq P3 (Polar Pl Al A))
(Setq A2 (Angle Pl P2)) (Setq P4 (Polar P3 A2 (Distance Pl P2)))
(Command "Break" Pl P3 "Break" P2 P4)
(Command "Line" Pl P2 "" "Line" P3 P4 "") (Princ))
```

MACRO
66 Corner Cleanup

PURPOSE: Cleans intersecting lines, such as corners of a wall or box, with a single selection.

TO CREATE:

```
[CORNERS ]^C^CFillet;R;0;;Intersection;\@;
```

TO INVOKE: Add this macro to a space in your menu file.

LET'S TRY IT: Draw two lines that intersect with a small overlap. Pick the **CORNERS** macro and touch the intersection. Voila!

TO REVISE: You can add various prompts to this macro.

Example:

```
^C^C(Setq A+
(Getpoint "Touch near intersection to clean up: "));\+
Fillet;R;0;;Intersection;!A;@;
```

TIPS: If you've **ZOOM**ed out too far from the desired cleanup area, you may get inaccurate results. However, you won't have problems if you can clearly see the intersection.

MACRO
67 Wall Cleanup

PURPOSE: Cleans up the intersection between two walls (or in a construction resembling walls). This is most useful in architectural drawing where, for example, a 6" horizontal wall intersects a 4" vertical wall.

TO CREATE:

```
[INTERSEC]^C^CBREAK;\@.001,.001;+
FILLET;R;0;;INTERS;\@;;INTERS \@
```

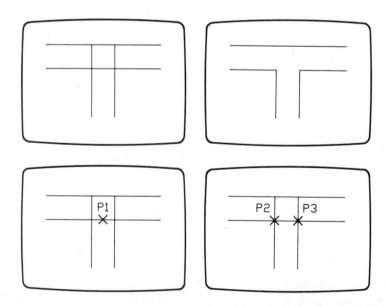

TO INVOKE: Add this macro to a space in your menu file.

LET'S TRY IT: Draw an intersection of two walls. Now let's clean it up. Pick the **INTERSEC** macro and touch three points, as shown.

First the macro will **BREAK** the first line you chose at one point (variation of Macro 9, "Break, 1 Point"); then it will **FILLET** the two intersections you chose (variation of Macro 66, "Corner Cleanup").

TO REVISE: To make it more user-friendly, you can edit the macro with prompts similar to those in the previous macro. You also can remove one of the required pick points and have the macro find it.

Example:
```
^C^C(Setq A+
(Getpoint "Pick first intersection on the line: "));\+
(Setq B(Getpoint "Pick second intersection on the line: "));\+
(Setq C(Polar A (Angle A B) (/(Distance A B)2))));+
Break;!C;@;+
Fillet;R;0;;Int;!A;@;;Int;!B;@;
```

TIPS: In order for the macro to work, all lines must truly intersect. Although you can accomplish this macro using the **TRIM** command, the **INTERSEC** macro illustrates how variations of other macros and routines can be borrowed and used to create new macros.

MACRO
68 Base Plates

PURPOSE: Allows you to generate a common baseplate by entering known data. It will generate the baseplate and all dimensions. This macro is explained in Chapter Eight.

TO CREATE:
```
(Defun C:Bplate () (Setvar "Cmdecho" 0)
```

```
(If (= SIDE1 nil) (Setq SIDE1 6.0))
(If (= SIDE2 nil) (Setq SIDE2 6.0))
(If (= BOLTHOLE nil) (Setq BOLTHOLE 1.0))
(If (= CHOLE nil) (Setq CHOLE 3.0))
(If (= CRADIUS nil) (Setq CRADIUS 0.5))
(If (= TAPSTRING nil) (Setq TAPSTRING ""))
(If (= INSET nil) (Setq INSET CRADIUS))
(If (= DS nil) (Setq DS 1.0)) (Initget "Y N")
(Setq X (Getkword "\nErase previous design? Y/<N>: "))
(If (= X "Y") (Progn (Setq A (Ssget "X")) (If A
(Command "Erase" A ""))))
(Setq X (Getreal (Strcat "\nEnter the baseplate width <"
(Rtos SIDE1 2 3) ">: "))) (If (/= X nil) (Setq SIDE1 X))
(Setq X (Getreal (Strcat "\nEnter the baseplate length <"
(Rtos SIDE2 2 3) ">: "))) (If (/= X nil) (Setq SIDE2 X))
(Setq X (Getreal (Strcat "\nBolt hole size <"
(Rtos BOLTHOLE 2 3) ">: "))) (If (/= X nil) (Setq BOLTHOLE X))
(Initget "Y N") (Setq TAP (Getkword
"\nAre the holes tapped <N>: ")) (If (= TAP "Y") (Progn (Setq X
(Getstring (Strcat "\nEnter tap specification<"
TAPSTRING ">: "))) (If (/= X "") (Setq TAPSTRING X)))) (If
(/= TAP "Y") (Setq HOLESTRING (Strcat "%%c"
(Rtos BOLTHOLE 2 3)))) (Setq X (Getreal (Strcat
"\nCorner radius <" (Rtos CRADIUS 2 3) ">: "))) (If (/= X nil)
(Setq CRADIUS X)) (If (> BOLTHOLE CRADIUS) (Progn
(Setq X (Getreal (Strcat "\nEnter bolt hole inset <"
(Rtos INSET 2 3) ">: "))) (If (/= X nil) (Setq INSET X)))
(Setq INSET CRADIUS))
(Setq X (Getreal (Strcat "\nCenter hole diameter <"
(Rtos CHOLE 2 3) ">: "))) (If (/= X nil) (Setq CHOLE X))
(Setq X (Getreal (Strcat "\nEnter the dimension scale <"
(Rtos DS 2 4) ">: "))) (If (/= X nil) (Setq DS X))
(Setq LOWER (List (* DS -5) (* DS -5)))
(Setq UPPER (List (+ (* 5 DS) SIDE1) (+ (* 5 DS) SIDE2)))
(Command "Zoom" "W" LOWER UPPER) (Command "Limits" LOWER UPPER)
```

```
(Command "Units" 2 2 2 4 "" "") (Command "Grid" (* 2 DS))
(Command "Dim" "Dimscale" DS) (Setvar "Blipmode" 0)
(Setvar "Ltscale" DS) (Command) (Setq Pl (List 0 0))
(Setq P2 (List SIDE1 0)) (Setq P3 (List SIDE1 SIDE2))
(Setq P4 (List 0 SIDE2)) (Command "Layer" "M" 1 "")
(Command "Pline" Pl P2 P3 P4 "Cl") (If (> CRADIUS 0) (Progn
(Command "Fillet" "R" CRADIUS) (Command "Fillet" "P" "Last")))
(Setq Cl (List INSET INSET))
(Setq C2 (List (- Sidel INSET) INSET))
(Setq C3 (List (- SIDE1 INSET) (- SIDE2 INSET)))
(Setq C4 (List INSET (- SIDE2 INSET)))
(Command "Circle" (List INSET INSET) "D" BOLTHOLE)
(Setq S1 (- SIDE1 (* 2 INSET))) (Setq S2 (- SIDE2 (* 2 INSET)))
(Command "Array" "L" "" "R" 2 2 S2 S1) (If (= TAP "Y") (Progn
(Command "Layer" "M" 2 "") (Command "Circle" (List INSET INSET)
"D" (+ BOLTHOLE (/ DS 16))) (Setq S1 (- SIDE1 (* 2 INSET)))
(Setq S2 (- SIDE2 (* 2 INSET))) (Command "Array" "L" "" "R"
2 2 S2 S1))) (If (> CHOLE 0) (Progn (Setq MPT (List (/ SIDE1 2)
(/ SIDE2 2))) (Command "Layer" "M" 1 "") (Command "Circle" MPT
"D" CHOLE))) (Setq P5 (List 0 (- SIDE2 CRADIUS)))
(Setq P6 (List SIDE1 (- SIDE2 CRADIUS)))
(Setq P7 (List (- SIDE1 CRADIUS) SIDE2))
(Setq P8 (List (- SIDE1 CRADIUS) 0))
(If (> CHOLE 0) (Setq P9 (Polar MPT (/ Pi 4) (/ CHOLE 2))))
(Setq P10 (Polar C4 (/ Pi 4) (/ BOLTHOLE 2)))
(Setq P11 (List (+ (Car C4) INSET (/ DS 2)) (+ (Cadr C4) INSET
(/ DS 2))))
(Setq P12 (Polar (List CRADIUS CRADIUS) (* Pi -0.75) CRADIUS))
(Setq P13 (List (- 0.0 INSET (/ DS 2)) (- 0.0 INSET
(/ DS 1.75)))) (Setq P14 (List 0 CRADIUS))
(Setq P15 (List Sidel CRADIUS)) (Setq P16 (List CRADIUS 0))
(Setq P17 (List CRADIUS SIDE2)) (Setq P18 (List (* DS -1.75) 0))
(Command "Layer" "M" 4 "") (Command "Dim" "Hor" P5 C4 (List
(Car P4) (+ (Cadr P4) (* 2 DS))) "") (Command "Cont" C3 "")
(Command "Cont" P6 "") (Command "Ver" P7 C3 (List (+ (Car P3)
```

```
(* 2 DS)) (Cadr P3)) "") (Command "Cont" C2 "")
(Command "Cont" P8 "") (If (> CHOLE 0) (Command "Dia" P9 ""))
(If (= TAP "Y") (Command "Lea" P10 P11 "" TAPSTRING))
(If (/= TAP "Y") (Command "Lea" P10 P11 "" HOLESTRING))
(If (> CRADIUS 0) (Progn
(Setq CRADIUSTXT (Strcat (Rtos CRADIUS 2 2) "R"))
(Command "Lea" P12 P13 "" CRADIUSTXT)))
(Command "Hor" P14 P15 P13 "") (Command "Ver" P16 P17 P18 "")
(Command) (Princ))
```

TO INVOKE: Create this macro as an AutoLISP file (**.lsp**).

LET'S TRY IT: To try this macro you must be in a new drawing and these layers must exist.

  Layer 1, Continuous
  Layer 2, Hidden
  Layer 4, Continuous

  Load **MACRO68 (Load "Macro68")**. Type **BPLATE**. You'll be prompted:

```
Erase previous design? Y/<N>: Y
Enter the baseplate width <DEF>: 4
Enter the baseplate length <DEF>: 6
Bolt hole size <DEF>: .5
Are the holes tapped <N>: Y
Enter tap specification <DEF>:
Corner radius <DEF>: .5
Center hole diameter <DEF>: 2
Enter the dimension scale <DEF>: 1
```

TO REVISE: You could have this macro create the layers if they don't already exist. You also could have it read the current drawing **DIM-SCALE** instead of prompting for it.

MACRO 69 Drill

PURPOSE: Lets you specify the size of a hole to be drilled according to its **NUMBER** or **LETTER** size. Normally, if you wish to use a No. 32 hole you need to look it up to find out it's 0.1160. This macro does the reading for you. It has a matching data file that it scans for specified data. When it finds the data, it reads the rest of the line to determine dimensions for objects. In this case it will retrieve only a single number representing the diameter of the hole (**CIRCLE**) to be drawn.

To use this macro, you'll need to create both the AutoLISP routine and the data file it will scan. The **TO CREATE:** section lists the AutoLISP routine. Now let's create the data file.

This macro must be created using a *space delimited data* file. Using any ASCII editor, create the file **MACRO69.DTA** that contains the necessary information. The following is a sample of the file included on the optional *AutoCAD Productivity Diskette*.

```
80 0.0135
79 0.0145
.

.
10 0.1935
9  0.1960
.

.
1  0.2280
A  0.2340
.

.
Z  0.4130
```

This file must be created in exactly the same format as above. The first two characters of each line represent the drill size. If the size takes up only a single character, **1,2,3,A,B,C**, then the second character should be left blank. The third character should be left blank on every line. And the fourth through eighth characters should contain the size of the hole. This chart can be found in most drafting manuals and machining handbooks.

TO CREATE:

```
(Defun C:Drl () (Setvar "Cmdecho" 0) (Setq P1 nil)
(Setq B (Open "Macro69.dta" "r")) (If B (Progn
(Setq A (Strcase (Getstring "\nEnter size of drilled hole: ")))
(Setq C (Strlen A)) (Setq D (Read-line B))
(Princ "Searching file.") (While (Boundp 'D) (Cond
((And (= (Substr D 1 C) A) (= " " (Substr D 3 1))) (Initget 1)
(Setq P1 (Getpoint "\nEnter center point: "))
(Command "Circle" P1 "D" (Substr D 4 6)) (Setq D nil))
((= nil P1) (Princ ".") (Setq D (Read-line B))))) (If (= nil P1)
(Princ "Item not found in MACRO69.DTA."))) (Princ (Strcat
(Chr 34) "MACRO69.dta" (Chr 34) ": Can't open file\n*Invalid*")))
(Princ))
```

TO INVOKE: Create this macro as an AutoLISP file (**.lsp**).

LET'S TRY IT: Get into an AutoCAD drawing and load **MACRO69** (**Load "Macro69"**). Type **DRL**. If it finds the file **MACRO69.DTA**, it will open it and begin. If it can't find it, make sure the file is in the directory in which you're working. When the file is found and opened, you will be prompted:

```
Enter size of drilled hole: (Enter a drill size.)
Searching file....................................
```

    If it finds the size you entered, you'll be prompted:

```
Enter center point: (Pick a point.)
```

    If it doesn't find the size you entered, you'll be prompted:

```
Item not found in MACRO69.DTA.
```

^{MACRO} 70 Pipe Elbows

PURPOSE: Lets you draw pipe elbows by specifying the nominal size of the elbow. It is similar to the above macro in that it takes user-specified data and scans a file to retrieve dimensions. In this case the routine will retrieve two dimensions necessary to draw a pipe elbow. This macro has the added ability to add new information to the file if it's not already there.

Note: This macro draws only 90 degree elbows.

As in the macro above, you must create the AutoLISP routine and data file that it will scan. The **TO CREATE:** section lists the LISP routine. Now let's create the data file.

You'll create this data file in a comma delimited format. Using any ASCII editor, create the file, **MACRO70.DTA**, that contains all the necessary information needed. The following is a sample of the file included on *The AutoCAD Productivity Diskette*.

```
1/2,.84,1.5
3/4,1.05,1.125
1,1.315,1.5
1 1/4,1.66,1.875
1 1/2,1.9,2.25
2,2.375,3
```

This file is not as picky as the previous data file. All information must be separated by commas with no spaces in between. Each of these pieces of information is considered a field. The first field is the reference number, or the number you wish to search for. The second field is the outside diameter of the elbow. The third and last field is the center-to-face dimension.

In this file you specify the reference number in fraction form and the dimensions in decimal form (this is the way it was specified in the manual from which we copied the data).

TO CREATE:
This routine is composed of several sections. The first section, **C:PIPE**, is the main body. It searches for the file, then opens it. The second section, **LOCDATA**, takes user-specified input from the user checks to see if what he/she's input is in the file. If the information is found, the third section will be invoked. If not, you'll be given the option to invoke the fifth section.

The third section, **EXT**, extracts the data needed from the file after the second section has located it. It passes this information on to the fourth section.

The fourth section, **DRAW**, uses all the gathered data to create the elbow.

The fifth section, **ADDDTA**, adds data necessary to append the .DTA file. After it completes this task, the fifth section will be invoked.

```
(Defun C:Pipe () (Setvar "Cmdecho" 0)
(Setq A (Open "Macro70.dta" "r")) (If (= Nil A) (Princ
(Strcat (Chr 34) "MACRO70.dta" (Chr 34)
": Can't open file\n*Invalid*")) (Locdta)) (Princ))


(Defun Locdta () (Setq B (Getstring t
"\nEnter nominal pipe size for elbow: ")) (Setq C (Read-line A))
(If (= nil C) (Setq C "")) (Setq D C) (Princ "\nSearching file.")
(While (/= "" D) (If (And (= (Substr D 1 (Strlen B)) B)
(= "," (Substr D (1+ (Strlen B)) 1))) (Progn (Setq D "")
(Ext 1) (Ext 2) (Ext 3) (Draw)) (Progn (Princ ".")
(Setq C (Read-line A)) (If (= C nil) (Setq C "")) (Setq D C)
(If (= "" D) (Progn (Princ "\nItem not found in file")
(Initget 1 "Y N") (Setq C (Getkword
"\nWould you like to input the data? Y/N: "))
(If (= C "Y") (Adddta))))))) (Princ))


(Defun Ext (N) (Setq D "T") (Cond ((= N 2) (Setq E ""))
((= N 3) (Setq F ""))) (While (/= D "") (Setq D (Substr C 1 1))
(If (Or (= (Ascii D) 44) (= D "")) (Progn (Setq D "")
```

```
(Setq C (Substr C 2 (- (Strlen C) 1))) (Cond ((= N 2)
(Setq E (Atof E))) ((= N 3) (Setq F (Atof F)))))(Progn (Cond
((= N 2) (Setq E (Strcat E D))) ((= N 3) (Setq F (Strcat F D))))
(Setq C (Substr C 2 (- (Strlen C) 1)))))))


(Defun Draw () (Setq P1 (Getpoint "\nEnter insertion point: "))
(Setq P2 (List (+ (Car P1) F) (+ (Cadr P1) (/ E 2.0))))
(Setq P3 (List (+ (Car P1) F) (- (Cadr P1) (/ E 2.0))))
(Setq P4 (List (+ (Car P1) (/ E 2.0)) (- (Cadr P1) F)))
(Setq P5 (List (- (Car P1) (/ E 2.0)) (- (Cadr P1) F)))
(Command "Line" P2 P3 "" "Line" P4 P5 "")
(Command "Arc" P2 "E" P5 "A" "90")
(Command "Arc" P3 "E" P4 "A" "90"))


(Defun Adddta () (Setq A (Open "Macro70.dta" "a"))
(Setq E (Getstring "\nEnter the actual O.D. of pipe: "))
(Setq F (Getstring "\nEnter center to face: "))
(Setq C (Strcat B "," E "," F)) (Write-line C A) (Close A)
(Setq E (Atof E)) (Setq F (Atof F)) (Draw))
```

TO INVOKE: Create this macro as an AutoLISP file (**.lsp**).

LET'S TRY IT: Get into an AutoCAD drawing and load **MACRO70** (**Load "Macro70"**). Type **PIPE**. If the macro can locate the file **MACRO70.DTA**, it will open the file and begin. If it can't find it, be sure the file is in the directory you're working in. When the file is found and opened, you'll be prompted:

```
Enter nominal pipe size for elbow:
Searching file...................................
```

If it finds the size you entered, you'll be prompted:

```
Enter insertion point: (Pick a point.)
```

If it doesn't find the size you entered, you'll be prompted:

```
Item not found in file.
```

Would you like to input the data? Y/N:

If you answer **Yes**, you're then asked;

Enter the actual O.D. of pipe:
Enter the center to face:
Enter insertion point:

When you enter the data to the file, remember the fields mentioned above.

3D MACROS

Macros 71 through 80 are designed specifically for Release 10. Each is an AutoLISP program designed to make you more productive in 3D.

MACRO
71 Distance
On and Off

PURPOSE: Turns **PERSPECTIVE ON** and **OFF**. When the **DISTANCE** command is issued through **DVIEW**, and **PERSPECTIVE** is turned **ON**, there are certain restrictions to edit, display and draw commands. Many commands, such as **LINE**, allow only coordinates from the keyboard. Picking points isn't allowed while **PERSPECTIVE** is **ON**. These commands, **disoff** and **dison**, quickly turn **PERSPECTIVE OFF** and then **ON** at the same distance as before.

A word of advice — be sure you've set your distance in a conventional way at least once before these commands are issued. Even though they'll work as the first command issued, you can get some unusual results.

TO CREATE:

```
(defun c:disoff ()
(command "dview" "" "off" ""))

(defun c:dison ()
(command "dview" "" "d" "" ""))
```

TO INVOKE: Create these macros as an AutoLISP file (**.lsp**).

LET'S TRY IT: Get into a new AutoCAD drawing and create a 3D object. Load **MACRO71 (Load "Macro71")**. Using the **DVIEW** command, select your entire object and confirm. Now use the **DISTANCE** subcommand. Set the distance to the object to turn **PERSPECTIVE ON**. Then exit the **DVIEW** commands.

Now if you issue the **LINE** command, you'll find you can't point to the objects. First turn **PERSPECTIVE OFF**.

Type: disoff (RETURN)

Now you can edit the drawing. When you're finished,

Type: dison (RETURN)

PERSPECTIVE is now turned **ON**.

MACRO
72 Distance
On and Off
with Saved View

PURPOSE: Many times after turning **PERSPECTIVE OFF**, you might **ZOOM** around or change your original view in other ways. This macro not only turns **PERSPECTIVE ON** and **OFF**, but saves your view to "tempview" before **PERSPECTIVE** is turned **OFF** and then restores "tempview" prior to turning **PERSPECTIVE** back **ON**.

TO CREATE:
```
(defun c:disoffv ()
(command "view" "s" "tempview")
(command "dview" "" "off" ""))
```

```
(defun c:disonv ()
(command "view" "r" "tempview")
(command "dview" "" "d" "" ""))
```

TO INVOKE: Save this macro as an AutoLISP file (**.lsp**).

LET'S TRY IT: Get into a new AutoCAD drawing and create a 3D object. Load **MACRO72 (Load** "**Macro72**"). Using the **DVIEW** command, select your entire object and confirm. Now use the **DISTANCE** subcommand. Set the distance to the object to turn **PERSPECTIVE ON**. Then exit the **DVIEW** commands.

Type: `disoffv` (RETURN)

This saves your view and turns **PERSPECTIVE OFF**. You can now use any draw or edit commands, as well as **ZOOMS** or other **VIEWS**. When you're finished,

Type: `disonv` (RETURN)

You're returned to your original view with **PERSPECTIVE ON**.

MACRO 73 Elevation and Thickness to 0

PURPOSE: Many times when you're creating 3D objects, you'll set **THICKNESS**. It's easy to forget to set **THICKNESS** back to 0. But you'll receive an abrupt reminder when you proceed to draw in 3D as your object is rotated. This macro provides you with a shortcut to turn **ELEVATION** and **THICKNESS OFF** (0).

TO CREATE:

```
(defun c:elth0 ()
(command "elev" "0" "0"))
```

TO INVOKE: Save this macro as an AutoLISP file (**.lsp**).

LET'S TRY IT: Set your **ELEVATION** and/or **THICKNESS** to some non-0 amount. Load **MACRO73 (Load "Macro73")**. Then issue the macro.

Type: elth0 (RETURN)

Both **ELEVATION** and **THICKNESS** are returned to 0.

MACRO 74 Set to UCS Entity

PURPOSE: Many times you'll try to edit an entity only to get an error message that says the entity isn't parallel to the current **UCS**. The easiest way to make parallel is to use **UCS ENTITY**. This macro sets the current **UCS** to **ENTITY**. You can now edit the entity.

TO CREATE:

```
(defun c:ucsent ()
(command "ucs" "e" pause))
```

TO INVOKE: Save this macro as an AutoLISP file (**.lsp**).

LET'S TRY IT: Get into a new drawing and create a 3D object. Set a new **UCS** using **3POINT**. Load **MACRO74 (Load "Macro74")**.

Type: ucsent (RETURN)

The **UCS** will be set to **ENTITY**. After you edit the entity, set **UCS** back with **PREVIOUS**.

MACRO 75 Set Icon for All Vports

PURPOSE: The **UCSICON** command requires multiple selections in order to set the icon on, off, on the point of origin and off the point of origin in all **VPORTS**. The **ALL** command must be issued prior to each option. This macro assumes that you want the icon changed in all **VPORTS** with one command.

TO CREATE:

```
(defun c:iconor ()
(command "ucsicon" "a" "on")
(command "ucsicon" "a" "or"))

(defun c:iconnor ()
(command "ucsicon" "a" "on")
(command "ucsicon" "a" "no"))

(defun c:iconoff ()
(command "ucsicon" "a" "off"))

(defun c:iconon ()
(command "ucsicon" "a" "on"))
```

TO INVOKE: Save these macros as an AutoLISP file (**.lsp**).

LET'S TRY IT: Get into a new drawing and create a 3D object. Load **MACRO75 (Load "Macro75")**. Using **UCS ORIGIN**, pick a point on the object as the new point of origin. Be sure the object is well into the center of the screen. Using **VPORTS**, split your screen into at least two **VPORTS**.

Now issue the following commands:

Type: `iconor (RETURN)`

This turns the icon on and places it at the point of origin.

Type: `iconnor (RETURN)`

This turns the icon on and places it in the lower left of the screen.

Type: `iconoff (RETURN)`

This turns the icon off.

Type: `iconon (RETURN)`

This turns it on.

^{MACRO}
76 Camera Vertical

PURPOSE: Offers a variation on a special purpose **DVIEW CAMERA** command. When you only want to tilt the object vertically rather than in both directions, this macro takes you directly into the vertical tilting of the object while maintaining the existing left-right rotation.

TO CREATE:
```
(defun c:dvcamv()
(command "dview" "c" pause pause "" "ca" pause ""))
```

TO INVOKE: Save this macro as an AutoLISP file (**.lsp**).

LET'S TRY IT: Get into a new drawing and create a 3D object. Load **MACRO76 (Load "Macro76")**. Using the **DVIEW CAMERA** command, set the object to an angle in each direction you want. Then exit the command with **(RETURN)**. You can now issue the macro.

Type: dvcamv (RETURN)

This macro maintains the horizontal rotation and lets you rotate the object vertically.

MACRO
77 Camera Horizontal

PURPOSE: Similar to Macro 76, except that it lets you rotate the object horizontally while maintaining the vertical inclination constant.

TO CREATE:
```
(defun c:dvcamh ()
(command "dview" "c" pause pause "" "ca" "" pause))
```

TO INVOKE: Save this macro as an AutoLISP file (**.lsp**).

LET'S TRY IT: Get into a new drawing and create a 3D object. Load **MACRO77 (Load "Macro77")**. Using the **DVIEW CAMERA** command, set the object to an angle in each direction you want. Then exit the command with **(RETURN)**. You can now issue the macro.

Type: dvcamh (RETURN)

This macro maintains the vertical inclination and lets you rotate the object horizontally.

MACRO 78 Origin, Positive X, Positive Z

PURPOSE: AutoCAD gives you virtually every option possible with **UCS**, but it doesn't let you use **3POINT** with a positive **X** and a positive **Z**. One of the most frequently used **UCS**s is **3POINT**, also called **Origin, Positive X, Positive Y**. Even though there are several options for the **Z** axis, this macro is an easy way to point to **Origin, Positive X, Positive Z**. It first does a **3POINT**, then rotates around the **X** axis -90 degrees.

TO CREATE:

```
(defun c:ucs3z ()
(setq o (getpoint "\nOrigin point  "))
(setq x (getpoint o "\nPositive X  "))
(setq z (getpoint o "\nPositive Z  "))
(command "ucs" "3" o x z)
(command "ucs" "x" -90))
```

TO INVOKE: Save this macro as an AutoLISP file (**.lsp**).

LET'S TRY IT: Get into a new drawing and create a 3D object. Load **MACRO78 (Load "Macro78")**.

Type: UCS3Z (RETURN)

Response: Origin point.

Pick the point of origin.

Response: Positive X.

Pick a point in the direction of positive **X**.

Response: Positive Z.

Pick a point in the direction of positive **Z**.

_{MACRO}
79 Turn On and Off Invisible 3DFACES

PURPOSE: It's possible to draw **3DFACES** where the lines are invisible. This macro will turn on any of the four lines if they're off or turn them off if they're on.

TO CREATE:

```
(defun c:3dfacei (/ b i d dl bl)
(setq b (entget (car (entsel))))
(setq i (getreal "\nEnter sum of the sides to make invisible"))
(setq d (assoc 70 b))
(setq dl (cons (car d) i))
(setq bl (subst dl d b))
(entmod bl)
)
```

TO INVOKE: Save this macro as an AutoLISP file (**.lsp**).

LET'S TRY IT: Get into a new drawing. Load **MACRO79 (Load "Macro79")**. Using the **3DFACE** command, draw a rectangle. Each of the four sides of the rectangle has a specific code number. The first side is 1, the second is 2, the third is 4 and the fourth is 8. The direction that determines each side is the same way the object is drawn.

By entering a code number as the sum of the sides, you can determine which sides are invisible. For example 1, 2, 4 or 8 will turn off sides 1, 2, 3 or 4 respectively. 0 will turn on all sides. 3 will turn off sides 1 and

2, because 3 is their sum. 6 will turn off side 2 and 3, since 6 is their sum (4 + 2). 15 will turn off all sides.

Type: 3dfacei (RETURN)

Response: Enter sum of the sides to make invisible.

Type: 12 (RETURN)

This will turn off sides 3 and 4, the sum of (4 + 8).

MACRO 80 Find Sides 1 and 2 of 3DFACE

PURPOSE: When using Macro 79, it's important for you to know which way the **3DFACE** was drawn and which is side 1. This macro asks you to pick the **3DFACE**, then makes side 1 invisible, then side 2. At the end, it returns the **3DFACE** to its original visibility. Once you know which is side 1 and the direction, you can set the visibility on any of the sides with Macro 79.

TO CREATE:
```
(defun c:3dfacet (/ b i d dl bl e)
(setq b (entget (car (entsel))))
(setq i 1)
(repeat 2
(setq d (assoc 70 b))
(setq dl (cons (car d) i))
(setq bl (subst dl d b))
(entmod bl)
(prompt "\nThis is side ") (princ i)
```

```
(setq i (+ 1 i))
(setq e (getstring))
)
(terpri)
(entmod b)
```

TO INVOKE: Save this macro as an AutoLISP file (**.lsp**).

LET'S TRY IT: Get into a new drawing and draw a rectangle using a **3DFACE**. Load **MACRO80 (Load "Macro80")**.

Type: 3dfacet (RETURN)

Response: Select Object:

Pick the **3DFACE**. The first side will disappear. **(RETURN)** and the second side will disappear. **(RETURN)** and the **3DFACE** will return to its original visibility.

DOS Commands and Compendium

This appendix covers most AutoCAD-related DOS commands and control characters featured in the book. Not written as a DOS tutorial, this appendix provides a description of each command's use. For further explanation, see your DOS manual.

When using the DOS operating system, you're limited in the way you can enter the filenames. A filename consists of two parts, always separated by a period: 1) the filename; and 2) its extension—denoted as **FILENAME.EXT**. Not all filenames contain both a filename and an extension.

A filename consists of one to eight characters, excluding the following characters that are considered invalid:

. " / \ [ ] : < > + = ; ,

and any ASCII character less than 20H.

The extension consists of a period followed by one to three characters. The above list of invalid characters also applies here.

Below is a list of filetypes you'll encounter when using AutoCAD:

.BAK Backup file

.CFG Current configuration file

.DOC Document file

.DRV Peripheral driver file

.DVP Peripheral initialization file

.DXB Binary drawing interchange file

.DXF Drawing interchange file

.DXX Attribute extract file (DXF format)

.EXE Executable file

.HLP **HELP** file in ASCII form

.HDX Index to **HELP** definition screens

.IGS IGES interchange file

.LSP AutoLISP file

.LST Spooled printer plot file

.MID Master identification file

.MNU AutoCAD menu file in ASCII form

.MNX AutoCAD menu file in compiled form

.OLD Original version of converted drawing file

.OVL Overlay files

.PAT Pattern file for hatching

.PGP External command definition

.PLT Spooled plot file

.SCR Script files

.SHP Shape definition file in ASCII form

.SHX Shape definition file in compiled form

.SLD Slide file

.TXT Attribute extract file in space- or comma-delimited form

.$$$ AutoCAD temporary drawing file

.$AC Another temporary file

.$RF AutoCAD's current working file, usually not seen

A.1 ## CONTROL CHARACTERS
To enter a control character, you must hold down the **CONTROL** key, then depress the desired character simultaneously.

A.1.1 **CTRL-C (^C)**: This is used to cancel almost any command you might enter.

A.1.2 **CTRL P (^P)**: This turns on the printer echoing. Any text displayed on the screen will be **ECHOED** to the printer as it's printed on the screen.

If you want to print a directory as it scrolls on the screen:

Type: ^P (This won't be displayed when you type it.)

Type: DIR

The printer will now **ECHO** the directory as it scrolls on the screen. When finished, remember to turn the **ECHO OFF,** or it will **ECHO** everything else you type. Another ^P will toggle the **ECHO OFF**. If you have a **PRINT SCREEN** key, you can type ^**PrtSc** and get the same results.

A.1.3 **Shift PrtSc**: Though this isn't a control character, we'll treat it as one. **Shift PrtSc** prints what's presently on the screen. It differs from ^**P** in that it prints only what's on the screen at any one time instead of everything that scrolls.

A.1.4 **CTRL-S (^S)**: Stops the screen scrolling action that you get when you call a **DIR**ectory or **TYPE** a file. After entering a command that causes the screen to scroll, type ^**S** to stop the scrolling. Hit any key to continue.

A.1.5 **CTRL-ALT-DEL (^ALT DEL)**: **REBOOTS** the system. To enter this command you must depress **CTRL**, **ALT** and **DEL** simultaneously. If your system has locked up, this command usually will unlock it. All memory will be cleared just as if you'd turned off the power.

A.1.6 **Global Characters**: Used as **WILDCARDS** to help you locate and manipulate files.
The ***** is used in place of any number of characters. **DIR *.*** will give you a directory of everything. **DEL *.*** will **DEL**ete everything. For a directory of files with extension **.DWG** only, type **DIR *.DWG**.

If you have a series of drawings that begins with the prefix **ABC**, followed by an unknown number of characters and a **.DWG** extension, you can view those files by typing **DIR ABC*.DWG**.

Suppose you have a series of drawings that begin with the prefix **ABC**, followed by any number of characters and extension **.DWG**. And suppose you want to list only those with two characters following **ABC**. Here's how: type **DIR ABC??.DWG.**

A.2 COMMANDS

A.2.1 **BATCH Files**: Store a series of DOS commands that can be executed with a single command. The files must be created with the extension **.BAT**.

A special **BATCH** file, **AUTOEXEC.BAT**, is executed automatically each time your system is booted.

These subcommands are used in batch files.

A.2.1.1 **ECHO**: Lets you display or turn off certain actions that take place when a **BATCH** file is executing.

A.2.1.2 **FOR**: Allows iterative execution of DOS.

A.2.1.3 **GOTO**: Lets you transfer control to another line of the **BATCH** file. Resembles the **GOTO** command in BASIC.

A.2.1.4 **IF**: Lets you test expressions in DOS.

A.2.1.5 **SHIFT**: Allows you to use more than 10 replaceable parameters.

A.2.1.6 **PAUSE**: Halts processing and displays the message **Strike a key when ready....**

A.2.1.7 **REM**: Displays a **rem**ark statement from within a **BATCH** file.

A.2.2 **CHDIR (CD)**: **CH**anges the current **DIR**ectory to one specified in the default drive, unless otherwise specified. Discussed in further detail in Section A.3 below.

A.2.3 **CHKDSK: CHecKs** directories, **DiSK** files and File Allocation Table for lost clusters and gives a disk and memory status report.

If your system locks up (or you shut off the power or reboot) while you're in a drawing file, files are created that never get closed. DOS treats that file area as a "lost cluster." Large drawings may take many clusters and render them useless to other files.

By using **CHKDSK**, you can obtain a report that tells how many lost clusters are on your disk. By using the **/F** option, you can change the lost clusters to files to be viewed for useful information or to be deleted to free space.

A.2.4 **CLS: CL**ears the display **S**creen.

A.2.5 **COPY: C**opies one or more files to a specified disk or directory.

A.2.6 **DATE**: Adds a date to each file as it's created. If not otherwise specified, most systems have a default date of **1-01-1980**. On booting, the system will prompt for the **Date** if no **AUTOEXEC.BAT** file is found. If **AUTOEXEC.BAT** is found, it won't prompt unless you add the **Date** command to the **AUTOEXEC.BAT** file.

Systems with internal clocks will keep the time and date even after the power has been shut down, so you don't have to enter the time and date each time you boot.

A.2.7 **DEL: DEL**etes a specified file or group of files.

A.2.8 **DIR:** Lists all files or specified files. Two parameters can be used with this command:

A.2.8.1 **/P: P**auses a full screen. Type **DIR/P**, and the screen will stop scrolling when full and prompt **Strike a key when ready . . ..** When you strike a key, the screen will scroll again until full.

A.2.8.2 **/W:** Causes the directory to print in a **w**ide format. It doesn't display attributes of the file such as date and size.

A.2.9   **FORMAT:** Sets the disk up so that it can be read by DOS. Six parameters can be used with this command.

A.2.9.1   **/S**: Copies the operating system to the formatting disk.

A.2.9.2   **/1**: Formats a diskette for single-side use only.

A.2.9.3   **/8**: Formats a diskette for eight sectors per track.

A.2.9.4   **/V**: Lets you give the disk a **V**olume label after the formatting process.

A.2.9.5   **/B**: Formats a disk for eight sectors per track, with space reserved for the **IBMBIO.COM** and **IBMDOS.COM** modules.

A.2.9.6   **/4**: Formats a double-sided diskette in a high-capacity drive.

A.2.10   **LABEL**: Lets you create, change or delete a volume label from a disk.

A.2.11   **MKDIR or MD**: Ma**K**es a **DIR**ectory or subdirectory in the current drive or directory. Discussed further in Section A.3 below.

A.2.12   **PATH**: Defines a set of directories for the system to search if the command given is not found in the current drive or directory. Searches for **executable** files only.

A.2.13   **PRINT**: Prints a list of data on the printer while you're working on another task.

A.2.14   **PROMPT**: Creates a new DOS prompt.

A.2.15   **RENAME (REN)**: Lets you **REN**ame a file or group of files.

A.2.16   **RMDIR or RD**: Re**M**oves a **DIR**ectory or subdirectory from the current drive or directory. Discussed further in Section A.3 below.

A.2.17 **SET:** Inserts strings into the command processor's environment. Sets AutoLISP's **stack** and **heap** large enough to handle many bits of information.

A.2.18 **TIME:** Lets you have the time of creation added to each new file. Most systems have a default time of **00:00:00** unless directed otherwise. On booting, a system will prompt for **TIME** if no **AUTOEXEC.BAT** file is found. If the file is found, the system will prompt for time only if you add the **TIME** command to the **AUTOEXEC.BAT** file.

An internal clock will keep the time and date even after the power has been shut down, so you don't have to enter them each time you boot.

A.2.19 **TREE:** Displays all directory paths found on a specified drive and optionally lists the files in the **ROOT** directory and each subdirectory.

A.2.20 **TYPE:** Displays the contents of a file.

A.3 **DIRECTORIES**

Directories and subdirectories are useful for helping you separate and organize information on your disk. They're listed in a tree-structured form, with the **ROOT** directory beginning at the top.

For example, if you're using your system for AutoCAD, WordStar and Lotus and want to separate files, directories can be a big help. You could create directories named **AUTOCAD**, **WORDSTAR** and **LOTUS**; or **ACAD**, **WS** and **LOT;** or any desired names.

Further, you may want to create directories within AutoCAD. From your **AUTOCAD** directory, you can create subdirectories named **PROJECT1**, **DRAWING2**, **FLANGE3** or any desired names.

Directories are created and maintained using the following five functions:

A.3.1 **MKDIR:** Enables you to create a new directory by typing **MKDIR**, or **MD**, followed by the directory name. If the directory already exists, DOS will report **Unable to create**

directory. If not, the directory will be created and you'll be returned to the DOS prompt.

A.3.2   **RMDIR**: Enables you to remove or delete a directory by typing **RMDIR**, or **RD**, followed by the name of the directory you want to remove.

If DOS finds no such directory, a multipurpose error will appear: **Invalid path, not directory,** or **directory not empty.** At times you'll get the above message even when the directory *does* exist and appears to be empty. This is because a file with a hidden attribute (an invisible file) resides in the directory but will not display. Delete that file, then remove the directory.

A.3.3   **CHDIR** or **CD**: Displays and **CH**anges the current **D**irectory. To change from one directory to another or show the current directory, type **CHDIR** or **CD**.

If you want your current directory to be displayed at all times, type **PROMPT = PG**. If followed by the name of one or more directories, **PG** will change the current directory to the one specified. Multiple directories must be separated with a backslash (\). You can get from one directory to another in three ways:

A.3.3.1 **CD**(space)(**directory name**): Advances you to the specified directory if it's a subdirectory of the current directory.

A.3.3.2 **CD ..**: Moves to the parent of the current subdirectory (back one directory up the tree).

A.3.3.3 **CD**\: Changes the directory to the **ROOT** directory. Typing another directory name immediately following the backslash moves to that directory under the **ROOT**. If you continue to string together directory names, separated by backslashes, you'll move to the directory at the end of the string.

By using combinations of the above options, you'll be able to navigate through directories with ease. You should be able to go from one directory to another with a single command.

A.3.4   **Directory (DIR)**: The **Directory** command will obtain a listing of all or a user-specified amount of the files contained in the current or specified directory. Type **DIR** to obtain a list of all files and subdirectories contained in the current directory. **DIR A:** will get you a list of all files and directories from the **A:** drive. Using global characters (see A.1.6), you can specify certain files you want to view.

A.3.5   **TREE**: Displays the directory structure. Type **TREE** to view all directories and their subdirectories in a "tree-structured" format.

Appendix B EDLIN Commands

EDLIN is a line editing program included with every DOS package. We've used EDLIN throughout this book because it's universal to AutoCAD users. EDLIN is an unadorned, hard-to-use word editor in a programming, or non-document, mode. If you intend to create and revise a number of macros, we strongly recommend that you learn to use another word editor to accomplish the task! (See Appendix D.)
   To begin EDLIN,

Type: EDLIN FILENAME.EXT

   If a file is found, you'll see:

End of input file
*

At this point you're ready to begin editing. If a file is *not* found, you'll see:

```
New file
*
```

B.1 Commands

With one exception, commands used in EDLIN are single-character entries:

B.1.1 **A** Appends lines and adds a specified number of lines to the file being edited. The lines are added at the end of the current lines.

B.1.2 **C** Copies a line or group of lines to other lines. The new lines are put above the line the user specifies.

B.1.3 **D** Deletes a specified range of lines.

B.1.4 **Edit Line**: Lets you revise an existing line of text. The command is the line number that you want to edit. For example, **1** brings up line **1** for editing.

B.1.5 **E** Ends EDLIN and saves the changed file.

B.1.6 **I** Inserts lines of text on the specified line. Use this to add lines of code when creating a new file.

B.1.7 **L** Lists a specified range of lines.

B.1.8 **M** Moves specified lines.

B.1.9 **P** Lists a specified block of lines.

B.1.10 **Q** Quits the editing process without saving the changes entered.

B.1.11 **R R**eplaces all occurrences of a string with a newly specified string.

B.1.12 **S S**earches a range of lines for a specified string of text.

B.1.13 **T T**ransfers the contents of a specified file into the file currently being edited.

B.1.14 **W W**rites a specified number of lines to disk from the file being edited.

Appendix C AutoLISP Notations

This appendix briefly lists and discusses the purpose of selected AutoLISP commands. It doesn't cover some of the more advanced functions of AutoLISP; those can be found in Autodesk's *AutoLISP Programmer's Reference*. I also recommend *AutoLISP in Plain English: A Practical Guide for Non-Programmers*, by George O. Head (Ventana Press).

C.1 **AutoLISP Expressions:** All AutoLISP expressions are in the form of (**Fun**ction [**Arg**uments] ...).

Each expression begins with a left parenthesis and consists of a function name and an optional list of arguments to that function (each can be an expression unto itself). The expression ends with a right parenthesis.

Every expression returns a value that can be used by a surrounding expression. If there's no surrounding expression, AutoLISP returns the value to AutoCAD. If an incorrect expression is typed or read from a file, AutoLISP may display the following prompt:

```
n>
```

This usually indicates that you failed to close the same number of parentheses or quotes as you opened during your AutoLISP operation.

C.2   **AutoLISP Variables:** Variables can be of four types: **real**, **integer**, **point** and **string**. They can have any name that begins with an alphabetical character.

The **setq** function is used to assign values to a variable. The format is:

```
(setq variable-name value)
```

The **list** function places together more than one item as a single variable. A point is a list of an **x** component and a **y** component.

car and **cdr** are used to retrieve parts of a list. **car** retrieves the first variable in a list and **cdr** retrieves everything after the first bit of data in the list.

To use a variable AutoLISP has stored in an AutoCAD command, add **!** to the beginning of the variable name **p1**.

C.3   **AutoCAD System Variables:** There are many predefined variables in any AutoCAD drawing file. To retrieve one, you must use the **getvar** function. To set a system variable to a new value, use **setvar**. Their formats are:

```
(getvar variable-name)
```

and

```
(setvar variable-name).
```

C.4   **Arithmetic Expressions:** Several arithmetic, trigonometric and geometric functions are available for use in expressions. The functions include:

(+ x y)	Returns the sum of **x** and **y**.
(- x y)	Returns the difference of **x** and **y**.

(* x y)	Returns the product of **x** and **y**.
(/ x y)	Returns the quotient of **x** divided by **y**.
(max x y)	Returns the **max**imum of **x** and **y**.
(min x y)	Returns the **min**imum of **x** and **y**.

The above functions can accommodate more than two arguments and will perform the associated function for the entire set of arguments. On the other hand, the functions listed below require the number of arguments shown.

(abs x)	Returns the **abs**olute value of **x**.
(sqrt x)	Returns the **sq**uare **root** of **x**.
(expt x p)	Returns **x** to the **p** **p**ower.
(log x)	Returns the natural **log** of **x**.
(float x)	Returns the promotion of integer value **x** to real.
(fix x)	Returns the truncation of real value **x** to integer.
(sin ang)	Returns the **sin**e of **ang**, where **ang** is an **ang**le in radians.
(cos ang)	Returns the **cos**ine of **ang**, where **ang** is an **ang**le in radians.
(atan x)	Returns the arc **tan**gent (in radians) of **x**.
(1 + x)	Returns the sum of **x** and **1**. Equivalent to **(+ x 1)**.
(1- x)	Returns the difference of **x** and **1**. Equivalent to **(- x 1)**.
(angle p1 p2)	Returns the **angle**, in radians, between points **p1** and **p2**.
(distance p1 p2)	Returns the **distance** between **p1** and **p2**.
(polar p1 ang d)	Returns the point a distance **d** from point **p1** at bearing **ang** (in radians).
(type a)	Returns the **type** of **a** (integer, real, list or string).

C.5   **String Functions:**

(itoa int)	Returns the integer value **int** converted to an ASCII string.
(atoi s)	Returns the integer conversion of string **s**.
(ascii c)	Returns the (integer) ASCII code for character **c**.
(chr int)	Returns the ASCII **character** represented by **integer int**.
(strcat s1 s2)	Returns the concatenation of strings **s1** and **s2**.
(strlen s)	Returns the length of **string s**.
(terpri)	Begins a new line on the display screen.

C.6   **Conditional Expressions:** You can construct conditional expressions that perform a given operation only if some condition is true. This is done using the **IF** function.

You must tell **if** what condition to test and what operation to perform if the test is successful. You may also indicate an operation to be performed if the test fails. The two forms of the **if** function are shown below:

(If condition do-if-true)
(If condition do-if-true do-if-false)

Several functions are provided:

(minusp num)	Returns **T** if **num** is negative, **nil** otherwise.
(zerop num)	Returns **T** if **num** is **0**, **nil** otherwise.
(numberp x)	Returns **T** if **x** is a number, **nil** otherwise.
(not a b ...)	Returns the logical **not** of **a**,**b**,. . ..

(or a b ...)	Returns the logical **or** of **a,b**,. . ..
(and a b ...)	Returns the logical **and** of **a,b**,. . ..
(= a b)	Returns **T** if **a** is equal to **b**, **nil** otherwise.
(/= a b)	Returns **T** if **a** is not equal to **b**, **nil** otherwise.
(> a b)	Returns **T** if **a** is greater than **b**, **nil** otherwise.
(>= a b)	Returns **T** if **a** is greater than or equal to **b**, **nil** otherwise.
(< a b)	Returns **T** if **a** is less than **b**, **nil** otherwise.
(<= a b)	**Returns T** if **a** is less than or equal to **b**, **nil** otherwise.
(listp a)	Returns **T** if **a** is a **list**, **nil** otherwise.
(null a)	Returns **T** if **a** is **nil**, **nil** otherwise.

C.7   **Data Input Functions:** Several functions let you prompt for input and use the response in an expression. These functions are most useful in custom menus.

Prompting for input: **(prompt "string")**

Obtaining a point   **(getpoint [base] [prompt])**

Obtaining a distance: **(getdist [base] [prompt])**

Obtaining an angle: **(getangle [base] [prompt])**

Obtaining a real number: **(getreal [prompt])**

Obtaining an integer: **(getint [prompt])**

Obtaining a text string: **(getstring [t] [prompt])**

Appendix
D Word Editors and Utilities

Although you can run AutoCAD straight from the box and create macros using EDLIN, some utility programs are useful and make life easier. Also, we strongly recommend you read and use the information about using AutoCAD's **.PGP** file — you'll save a lot of time using your word processor within AutoCAD, particularly when debugging.

WORD EDITORS

In Appendix B and throughout the tutorial chapters, we described a universal but limited way to create macros using EDLIN. The task can be accomplished more easily by using almost any word processor, as long as a few simple rules are followed.

This appendix covers some common editors — Word-Star, WordStar 2000, WordPerfect and the Norton Editor — and how to use them to create the **MY1ST.MNU** macro from Chapter One.

If you're using a word editor not described below, get into the nondocument (or programmer's) mode and create **MY1ST.MNU** as shown.

WordStar

To create a macro using WordStar, you must enter **nondocument** mode.

First, enter WordStar by typing **WS**, which brings up WordStar's main menu. One of the options is **N (Open a nondocument** file). Enter **N** and WordStar will prompt you for a filename. Enter **MY1ST.MNU**. If the file doesn't exist, it will report **New File**. If the file exists, a new file will be opened for editing. (We assume the file is a new one.)

Once you're in the new file, you may begin entering lines. Unlike EDLIN, this editor doesn't give line numbers. *Line numbers aren't needed; don't add them or your macros won't work.*

When finished, your screen should look like this:

```
[MY FIRST]
[ MENU ]
[LINE]
[ERASE-L]
```

If your screen doesn't read as shown above, use the arrow keys to correct mistakes. (With EDLIN, you must recall a line before editing it, a cumbersome and error-prone process.)

Now that you've created the menu, save it to a file. Enter **CTRL K (^K)**. This brings up the **BLOCK MENU**, which has options for **saving** and **quitting** the file. Type option **D** to save the file, or option **X** to save the file and exit Word-Star. Now the file is ready to use, just as described in Chapter One.

WordStar 2000

To get into WordStar 2000, type **WS2**, which brings up its main menu. Pick **E**, the Edit option, which prompts for a file to open. Type **MY1ST.MNU**. If it exists, you can begin editing that file. If it doesn't, you'll be asked which form to use. Use **UNFORM.FRM**, the nondocument or programmer's mode.

After you pick **UNFORM.FRM**, a large screen will prompt you for information about the file you want to edit. You can fill in the blanks or hit **CTRL Q (^Q)** to exit that screen. You're now ready to begin entering code.

```
[MY FIRST]
[ MENU ]
[LINE]
```

```
[ERASE-L]
```

The full screen editor, unlike a line editor, lets you move freely about the screen to make revisions. When you want to save your work, type **CTRL Q** (**^Q**) to retrieve the **QUIT EDITING** menu. Hit **S** to save the file. Once the file has been saved you'll be returned to the main menu, which you can exit by entering **Q**.

WordPerfect

This popular program works a little differently. First, you create your document in the normal manner. When you're finished, and before you save it,

Type: CTRL-F5 (**ConTRoL** key & **F5**)

and you'll see the following menu:

   1 - Save current document at a DOS text file
   2 - Retrieve a DOS text file
   3 - Lock a current document
   4 - Unlock and retrieve a locked document

Hit **1**, and your EDLIN file will be saved in ASCII.

Norton Editor

The previous examples involved word processors used as editors. We'll now show you the Norton Editor, an inexpensive full-screen editor made just for programmers.

To enter the Norton Editor, type **NE**. You'll be asked for a file to edit. Type **MY1ST.MNU**, and you're ready to begin entering code.

```
[MY FIRST]
[  MENU  ]
[LINE]
```

[ERASE-L]

Again, if changes are necessary, you can access the full screen. To save your work, hit **F3**, which brings up an **exit** menu. Pick option **E**; this saves the macro and returns you to your operating system.

AUTOCAD'S ACAD.PGP FILE

AutoCAD's **ACAD.PGP** file is a way to automate DOS and other program commands. If you want to run a text processor other than EDLIN within AutoCAD, you can easily modify the **ACAD.PGP** file to do so.

The **ACAD.PGP** file that comes with AutoCAD has the following lines:

```
CATALOG,DIR /W,25000,*Files: ,0
DEL,DEL,25000,File to delete: ,0
DIR,DIR,25000,File specification: ,0
EDIT,EDLIN,40000,File to edit: ,0
SH,,25000,*DOS Command: ,0
SHELL,,125000,*DOS Command: ,0
TYPE,TYPE,25000,File to list: ,0
```

The only line that interests us is:

```
EDIT,EDLIN,40000,File to edit: ,0
```

This line lets you use EDLIN from inside AutoCAD. Each item in the line is separated by a comma. The first item, **EDIT**, is what you type at the AutoCAD command line to bring up the program. The second item, **EDLIN**, is the name of the program. The third line, **40000**, is the number of bytes needed to run the program. The fourth item, **File to edit:**, is the prompt statement. Anything you type here will be appended to the program called up. In other words, this is the name of the file you're editing. If there's no prompt, use two commas. The final item, **0**, is a bit-coded integer that doesn't concern you. Therefore, it will always be **0** for our purposes.

As an example, if you want to use WordPerfect as your text editor, change the **.PGP** line as follows:

```
EDIT,WP,145000,,0
```

Or, using WordStar:

```
EDIT,WS,80000,,0
```

Note there's no file to edit. To revise **ACAD.PGP**, you must first bring up WordStar or WordPerfect, go into **non-document** mode in WordStar or **Edit Dos File** in Word-Perfect, then load the file. If you edit **ACAD.PGP** directly and save it, the word processing control codes may be embedded.

Different word processing programs and text editors have various memory requirements. The suggestions made above will work in most cases. Depending on your machine, configuration and the program you're using, you may have to experiment with the number of bytes to be reserved in memory.

OTHER UTILITIES

In this section we list a few useful products for a CAD operator.

Norton Utilities—A set of programs that enhances DOS. Includes functions for rearranging directories alphabetically or by date, time, extension, size of file and other criteria. A routine for recovering most deleted files is included.

Disk Optimizer—Lets you quickly reorganize fragmented files into contiguous sectors of the disk.

Fast Back—Backs up your hard disk to floppies. Using this program, a 10 Mbyte hard disk can be backed up to 360K floppies in about eight minutes (this creates a file backup, not an image backup).

CADD Clock—Lets you track the amount of time spent on parts of a project and the whole project for better system management. Prints reports of specified activities and acts as a system manager.

Norton Editor — This is a programmers' editor that is practically made to write LISP code. It is a pure ASCII editor that does not use control codes. It has bracket and parenthesis matching, auto indenting and split screen editing. It is also small enough to run under AutoCAD's **SHELL** environment.

PLUMP — This is a background plot spooler that sends data from a plotted vector file to your plotter. This will free your CPU in much less time than normal plotting.

SOFTWEST D2D — This program converts AutoCAD drawing files (**.dwg**) to drawing exchange format (**.dxf**) without the use of AutoCAD. It will convert the drawing even if AutoCAD is not installed on the machine.

TkSolver — This package does engineering calculations much more efficiently than by writing programs to do this. It also has a link to AutoCAD called TkLink that will update attributes in the drawing file.

Synthesis — This program will create true scaled drawings by linking together spreadsheet data and an AutoCAD master drawing file.

Your authorized AutoCAD dealer can provide buying information on these programs.

PUBLIC DOMAIN "SHAREWARE"

Other useful items exist in the public domain and can be found in trade magazines and electronic bulletin boards or obtained from user groups. We've outlined a few here:

Vtree — Shows a schematic of your DOS directory structure instead of scrolling all the directories and subdirectories on the screen.

Move — Lets you move files instead of copying them from one place to another, then deleting the original files.

Browse—Lets you scan a file forward and backward, but can do no editing.

Equip—Reports all presently installed equipment, including memory.

BOOKS

PC-DOS, Introduction to High-performance Computing, by Peter Norton. A nontechnical introduction to DOS.

LISP, Second Edition, by Patrick Henry Winston and Berthold Klaus Paul Hornor. A general guide to the LISP language, though not as applied to AutoCAD.

AutoLISP in Plain English: A Practical Guide for Non-Programmers, by George O. Head. For those who want to learn the basics of AutoLISP to solve everyday drawing problems (Ventana Press).

The AutoCAD Database Book: Accessing and Managing CAD Drawing Information, by Fred Jones and Lloyd Martin. Chapters Five through Eight show how AutoLISP can be used to work with AutoCAD's nongraphic data.

The AutoCAD 3D Book, by George O. Head, Charles Pietra and Kenneth Segal. A guide to AutoCAD's powerful new three-dimensional capabilities. (Ventana Press).

Index

Boldface entries indicate macros and AutoLISP routines featured in Section II, The AutoCAD Productivity Library.